The beginning *inden Girl* emerged whilst Pamela Rajkov earching her first book *In the Tracks* alarming details, formerly sup of the Akbars of South Aus and led Rajkowski on

Born in Hors ents, Rajkowski moved y as a young child. Trained a teacher, she has also pursued an i rnalism while travelling extensively i ralia and overseas. Rajkowski currently combines her writing with secondary school teaching and her role as Education Department Project Officer in Adelaide.

LINDEN GIRL

LINDEN GIRL

a story of outlawed lives

PAMELA RAJKOWSKI

UNIVERSITY OF WESTERN AUSTRALIA PRESS

First published in 1995 by
University of Western Australia Press
Nedlands Western Australia 6709

National Library of Australia
Cataloguing-in-Publication entry:

Rajkowski, Pamela, 1950– .
Linden girl : a story of outlawed lives.

Includes index
ISBN 1 875560 25 4.

Matbar, Lallie – Marriage. 2. Akbar, Jack – Marriage.
3. Neville, A. O. (Auber Octavius), 1975-1954.
4. Aborigines, Australian – Western Australia – Biography.
5. Aborigines, Australian – Western Australia – Treatment – History. 6. Afghans – Western Australia – Biography.
7. Interracial marriage – Western Australia. 8. Cameleers – Western Australia – Biography. I. Title.

305.899150941

Publication and promotion of this title was assisted by the South Australian Government through the Department for the Arts and Cultural Development.

Consultant editor: Helen Bradbury
Designed by Brown Cow Design, Perth
Typeset in 10pt Palatino
Printed by Scott Four Colour Print, Perth

LINDEN GIRL

a story of outlawed lives

PAMELA RAJKOWSKI

UNIVERSITY OF WESTERN AUSTRALIA PRESS

First published in 1995 by
University of Western Australia Press
Nedlands Western Australia 6709

National Library of Australia
Cataloguing-in-Publication entry:

Rajkowski, Pamela, 1950– .
Linden girl : a story of outlawed lives.

Includes index
ISBN 1 875560 25 4.

Matbar, Lallie – Marriage. 2. Akbar, Jack – Marriage.
3. Neville, A. O. (Auber Octavius), 1975-1954.
4. Aborigines, Australian – Western Australia – Biography.
5. Aborigines, Australian – Western Australia – Treatment – History. 6. Afghans – Western Australia – Biography.
7. Interracial marriage – Western Australia. 8. Cameleers – Western Australia – Biography. I. Title.

305.899150941

Publication and promotion of this title was assisted by the South Australian Government through the Department for the Arts and Cultural Development.

Consultant editor: Helen Bradbury
Designed by Brown Cow Design, Perth
Typeset in 10pt Palatino
Printed by Scott Four Colour Print, Perth

This book is dedicated to the
children of Jack and Lallie Akbar:
Mona Wilson, Shirly Wilson, Jimmy Akbar
and Johnny Akbar and their
descendants

A C K N O W L E D G E M E N T S

With deepest affection and greatest appreciation I offer my thanks to those people who gave me much of their precious time and advice during the writing of this book. Many thanks go particularly to the two Akbar daughters, Mrs Mona Wilson and Mrs Shirley Wilson, who showed me trust, generosity and goodness of heart and who never failed me when I sought their advice and cooperation.

I would like to acknowledge the assistance I was so kindly and trustingly given by some descendants of the Western Australian Wongai people: Laurel and Norman Cooper, Verna Voss, Les Wilson and Ranji MacIntyre.

Other Western Australians I would gratefully like to acknowledge are, from Perth: Margaret Morgan, John Priestley, Jenny Carter, Penny Tingsley, Tom Reynolds and Dr John Stanton at The University of Western Australia; from Esperance: Gordon and Jenny Leaney and Will and Marjorie Sharpe; and Dora and Claude Cotterill from Leonora.

In South Australia thanks go to Judy Lucas and Mona Tur.

A special thanks to Mr R. M. Williams who brought Mona Wilson and me together.

CONTENTS

INTRODUCTION

On 23 May 1928 an Afghan storekeeper named Jack Akbar and an Aboriginal woman named Lallie Matbar fled together from the eastern goldfields of Western Australia to South Australia so that they could be married. Their marriage was forbidden in their own State. From 1928 Mr and Mrs Akbar lived in South Australia in exile. To return would mean facing charges. The wording of the Bond held over Lallie distinctly discouraged her return to her people.

Jack and Lallie Akbar never told their four children about the Western Australia period of their lives. Their children never knew why their parents were so reluctant to talk about their past.

Sixty years later I commenced research into the lives of Lallie and Jack Akbar before their marriage when they lived in Western Australia. I had developed a vague curiosity about a South Australian Afghan family named Akbar as a result of researching, during the 1980s, the history, society and culture of the Afghan camelmen and their families. In 1987 the comprehensive manuscript I completed was published as the book titled, *In the Tracks of the Camelmen* (Angus and Robertson). One outcome of my research was a knowledge of the names of many Afghan families and of their family trees, and where these Afghan families tended to be located or to originate from. Why there were descendants of an Akbar family around Lyndhurst in the far north of South Australia had never been resolved in my investigations. This puzzle was irregular. Most of the surviving Afghan descendants, whom I had met, knew each other, either by being related by blood or marriage, or by having lived in the same 'Ghan' communities. Those that I interviewed knew very little about the family of the Akbar brothers of Lyndhurst. This was because the brothers Jimmy and Johnny Akbar rarely talked about their parents, their father's people, their mother's people or where they themselves grew up. When many of the Afghan descendants came together in 1986 to attend a rare reunion (called a 'charity' in the Afghan culture)[1] in Port Augusta in South Australia, my queries amongst them regarding the genealogy of the name of Akbar brought no resolution. The single piece of information I did glean from my enquiries was that there was a sister to the brothers living under a married name in Victoria. She had been collecting what details she could to attempt to resolve the mystery in her family's history.

The desire to both solve the mystery and complete my collection of Afghan genealogies compelled me to find the sister in Victoria. When I met Mrs Mona (nee Akbar) Wilson in 1987 near Bendigo, Victoria, I learned that she had been harbouring a number of questions about her parents for over fifty years. I was surprised to learn that what was for me technically a puzzle in my research was for the four Akbar descendants - Mona, her sister Mrs Shirley Wilson in Perth, Western Australia and their two brothers around Lyndhurst - an absence of family history and heritage that had been in the back of their minds all their adult years. Though Mona and her siblings remembered their parents with great affection, love, pride and respect, they were haunted by the absence of any explanation of why their 'long-suffering parents who gave [them] a loving and secure home and lifestyle said nary a word about all the trauma that led up to them establishing a home to rear a family'[2]. The only significant fact that Mona could give me as a starting point to commence research was that her Afghan father and Aboriginal mother came from the eastern goldfields in Western Australia. Neither of us had any preconceptions or theories about the circumstances of the lives of her parents before their marriage or what my research in Western Australia would uncover.

Chasing clues and suggestions around Perth, the capital city of Western Australia, led to a discovery about Mona's mother that stunned me. When I found a way to tell the descendants of Jack and Lallie Akbar of this discovery they were shocked. There existed a comprehensive, personal file on Lallie. It had been kept by the government for over fifty years and Lallie's children, now in their fifties, had never known of it.

Lallie's file sat amongst several hundreds of files on Aboriginal individuals which had been collated by the government over many years. At least until 1988 (when I learned of their existence) there would have been many descendants of the subjects of these files who did not know that a part of their genealogy, their personal heritage perhaps unknown, rested there. Only immediate descendants, who had to be aware of their existence, could apply for access to the file on their relative. The office responsible for these files provides an Aboriginal counsellor to support those people who are emotionally upset, distraught or need to grieve because of the information contained in those files. The files had been collated on these people, not because they were criminals, but because they were Aborigines.

The department which initiated the project of compiling files on Aboriginal people in Western Australia, the Aborigines Department, was established in 1898 when its predecessor, the Aborigines Protection Board, was abolished. The Aborigines Protection Board was founded in 1886 under the Aborigines Protection Act of that year. The Board's responsibilities included providing Aboriginal people with food and clothing, education of Aboriginal children and assistance in the preservation and well being of Aboriginal people. As Aboriginal affairs were the responsibility of the British Government, the Board reported directly to the Colonial Secretary. The Act of 1886 instituted the regulation and control over the entire Aboriginal population in Western Australia. The changes in 1898 transferred the responsibility of Aboriginal affairs to an Australian State government and the head administrator of the Aborigines Department, the Chief Protector of Aborigines (CPA), became responsible to the Premier of Western Australia.

A Royal Commission conducted in 1904 into the effectiveness of the administration of the Aborigines Department revealed many abuses of Aborigines. The Royal Commission perceived that the most effective way to deal with Aboriginal affairs was to provide for stricter control over this population. The Roth Royal Commission, named after its head Dr W.E. Roth, prompted the passing of the 1905 Aborigines Act which started a new phase in Aboriginal history. One provision of this Act increased the power of the Chief Protector of Aborigines over the lives of Aboriginal people. All Aboriginal children aged sixteen and under were made the wards of the Chief Protector, and the definition of 'native' in the terms of the Act was extended from referring to 'full-bloods' to include 'half-castes' as well. The Act also legalised the forced removal of Aboriginal children from their biological families and banned Aboriginal children from attending State schools. The keeping of files on Aboriginal people commenced after 1905 but was upgraded in 1915 to be more thorough.

In 1920 the Aborigines Department was divided into two parts. The Department of the North West was responsible for Aboriginal people living north of 25 degrees latitude and the Department of Aborigines and Fisheries was responsible for the Aboriginal people south of 25 degrees. When the Aborigines Department was re-established as one department in 1926 the collating of the Department's files on Aboriginal persons was attended to with renewed vigour. Lallie's file commenced in 1926.

A second Royal Commission in 1934 into Aboriginal affairs, headed by Mr M.D. Moseley, led to amendments to the 1905 Aborigines Act. It was retitled in 1936 as the Native Administration Act and the Aborigines Department was renamed the Department of Native Affairs. The Chief Protector of Aborigines was retitled the Commissioner of Native Affairs. The changes to the Act resulted in even greater control of the Aboriginal population. For instance, the Commissioner was made the legal guardian of Aboriginal children under the age of twenty-one, and the definition of 'native' was reviewed so as to include 'quadroons' as well as 'half-castes' and 'full bloods'.

In 1954 the Native Administration Act was replaced by the Native Welfare Act and the Department of Native Affairs was renamed the Department of Native Welfare. In 1972 the Native Welfare Act was repealed and the Department of Native Welfare was replaced by the Aboriginal Affairs Planning Authority (AAPA), with some of its functions being taken over by the newly created Department of Community Welfare[3]. The files on Aboriginal people are today housed in the Department of Community Services (DCS).

Perhaps the most notable personality in the history of the Aborigines Department in Western Australia was the man who in 1915 took up the office of Chief Protector of Aborigines, became the Commissioner of Native Affairs in 1937 and held the position until 1940, Auber Octavius Neville. Soon after his appointment he ordered the reorganisation of departmental records. Some of the earliest surviving files kept on individual Aboriginal people date back to 1910[4], but the purpose of the files took on a more fundamental role to the Aborigines Department when Mr Neville was reinstated as the overall head administrator of the department in 1926. In that year he argued the practicality of his having control of the files of the department that he was appointed to administer[5]. The files kept on the Aboriginal people were used to trace children who had been forcibly removed by police from their natural families, relocated into alien districts and interned into institutions 'for their own good'[6] or placed with foster families. The movements of these people would be monitored from the time they found employment and during their adult lives. The names of their children would be included in their file. It was intended that the removed children would forget their Aboriginal heritage and ultimately, particularly the fairer 'half-castes' and 'quadroons', would assimilate into the wider Commonwealth society. Many of these children did lose contact with and memory of their Aboriginal families. The practice of the forced removal of children from their biological mothers, which occurred on a national scale, left such a degree of emotional and psychological scarring in the Aboriginal population that it has endured in families over several generations. Some people who have received access to the file on their immediate relative in the Department of Community Services have been shocked or disturbed by what they have learned of their earlier lives, as well as the lives and circumstances of their natural parent(s). Some did not realise who their own people were until they saw the file[7].

Shirley and Mona applied for and obtained a copy of their mother's file. They needed time to deal with whatever they learned about their parents, or themselves, from the contents of the file, and to inform other family members of its existence and its contents. For them a gap in the family's history that had been a part of their lives was finally being filled. There could be details that could upset them. They were kind and trusting enough to allow my access to a copy.

As I researched beyond the file for what became essentially the biographies of Jack Akbar and the Aboriginal woman Lallie I learned of the social and political context in which Jack and Lallie's lives evolved before their marriage. The compilation of factual information from about 1900 to 1930 revealed the terrible treatment experienced by the indigenous population and the circumstances in which Lallie spent her infancy, childhood and teenage years. That treatment seemed to be acceptable in the broader context of the popular biological, evolutionary theories of the nineteenth to the early twentieth centuries up until the 1940s. To the well-educated, informed and widely read citizen of today it may seem inhumane and unjust.

The early years of the biographies of Jack and Lallie had to be researched after their deaths. What complicated the task further was that both persons came from communities in Australia which were not highly literate. The method I have used to account for their historical, social and political backgrounds is to piece together facts which provide substantiation and to support these with supposition. Facts were taken from the DCS file on Lallie, interviews of Aboriginal and non-Aboriginal people who knew Jack and Lallie and were part of their lives, the written works of academic people who work in the field of Aboriginal studies and interviews with some of these, my research on the history of the Afghan camelmen of Australia, and government and archival records and papers kept in the Australian Aboriginal Planning Authority (AAPA), the Battye Library and State Archives in Perth. By learning of the treatment of Aboriginal people, particularly Aboriginal women, and the difference in experiences of women categorised as 'full-blood' as opposed to 'part-Aboriginal', we can gain insight into what were the most likely determinants of Lallie's lifestyle, and how significantly her life changed when Jack Akbar decided to marry her.

Interviews with Aboriginal descendants had to be conducted with sensitivity, particularly when enquiries were made about infanticide, the experiences and feelings of the Aboriginal mothers who lost their babies and their children to the authorities, and sexual experiences and exploitation of Aboriginal women. I was informed by several Aboriginal women that 'there are some things that they do not talk about amongst themselves'[8].

In order to work towards eliminating travesties of justice in our past and to achieving reconciliation between Aboriginal and non-Aboriginal people, one of the modern requirements expressed by the Aboriginal people of Australia is that certain terms referring to them no longer be used. Such terms include 'half-caste', 'full-blood', 'coloured', 'mixed blood', 'quadroon', 'native', 'gin', 'fairer skin' or 'darker skin', 'tribal', 'black' and 'white', and 'part-Aboriginal'[9]. This vocabulary was part of the language that was popular with the British and other colonising settlers before and during the time of Jack and Lallie's lives, as well as reflecting the terminology of the years covered by Lallie's DCS file. It manifests the power felt by the Europeans over the indigenous people, the segregationist and assimilationist policies, the biological evolutionary theories, and the racist attitudes of those days. Today the Aboriginal people prefer all of these terms to be replaced with one, 'Aboriginal people'. In addition to this they have introduced into the wider Australian society some terminology of their own, of referring to people of Aboriginal descent: for example, *Nunga* (South Australia), *Nyungar* (South-West Western Australia) or *Koori* (used in the eastern States). Throughout the text I have attempted to avoid the word 'white' by using the terms 'colonist', 'Anglo-Saxon', 'European' or 'Caucasian'. Because the story of Jack and Lallie's early lives is set in the first quarter of the twentieth century words such as 'half-caste' or 'mixed blood', 'full blood', 'tribal', 'native' and 'part-Aboriginal' have been retained in the text to indicate verbatim the philosophies and attitudes of the wider Anglo-Saxon dominated society of their times, the holding of power by the dominant group and the lack of power of the minority groups.

This story focuses on an Aboriginal group in the eastern goldfields of Western Australia who have been referred to as the *Wongai*. The word 'Wongai' is not an Aboriginal word. It is derived from a combination of

Anglo-Saxon and Aboriginal words and loosely translated means 'a group of people'[10]. The Wongai were not of one language group, which was a traditional way of identifying the area from where Aboriginal people came. It consisted of human remnants of a number of language groups driven together by the Europeans who had forced them out of their traditional tribal areas.

It is understood that Lallie was born near Linden, an old mining settlement in the eastern goldfields. There was a ration depot for Aboriginal people at Linden, and those who tended to congregate around it over time were labelled by the police as the *Linden mob*[11]. They also were not all of the same language group. Because of the forced displacement of the Wongai from their tribal lands, the source of their identity and dignity, descendants of the groups will take a long time to retrieve their tribal knowledge and feelings of completeness.

The compilation of this story was a revelation for one family and raised their awareness of their cultural heritage. For the wider community of this country it provides a lesson. To understand the truth of Lallie's life is to learn about the experience of European colonisation from the point of view of the conquered, subjugated, indigenous people. Until recently the thoughts, experiences and memories of Aborigines were neither genuinely nor academically sought. Only now is their 'side of the story', being recorded and made public.

This new comprehension of the discrepancies between 'history' and 'the truth' may induce us all to think about ourselves and the complexity of our cultural heritage. Remembering to think about the other person's side of the story could produce a more tolerant, humane Australia.

Pamela Rajkowski, 1994.

Jack Akbar as a young man before he proposed marriage to the Linden girl, Lallie. Photo courtesy of Mona Wilson.

CHAPTER ONE

The pursuit of marriage

The quest of Jack Akbar, an Afghan, to marry Lallie Matbar, an Aboriginal woman, was intended as a genuine act of commitment. He had in mind the well being of Lallie whom he had admired for some time. However, his decision to actively seek authority for their marriage drew into their lives the forces and factors that had created over a few decades the disadvantage of both their races in Australia. Their choice to marry, to uphold an institution valued by their own cultures, the Moslem faith and Aboriginal beliefs, and by the Christian faith of the colonists, altered the course of both their lives. To understand how their relationship made their lives take an extraordinary turn requires an understanding of the circumstances impacting on their people before, as well as during, the time Jack sought permission to marry Lallie.

There is no literature on Lallie's infancy and childhood. By learning about aspects of Aboriginal society and experiences from the turn of the nineteenth century, in particular, aspects relevant to women, an understanding may be gained of how Lallie's life was likely to unfold and how Jack's wish to marry her changed its direction. Lallie's birth occurred in times of tremendous upheaval for her people. The non-Aboriginal people who commenced, from about the 1880s, to populate the country which had been inhabited by Lallie's people for tens of thousands of years came to this western colony in various occupations but all to settle. They came as miners, prospectors, sandalwood pullers, wood cutters, road builders and railway workers, as merchants and entrepreneurs. They were attracted to the lands of Lallie's people particularly by the prospect of finding gold. The earliest discoveries of gold in this colony had been west of the lands of Lallie's people. By 1888 gold was gathered in the Yilgarn district, of which Southern Cross was the chief town, and in the Pilbara goldfields. In 1891 gold mining commenced in the Murchison goldfields where the chief town was Cue. During the 1890s several, significant discoveries of gold occurred east of Southern Cross within the tribal lands of Lallie's people. Their proximity lead to the geographical definition of that region as the 'eastern goldfields'. The settlements of Coolgardie (1892), Kalgoorlie (1893) which developed into the regional centre of the goldfields, Broad Arrow (1896), Kanowna (1897), Wiluna (1897), Laverton, Menzies (1894), Mount Margaret goldfield (1897), Mount Malcolm (1899), Malcolm (1897), Mount Morgans, Linden, Burtville (1898), Leonora, Murrin Murrin, Yerilla (1896), Kurnalpi (1893), Edjudina, Yarri, Bulong (1899) and Pinjin sprung up where for tens of thousands of years previously Aboriginal men had hunted wildlife, Aboriginal women had gathered native edible vegetation, families had walked between waterholes (called 'gnamma holes' by the Aborigines) and Aboriginal groups had held their sacred ceremonies in sacred sites.

The colonists compounded the extension of their government's culture into the Western Australian goldfields by the laying of a railway over 560 kilometres from the State's capital coastal city, Perth, through Southern Cross to Coolgardie by March 1896, and over a further 40 kilometres to Kalgoorlie by September of that year. A branch line was laid from Kalgoorlie to Laverton, a further distance of about 350 kilometres. The railway line facilitated the invasion of the gold seekers and their support services into the traditional areas of the eastern goldfields' indigenous people.

Another group to entrench the Anglo-Saxon society in the interior of Western Australia was the pastoralists. These people were attracted from Great Britain by the offer of cheap leases of land and so took up very extensive pastoral holdings. They introduced domestic cattle to provide fresh meat to the miners and other settlers, and sheep for the export of wool to Great Britain and Europe.

The pastoralists' introduced stock bred by the millions, and in turn consumed millions of hectares of native vegetation. As well as being a food source for the indigenous people, the native vegetation was the traditional food supply for native animals which in turn provided sustenance for the indigenous people. The 'bush tucker' for Aboriginal people included witchetty grubs, goanna, lizard, kangaroo, and emu

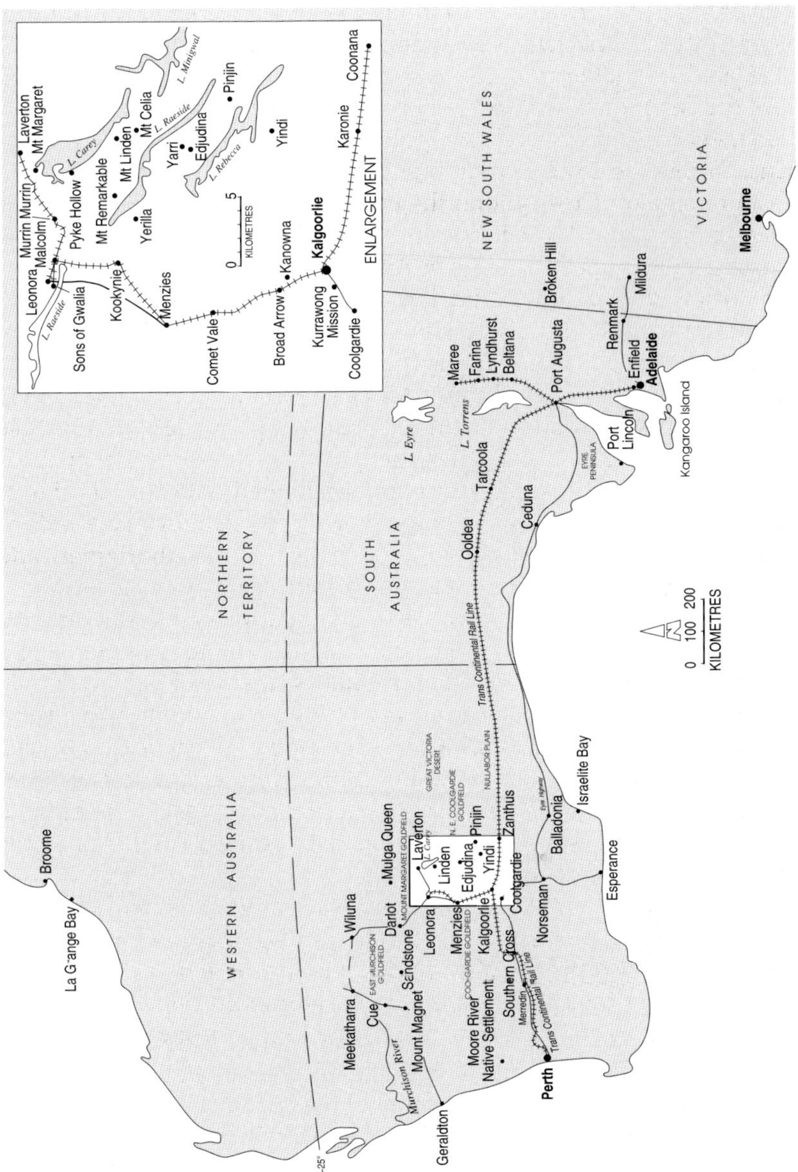

Western Australia, featuring the area of Lallie's birth, and South Australia.

eggs. When rabbits, which consumed much native grass, were introduced by the colonists the Aboriginal people learned to eat these[1]. The diminution of the native vegetation forced the Aboriginal people to seek alternative, supplementary sources of sustenance.

The pastoralists' occupation reduced access for the Aboriginal people to much of their traditional sources of drinking water. As water from the huge sub-artesian basin located towards the centre of the Australian continent did not extend to the eastern goldfields, both native wildlife and the Aboriginal people depended for their drinking water on the rare sources of precious surface water such as gnamma holes and soaks. The pastoralists fenced in most of these water sites as they occupied their leases, and drove Aboriginal people away from them so that their cattle would not be too frightened to drink at the waterholes or soaks. Aboriginal people during the nineteenth and early twentieth centuries were regularly driven away from their precious drinking sites and their hunting grounds by the 'whips and chains and the gun' of the police and pastoralists[2].

The colonising authorities understood their tasks as ones of economic progress, of development of the colonies and expansion of the largest empire the world had ever seen, and of the Anglo-Saxon civilisation, rather than the invasion of another culture and occupation of its lands. What was not visible to them were the many ways in which their 'progress' contributed to the detriment of the natural landscape and the destruction of the indigenous people. The occupation by the British empire-builders of the traditional lands of the Australian Aboriginal people initiated their disintegration as a culture and a race. Deprived of their traditional food and water sources, Lallie's ancestors and contemporaries had to combat hunger and starvation. The place of their birth gave Aboriginal people physical and spiritual life. By removing them from their religious and birth sites the colonists severed their links to their spiritual and ancestral heritage. Aspects of their culture such as language, art, dance and music deteriorated, only to survive in remnants. Many Aboriginal people, as did Lallie in her own life time, had to struggle with the disintegration of their families and tribal groups[3]. These were some of the circumstances which were part of the experiences of Lallie in her earlier years. She was born in a time when her people were reduced to the situation of having to resort to a range of options to acquire food, stave off hunger, seek ways and devise desperate measures to hold their families together and be safe.

The date of Lallie's birth has been calculated by examining details in the file maintained on her by the Aborigines Department of Western Australia from 1926 to 1970[4]. Lallie was born between 1908 and 1910 to a 'full-blood'[5] mother named Tjirrgulu whose tribal group had settled in the Linden-Laverton district of the eastern goldfields[6]. It is most likely that it was the local police constabulary out on patrol making further enquiries into the event of Lallie's bush birth who calculated that the nearest settlement to Lallie's birth was Linden, and for their records noted it as such. This settlement was in the North Coolgardie district and the nearest rail stop was Murrin Murrin. It was 113 kilometres from Laverton, the largest centre and railhead town of the district. The proposition that Linden was the place of Lallie's birth was supported by Ranji McIntyre, an elderly full-blood Aboriginal resident of Kurrawang Mission situated midway between Kalgoorlie and Coolgardie, and a descendant of the same tribal group as Lallie and her mother. He knew Lallie and her mother Tjirrgulu in the 1910s and the 1920s and learned then that Lallie was born near Linden, if not around Burtville[7].

The physical environment of Lallie's birth was a creek bed in her mother's traditional land and place of her ancestral spirits. Her mother was also born in a creek bed[8]. It was valued by Aboriginal people that their children were born on or as close as possible to their tribal land. The safest place for the birth of Tjirrgulu's daughter would be amongst her own people. After 1905 Aboriginal people were banned from the colonists' hospitals[9], and they also had a fear that if they were admitted for a delivery there was a chance that their baby might be taken from them.

As a manifestation of their upheaval and social fragmentation, an increasing number of Aboriginal mothers did not have a husband to assist them in the protection and feeding of their children. Tjirrgulu was a single mother with two children for whom she had to find food and whom she had to keep safe. Lallie's brother was, like herself, born of a non-Aboriginal father. Calculations made from entries in the DCS file on this Aboriginal male record his name as 'Snowy' and that he was born around Burtville[10] about 31 kilometres from Laverton. Single mothers of part-Aboriginal[11] children, like Tjirrgulu, had to find food by moving between two cultures, seeking charity in the colonists' settlements when not accompanying other families on the traditional nomadic routes.

The traditional migratory route of the Burtville-Linden Aboriginal group kept essentially to the south of the Kalgoorlie-Laverton rail branch. The northern point was Ida H, a mining settlement to the south of Laverton. Tjirrgulu's people circled Lake Carey and travelled southward to Burtville, the Granites and Linden, then returned northward passing Pikes Hollow to arrive at Morgans[12]. Another common route of movement of this group was from the Mount Margaret and Morgans area to Kurnalpi via Tindin[13]. The Linden-Burtville tribe would meet the Kanowna and Karonie tribes for corroborees[14]. Many years later, by the 1950s, as most mining settlements in the eastern goldfields became deserted and the lives and culture of Lallie's people was changed more by the missionaries and authorities, the Burtville-Linden descendants migrated to settle around Menzies and Kalgoorlie.

There were a number of reasons for the nomadic tradition of Aboriginal people. Their families migrated according to the seasonal cycle of plants and wildlife and availability of water. They would decamp and walk 70 to 90 kilometres at certain times annually to assemble with other members of their language group for corroborees and other ceremonies. They would visit religious sites or their totem places.

By the turn of the twentieth century the Aboriginal people of the goldfields had additional reasons for moving about the bush, and these were the product of their interaction with the European settlers. One was the loss of their access to traditional sources of drinking water. Driven away from water sources by the pastoralists, Aborigines congregated more and more in places where the government had established wells, tanks and water condensers. Another reason for migration was the lack of employment offered to Aboriginal men. They wandered with their families from one mining settlement to another, camping on the fringes of places such as Mount Margaret, Kalgoorlie, Linden, Morgans, Murrin Murrin, Burtville, Laverton and Leonora. Some Aboriginal people camped close to rubbish dumps, such as on the outskirts of Laverton, to scavenge for food[15]. These 'fringe dwellers' obtained food by various means, such as begging, pilfering and even by bartering their women[16].

Another reason for Aboriginal people moving to and camping on the fringe of settlements like Linden, Burtville and Laverton was to use the ration depots located there. The Aboriginal people who fitted the criteria of needing government rations had to be seen to be 'utterly destitute and incapable of seeking their own livelihood'[17]. This was the situation in the goldfields with many full-blood and half-caste[18] people and where employment for Aboriginal people was limited. The rations distributed for adults at the depots were '16 pounds of flour, five and a quarter pounds of meat, one and a half pounds of sugar, and one and a half ounces of tea, plus an occasional stick of tobacco. Blankets and clothing issued to Aboriginal people remained the property of Her Majesty'[19].

By the 1910s, the childhood years of Lallie, her people were dislocated, hungry, finding it very difficult to get employment and banned from many places by the laws of the colonists. Increasingly dependent on the colonists' gestures, the Aboriginal people were forced into acquiring food by resorting to a dual economy. One source of food was based on hunting and gathering in the bush. The Aboriginal people who tended to retain their nomadic practice were labelled by the colonists as 'bush natives'[20]. However, with the occupation of the land by pastoralists it became more difficult to retain their hunting and gathering skills. The other source was to move to settlements and camp on their fringes and from there enter the towns. As fringe dwellers they became more dependent on the odd opportunity for employment, on favours and charity provided by the Europeans. Both bush natives and fringe dwellers needed the government distributions of rations. The lifestyle of regularly decamping and living on the fringe of settlements, induced by the colonists' dispossession of these people from their traditional hunting land and their legislation to keep Aboriginal people out of their settlements, was viewed by the Anglo-Saxon colonists as demeaning, criminal and offensive. The Aboriginal people themselves were regarded as 'a nuisance, as a degraded remnant population'[21].

Another aspect of the disintegration of Aboriginal culture was the loss of the traditional way of giving people names. Their tribal-given name was used less and their colonist-given name was used more. By the early twentieth century government officials were attempting to be more precise in their record-keeping of the names of Aboriginal children and adults. The more thorough officials provided the indigenous name of the Aboriginal person as well as their colonist-given name. However, the spelling by the officials of the tribal-given name was often not consistent and was distorted by their various arrangements of the letters or syllables. The tribal name of Lallie's mother was spelt several ways. The missionary couple who managed the Mount Margaret mission from the 1920s to the 1940s attempted to retain the sound of Lallie's mother's name and called her 'Tjirrgulu'[22]. The police who monitored her attendance at the Linden ration depot entered her name on their check list as 'Chilgoo' and 'Chilgooloo'[23]. Her name was anglicised and sometimes she was referred to by the police as 'Polly'[24]. Lallie's tribal-given name was 'Nilba'[25], but when she was amongst the missionaries, the police or was referred to in reports by the staff of the Aborigines Department, her Christian-given name was used. Another method of substituting Aboriginal names was to give them a nickname. The nickname could be that of an inanimate object such as the colour or texture of flour or a quartpot mug[26]. Rodolphe Schenk, who managed the mission settlement at Mount Margaret out of Morgans from 1921, had a practice of giving Aboriginal men Anglo-Saxon names. This was because the pastoralists in the eastern goldfields would not employ an Aboriginal man who only provided his tribal name[27]. It has not been possible to uncover the Aboriginal name of Lallie's brother. He is remembered by his English given name 'Snowy' which compares him to the colour of snow or flour. This practice of altering or substituting Aboriginal names contributed to the denigration of the Aboriginal person[28].

Another aspect of the disintegration of Aboriginal families was the absence or anonymity of the non-Aboriginal biological father. Lallie's file contains two possible maiden surnames for Lallie, suggesting that her natural non-Aboriginal father was not confirmed. One of these surnames was reported on a form filled in by Lallie in her later years to claim maternity allowance for one of her own children. The maiden surname recorded for Lallie was 'Bradley'[29]. It is apparent that this surname was adhered to only by her brother Snowy, who is regularly referred to as Snowy Bradley. There is no evidence that Lallie used that surname herself elsewhere. It was entered on Lallie's file that Snowy's father was 'Arthur Burghley, now deceased'[30]. No details on this person were uncovered. It could also be a case of an official transferring a name between forms and not observing the spelling accurately, thus reforming the name.

The maiden surname that is used most often in Lallie's file to address her is 'Matbar'. Investigation into the origins of this surname did not reveal any evidence of a man with such a surname immigrating to Australia. It has been proposed by staff of the Department of Community Services who look after these files today that 'Matbar' is a distorted spelling of the surname 'Akbar' who is the man she later was associated with and married[31].

The lack of clarity about who was their biological father is partly reflected by the details in Lallie's and Snowy's DCS files suggesting that their fathers were two different men and thus they were step-siblings. However, details gleaned from interviews with Aboriginal descendants lead to the proposition that they had the same biological father. In Snowy's file another name is given for his father, 'Tommy Lowe', and there is a range of information on this man. Tommy Lowe, the owner of Mount Remarkable pastoral station in the north-west of the goldfields, is supposed to have raised Snowy for a number of years[32]. Gordon Leaney, now a retired missionary, knew Snowy Bradley during the 1920s and could recall some details about where Snowy spent some of his childhood. According to Leaney Mrs Lowe started raising Snowy, and when he was old enough to be employed he worked for some years for Tommy Lowe at Mount Remarkable station[33]. It is known that Snowy was not always with Tjirrgulu and Lallie in the bush and that he lived with some non-Aboriginal people for several years before 1926, including spending some time around Laverton[34]. In 1928, when he was stated to be 25 years old, his name was recorded as 'Snowy Lowe' and his address was given as 'c/o Mr Lowe of Yundamindra'[35]. As Snowy was called for a while by Mr and Mrs Lowe's name it is possible that that couple treated Snowy as their foster child.

Ranji McIntyre came to understand in his earlier years that 'Tommy Charlie', which was the name used by the Aboriginal people when talking about Tommy Lowe, was the biological father to both Snowy and to Lallie. He recalled that Tommy Lowe was in Burtville in about 1908, which was about the time of Lallie's birth and the place of Snowy's birth. Ranji claimed that when Tommy Lowe died he left half his station to 'Uncle Brad', the Aboriginal people's term of respect for Snowy Bradley[36].

The alien system of naming and labelling individual or groups of Aboriginal people extended to the loss of the names of many language or tribal groups. Since this new system was associated with how they acquired food, the Aboriginal people themselves became accustomed to using it. Aborigines named on a ration depot list became referred to by the police, who managed that depot, and the nearest missionaries, as that group or 'mob'. The names of Tjirrgulu and Lallie, who remained bush natives while Snowy was being raised on a station, were placed on the list at the Linden ration depot. They became known as members of the 'Linden mob'. The wider Aboriginal group to which the Linden mob was identified in the eastern goldfields had lost their original languages and had evolved their own language to make a common one that they could all understand. They were given the name

'Wongai', which loosely translated as 'a group of people'. This term was also not an Aboriginal word[37].

Before and during the years of Lallie's childhood it seems that Aboriginal children were menaced with laws, risks and dangers from the time of their birth, particularly if the child was a half-caste or of 'mixed blood'[38]. The threats to their life or future came from the societies of both their non-Aboriginal father and their Aboriginal mother. Most often mothers of children conceived by a non-Aboriginal father were deserted or disowned by that man. Their desertion put them at a disadvantage, particularly when they were in an advanced state of pregnancy and could not so easily obtain food for themselves. These women had only their own people in the bush for reliance on sustenance, care and support.

Amongst her mother's people children of mixed blood were not as highly valued as full-blood children[39]. Full-blood children were perceived to have the right to be given the knowledge of ancient beliefs, laws, traditions and customs. Their education on how to find food and water and distribute it in the family was provided by their full-blood father, a skilled hunter, and their full-blood mother, a competent gatherer of seeds, roots, berries, eggs, small reptiles and marsupials. On reaching puberty these children were shown the location of the sacred and corroboree sites. Full-blood children were taken deeper into the stories of the spiritual origins of themselves, their people and the elements of their environment, be given access to certain information that part-Aboriginal children had lost a right to know. When food sources or water became scarce in the bush, as in drought times, the full-blood parents would go with their children deeper into the bush, closer to the edge of the western desert or the spinifex country where they were apt at feeding their children and themselves for long periods of time.

When food sources for half-caste children and their unmarried Aboriginal mother were scarce they did not have a hunter to find sustenance for them, or who could take them deeper into the country to seek out traditional game food. Hunger would drive the single mother with her part-Aboriginal children into less safe settlements where they would beg for food or scavenge until the mounted police hounded them out. If there were no donations of food, sometimes the children or parents resorted to stealing.

The distinction between the full-blood and the mixed-blood children was maintained by the elders. These were generally middle-aged men who had the responsiblities of representing, interpreting and enforcing the laws. They held council meetings to discuss matters that affected their people[40]. They made communal decisions as well as wielded the power to enforce social sanctions[41]. They supervised the raising of the full-blood and half-caste children, as ancient laws and traditional practices had to be applied to them differently. The elders believed that a part-Aboriginal child did not have the spiritual connections that a child with a tribal father had[42], and thus broke the family's link with their ancestral spirits. The authorities and the missionaries further interfered with this spiritual link by preventing some Aboriginal children from undergoing initiation rites, and arranging the baptism of many of these children. It was the view of the elders that uninitiated and baptized children lost their rightful heritage[43]. It is most likely that these children were not told all the stories of the Dreaming and their origins, their people's ways, and were not shown all the sites of religious and sacred ceremonies. This compounded the disintegration of their people's culture and heritage.

It was considered that a female born of two full-blood parents would be the better wife for an Aboriginal man. Full-blood women were able to provide the more substantial and consistent food supplements. They were the more dependable providers of food for their families[44]. These females were more ammenable to travelling with their husbands. They knew about the tribe's traditions and laws and why their husband needed to travel traditional routes. Full-blood women were more familiar with the ceremonial and totem sites. They would be less likely to reject or run away from their husbands.

It was found to be more difficult to arrange marriages of the children who were part-Aboriginal. There were implications which the elders had to consider. Each tribal group had distinctly delineated family structures. A girl would be given to the man with whom, according to the process of delineation, she would be most appropriately partnered. By this arranging of marriages the social order, cohesion and stability of the tribal group was maintained. The children of Caucasian and Asiatic fathers did not quite blend into the delineation. They fractured the fibres that knitted and maintained social order and cohesion. They threatened the continuity and survival of the tribal group and its culture. Though accepted and loved by their mother's people it was more difficult at times to find an appropriate spouse for the part-Aboriginal children. In adhering to her people's ways Tjirrgulu hoped that the elders would find her part-Aboriginal daughter a husband.

The missionaries' attitude to marriage further frustrated the Aboriginal people's attempts to arrange marriages the way they believed was most suited to the survival of their culture and race. Missionaries viewed marriage as an act of choice which could be influenced by the romantic notion of love. They advocated that an Aboriginal girl could marry whom she chose. Aboriginal girls who were raised on a mission would be encouraged to consider not going with a tribal husband. Often missionaries would not release a girl to go with her people if they knew she was to be married to an older man and she was at what was deemed a suitable age[45]. It was known that the older men beat their younger wives. Amongst the Aboriginal tribes a marriage based on Christian influence upset the lineage structure and the guidelines on which arrangement of partners was made[46].

Because Lallie was of mixed blood there was a chance in her infancy that she, like other half-caste children, would be allowed to die. The decision by the elders to allow any one of their babies to die, termed by the colonists as the practice of 'infanticide', was based traditionally on economics. While the Christian colonists labelled the practice of infanticide as immoral, heathen and murderous, the Aboriginal people perceived it as a desperate means to preserve their physical and cultural survival and to maintain a balance between the human population and a delicate natural environment. The full-blood people inhabiting the more arid interior were conscious of the limited natural resources that existed in their lands. By practising population control they maintained the regeneration potential of vegetation and wildlife and the quality of their water. When there was a drought, or if a man had too many children at one time to feed, or if the number of children slowed down a nomadic tribe from getting to another area where food or water would be available, rather than over-hunt or over-harvest native vegetation and thus put pressure on the limited flora and fauna of an area, a few new born infants could be selected for infanticide. Which baby died was never a random choice or an irresponsible act. Sometimes babies who were born with some physical weakness or disability were selected to die.

The increase in the number of births of part-Aboriginal children made the Aboriginal population in some areas disproportionate to the resource base in their natural environment. The pressure of this was felt particularly when the 'bush natives' were forced to retreat from police in pursuit to the more semi-arid desert fringe and spinifex country for safety and food, or when there was a shortage of native wildlife, as in drought times. Having two or three small children to either carry or hold made it more difficult to outrun the police should they be chased out of a settlement or pursued into the bush. By the early years of the twentieth century, the basis for elders giving consideration to infanticide was altered to include criteria additional to economics. The consideration of infanticide, either before or after birth, was more noticed in areas where Aboriginal people had a significant degree of contact with Europeans[47].

The contemporary government officer in charge of Aborigines, the Chief Protector of Aborigines, who travelled the State intermittently to make personal observations and inspections of his indigenous charges, collected details on the practice of infanticide. He recorded that more often half-caste girls were chosen for infanticide than were half-caste boys. The male infants were regarded as having more value, particularly after their initiation, than were girls entering womanhood[48]. So, for Aboriginal infants like Lallie, who was born as a female and a half-caste, there was greater risk of death.

Explanations for why the Aboriginal mothers did not act to prevent the number of infant deaths among babies of non-Aboriginal fathers have surfaced through interviews with the Wongai women descendants now settled around Menzies and Kalgoorlie. Though the practice of cohabitation by the Aborginal female with a non-Aboriginal male, which produced children of mixed blood, had been sanctioned and advised by the elders and was not of the choosing of the Aboriginal female, the females concerned were still conscious of the ancient ways which determined which female should be given as a wife to which male. They were mindful of how more valued a full-blood child was with regard to the continuation of their tribal group and culture. These young mothers felt that infants of European blood attested openly to their act of dishonouring ancient beliefs and traditions. Yet they could not protest or prevent their involvement in activities with which they did not agree, such as cohabitation or the selection of their part-Aboriginal baby for infanticide. 'The young Aboriginal women or the children in those times had no choice', stated one of these women, named Laurel Cooper who, like Lallie, grew up as a child under such circumstances[49]. If the man with whom they slept was not their promised husband, was not tribal, or was a man with whom they had been forced to have intercourse, these women felt that in some way they had offended the laws of their people. As well as feeling they had no right to protest, they felt shame about their behaviour and their children who were an outcome of these acts[50].

Though the mothers of part-Aboriginal children generally felt it inappropriate for them to protest against the practice of infanticide, not all children who were selected for infanticide, did die. Some Aboriginal mothers found a way to save their child. When Laurel Cooper was an older child her mother told her that she was supposed to leave her, when an infant, to die. Laurel's mother could not do that and so fled her people with her baby daughter to be away from them for some time, thus ensuring Laurel's survival[51].

Mothers like Tjirrgulu of daughters like Lallie and Laurel had to be alert constantly to the safety of their children throughout their childhood. After infancy, the main threat to the safety of a half-caste child particularly was from its biological father's society. It was a constant fear that if the police sighted, or caught up to the children of bush natives, they could be seized and forcibly removed from the district, probably for ever. The police raids compounded the need for Lallie and her people to maintain their nomadic lifestyle.

The police raids increased significantly after the passing of the 1905 Aborigines Act. Before that time the definition of 'native' used in legislation was in reference to 'full-blood' indigenous persons. According to the 1905 Act the definition of 'native' was extended to include half-castes who habitually lived or associated with Aboriginal people, and all half-caste children aged sixteen and under[52]. This amendment to the definition 'native' facilitated the Aborigines Department's practice of forced removal of Aboriginal children from their families in the bush, or from circumstances that were considered to leave the child in neglect. The police did not consider their actions to be denigrading, though the term they used to apprehend the children, to 'catch' them[53], was comparable to catching animals by trapping them. Whether the child was in neglect was a subjective opinion, but it was a criterion used to make it convenient to choose the half-caste more so than the full-blood child for removal. Though the 1905 Aborigines Act covered full-blood and part-Aboriginal children, over time the forced removal of children focused less on full-blood children and more on part-Aboriginal children like Lallie and Laurel. The police raids were the main medium for the effective removal of many Wongai children from the eastern goldfields.

The Aboriginal children of the eastern goldfields who were seized by the police were transported to a native settlement hundreds of kilometres away on the Moore River, to the north of Perth. The intention of the government was to use this institution to separate the part-Aboriginal children from their Aboriginal people, give them a new culture and religion and prepare them for assimilation into the European society. It was intended that these children would go from the institution to productive employment and be assimilated into the European culture.

It was also intended that the 'inmates', the term used by the Aborigines Department to refer to the young residents of Moore River Native Settlement, remain geographically isolated. There was discouragement of visitors who could remind them of their cultural and family origins. Visitors had to acquire written permission from the Chief Protector of Aborigines in Perth before visiting there, and inmates had to gain written permission from the same authority to leave the settlement[54]. Removal to Moore River Native Settlement became a real fear and ever present threat. Aboriginal parents, particularly those without partners, would do all they could to avoid the apprehension and institutionalisation of their children.

The Wongai were aware that the police used other methods as well as police raids to capture their part-Aboriginal children. When ration depots were open the police could observe the Aboriginal families who came out from the cover of the bush. When collecting their portion of rations the adults would have to appear with the child whose name was on the list. This exposed the children who were fairer than full-blood, or a child who was not listed, to the police. The police would move either immediately, attempting a surprise raid, or at their convenience to catch the child[55]. Receiving rations became laced with fear for single mothers with part-Aboriginal children. Tjirrgulu must have experienced several times the fear of losing her daughter when she walked into the Linden depot to collect their rations.

Police also used informants in their efforts to locate children for removal. Pastoralists, miners, storekeepers, other itinerant workers or Afghan camelmen who worked their camel strings throughout the goldfields were in a position to observe Wongai groups when they passed by mining camps seeking jobs or food, pastoral homesteads or along bush tracks or old mining tracks. Details of the Wongai could be collected so as to supply the police with enough information for them to catch the child or children they were seeking. It would be particularly hurtful and confusing for the Wongai people when they learned that the informants who were collaborating with the police were other Wongai[56].

Over decades of experiencing police raids the Wongai developed a range of strategies to seclude their children from the view of police or their informants. The Wongai had become familiar with certain places where they could hide their children. One of these places was a group of caves in the hills beyond Laverton[57]. These were invisible from the plains below and only the Wongai knew of their location and existence.

Another place was the spinifex country. This was beyond the hills of Laverton and stretched from 40 kilometres north-east of Laverton and as far eastward as Alice Springs in the Northern Territory[58]. Aboriginal people knew which plant and animal was edible and where water sources were located. Women converted seeds such as black seed and wanderi seed with a grinding stone into flour, added water to the flour, mixed the two ingredients together with a piece of bark and made a dough. The dough would be patted into a round shape and baked in a camp fire[59].

In the spinifex country the children were free to play with siblings and other children of their group and learned the customs and beliefs of their Aboriginal relatives. Though they lived in exile in their own country the children in the spinifex were well beyond the reach of the police and the Moore River net.

Laurel was a girl in Tjirrgulu's tribal group who spent her first few years growing up in the spinifex country before she and her mother rejoined the Linden group when she become a friend of Lallie. Laurel's skin colour was fairer than that of Lallie. Laurel's mother was known as both Yundabrah and Adelaide Johnston. Adelaide, like Tjirrgulu, had two Aboriginal parents and they had taught her how to gather food and feed a family. When Adelaide became pregnant to a colonist she gave birth to a particularly fair girl. The tribal name of this girl is not known, but she was called Laurel. Adelaide was afraid constantly that the police would learn of her and would want to catch her. Driven by both that fear, and the potential for her daughter to be selected by the elders for infanticide, Adelaide took baby Laurel into the spinifex country. Unlike Lallie, Laurel spent the first five years of her life living safely and freely[60].

The Wongai adults used tricks to conceal their children when they had insufficient warning of the approach of the police and could not make a head start to the caves or the spinifex country. One trick was to cover their fairer children's skin with a skin-darkening agent. Sandalwood kernels were crushed, made into a paste and mixed in charcoal. When this paste was rubbed onto the child's body the charcoal would provide the darkener and the oil seeping out of the crushed kernels would help the paste to adhere to the child's skin. The colour gave the child the appearance of a full-blood. When Adelaide brought her five-year-old daughter out of the spinifex country the first skin darkening agent she could procur was black boot polish. She rubbed it all over Laurel, then put her out in the sun to dry it out[61]. Many mothers like Adelaide and Tjirrgulu found that boot polish was not as effective as the crushed sandalwood paste. When the boot polish dried out it tended to crack and flake off.

The resourceful, anxious mothers like Tjirrgulu and Adelaide had other tricks. Tjirrgulu rubbed ashes over the face and arms of her daughter when she was very young[62]. Laurel remembered her mother telling her when she was a little girl that it would be better for her to sit with her back to the camp fire. That way the flames would not highlight the fair skin of her face[63].

When the Wongai people came out of the bush to visit their ration depot, a mining camp or rail or road settlement, a ploy of concealment was to put the smaller children into hessian sugar bags. Once the child was in the bag the opening would be closed and the mother or adult would then sling the bag over their shoulders or on their back and behave as if the contents were inert[64]. To make the act more convincing for the colonists or their police, an Aboriginal adult would throw the full sugar bag about or drop it, apparently carelessly, to the ground. The children were taught that when they were put into these bags, it was crucial that they did not make a noise[65].

Another way that mothers or teenage girls concealed the smaller part-Aboriginal children was to hide them under the long skirts of their dresses. The little children would cling closely to the body of the woman protecting them and attempt to tread in rhythym with their feet. Tjirrgulu and Adelaide both resorted to this method when their girls were small[66]. Another ruse Adelaide employed was to cover herself with a big blanket, then place her little girl against her body under it[67].

By the early 1920s the Wongai around Linden and Laverton gained another option to keep their part-Aboriginal children from police capture and relocation. In 1921 a mission had been opened in the Wongai district near the old Mount Margaret mining site, which was about 113 kilometres from Laverton and 10 kilometres from Morgans. The local indigenous people had their suspicions of the missionary's intentions and the mission's impact on their society and culture. The missionary who managed the settlement was telling them that he wanted the parents to leave their children with him. He too wanted to separate the children from their families but in a way that was different to the police. Over time the Wongai noticed that the mission was not raided as often as the bush and so they weighed up the advantages of the mission near Morgans for them. If the colonists were going to take their children from them the Wongai children would be closer to them on the Mount Margaret mission than at Moore River Native Settlement. To put their children there would at least keep them in their district. The missionary allowed the parents to visit their children and talk with them, though he strongly discouraged them from removing their children from the mission. When Adelaide returned from the spinifex country with little Laurel she remained worried about Laurel being removed from the district altogether should the police finally catch her. Adelaide was one of the parents to leave her daughter at the mission. Tjirrgulu did not choose to take her daughter to the mission and Lallie remained a bush native.

Lallie and Laurel did not see much of each other. As a bush native Lallie's mother was on guard regularly to maintain her daughter's safety and liberation. When she became an adolescent Lallie would have to resort to means to find food that the elders would direct her to, and she may have had to face forms of violence towards herself. The risk that she could be removed forever from her people stayed with her. As an Aboriginal child on the mission Laurel was more fortunate in that she and her mother would no longer have to fear her forced removal or her participation in cohabitation. Later Laurel married Norman Cooper who was an Aborigine raised on a mission[68].

Many goldfields Aboriginal women alive today hold memories from their youth about the hurt, suffering, sadness and loss they and their people experienced in the 1910s and 1920s. The experience of the Aboriginal people of colonisation has not been fully accounted. One can wonder, as most probably the Aboriginal mothers do privately, about what became of the children who were forcibly removed, institutionalised, fostered or adopted out and did not find their way back to their Aboriginal families. Very little is known about the burial sites and rites of the children lost to infanticide. As many Aboriginal tribes had a belief that the dead should not be talked about, infanticide is one of the subjects not freely or openly discussed amongst the descendants of Lallie's people. The implications for Aboriginal people are that there is most likely much grieving and searching for family members to be done, and feelings of 'incompleteness' and 'not belonging' to be resolved.

The traditional rules about marriage amongst the Wongai would more likely apply to Lallie than to Laurel. The Aboriginal traditions still functioning in Lallie's adolescent years included rules regarding to whom females would become partnered, and the females had no choice about these arrangements. As a wife they were given to the tribal man to whom they were promised. One of the elders' roles was to work out, after a child was born and its sex identified, who would be the most appropriate person to whom to promise that boy or girl. Such decisions had social motives and were governed by certain social rules[69]. They were aimed at keeping the family lineages intact and thus preserve the cohesion of the tribal group, maintain the links to the ancestral spirits and keep safe the sacred and ceremonial sites for which that tribal group was responsible.

There were also economic motives[70]. An arranged marriage guaranteed that, in the long term, each family, or each woman, had a man who could hunt for them and provide the family group with substantial sustenance. By giving a younger wife with agile legs to an older man[71] who could not run, dodge, see or hear as quickly as he used to, his well being was provided for[72]. The relationship between an Aboriginal man and an Aboriginal woman was regarded as a practical arrangement. In camp the wife prepared the food she had gathered for her hunter husband while he rested or he roamed the bush after game. Women educated the children in almost all matters, except those pertaining to certain men's business such as the hunt, male initiation, warfare and certain ceremonies which were taboo to women[73].

Betrothal at infancy was not unusual. The power of the elders allowed them to 'acquire female children as subjects of pre-natal promises' for the older men[74]. When it was decided who would be the future husband of a girl, she would be taught that she belonged to that man and would be given to him when she was thirteen or fourteen[75], or younger, such as twelve[76], or even as early as eight or ten. The right to that girl by that man was referred to by some colonists as the girl being 'sold' or 'bought'[77].

The young wife could also be the second or third wife of her older husband. The colonists labelled such an older man with two or three wives as a 'polygamist'. The youngest wife was valuable in supporting the older wives and husband in acquiring food.

Because marriage was based on social and economic motives a woman was not left with any rights in the saying of whom should be her husband or sexual partner[78]. Ordinarily an Aboriginal wife was true to her husband, 'laudably loyal to the moral principles which [were] taught her', and accepted her position, whether that be to go to her promised tribal man, or to another tribal man as a lend or in an exchange of wives, or to a non-Aboriginal man if the elders so directed. It was considered an expression of goodwill and friendship towards a visitor for a husband to offer him one or two of his younger wives. Provided always that relationships on both sides were within the sub-divisions allowed by tribal law, a wife could be lent to a man who, through scarcity of the opposite sex in their particular group, had remained single. In cases to do with marriage or sexual partners it was compulsory to obtain the sanction of the 'medicine man'[79]. A woman could not refuse to be lent, neither could she divorce herself from her husband and the other wives[80].

One can appreciate how offensive to her mother's people it would have been if Lallie, living within traditional laws, married or cohabited with a man either of her choosing or not of her tribe, apart from any act of cohabitation sanctioned by the elders. Actions such as two people eloping, committing adultery or having a sexual affair with a person within the tribe or of another tribe were not condoned. Occasionally a man eloped with a girl who was outside the permissable inter-marrying lines, or a young man 'stole' an old polygamist's young wife. To go against any of the rules governing marriage, arrangement of partners or sexual relationships would incur a severe punishment. As elopement was considered to be a serious offence the tribe would make every effort to capture the couple so that both individuals could be punished. The punishment was carried out in the camp, or beyond, if the couple had fled for fear of extremely painful or even lethal punishment. An unfaithful promised girl or wife could be beaten or severely battered about with sticks and clubs[81]. One punishment witnessed by missionaries during Lallie's time was for the older husband of a runaway wife on her return to smash one of her legs with a nulla so that she could not run, and when that leg healed her other leg would be smashed. Another punishment they witnessed was for the old men to hold her leg to a fire so that it was charred to the bone[82]. The offending man was more likely to be speared.

It was not unusual for the form of punishment to lead to the death of either or both of the couple, but particularly the woman. The death would be the result of a spearing, of either the woman or the man, or of both of them. A couple who had fled could be tracked by a spearman until he reached them, then he would injure to wound or kill. If eloping couples managed to avoid discovery or capture, the fear of punishment which awaited them kept them from returning to their tribe[83]. Living as an adolescent Aboriginal female in the bush under the traditions of her people, Tjirrgulu would have taught her daughter the rules of relationships and the consequences, to herself as well as to Lallie, if they were not adhered to.

The spearman was the most common dealer of punishment. One aspect of Aboriginal culture that persisted when many other aspects were disappearing with colonial contact was the genuine fear of the spearman, the mystical attributes of whom were still taught by the 'medicine man'. Fear of reprisal from the spearman, the executor of justice, was constant[84]. The young male inducted as a spearman was selected for his expert ability to track and stalk. He followed the instructions of the elders and the tribal 'medicine man' and did not cease his pursuit of the escaped offenders until he located them and carried out his orders. If he returned to his people without accomplishing his mission he himself could be punished for his failure. In some tribal groups the spearman was identifiable by the breaking of the little toe on each foot and the wearing of emu feathers around the ankles, the purpose of which was to camouflage his footprints. Thus he was called the featherfoot man or emufoot man[85]. The degree of injury caused by the spearing, which could range from a maiming to death, was determined by the kind of offence committed by the target. If the featherfoot man could not trap and punish the intended victim any proxy from the family or camp could do[86]. Within the laws determining the punishment for elopement the mothers of the female who eloped could be speared too[87].

The structuring and maintenance of the social order of the Aboriginal families, and the arranging of marriages and sexual partners, was disrupted by the arrival of the colonists. The majority of male colonists in the goldfields did not have the company of their own womenfolk. Very few of the unmarried European women who migrated into this western colony were prepared to move from the more comfortable coastal areas into the harsher interior to start a family life with an itinerant miner, prospector, wood cutter, sandalwood puller, or railroad fettler. Arriving with the mentality of conquerors and members of the superior race as outlined by Darwin's biological theories of evolution, the colonists expected to have use of the daughters of the inferior indigenous people. Extra-marital cohabitation between male colonists and pubescent Aboriginal girls in interior locations was common. The men kept these girls around their camps or homesteads for a time and changed them periodically. The girls worked on domestic chores such as cooking, washing dishes or clothes, house cleaning and fetching fire wood, and were expected also to fulfil the sexual desires of these men. The male colonists may have considered that they were not exploiting these girls, nor harming them in any way when they used them for sexual intercourse, nor committing any significant offence, at least morally. Darwin's theory of evolution, outlined in his book, *The Origin of the Species*, which helped to determine the climate of thinking at this time, advocated that indigenous people were an inferior human species, on the lowest level of human development, and the European Caucasian was on the highest level and the most superior human race. With this framework of thinking the latter was not very sensitive to the former[88]. Consequently, many of the colonists in those times believed that the full-blood Aborigines were childlike, of limited intelligence[89] and therefore uneducable, and without feelings or human emotions[90]. It was accepted by the colonists that if a 'white man' had a 'fresh native girl' every week he 'does her no injury ... People cannot be robbed of what they do not possess nor native girls of chastity'[91].

Colonists had misinterpreted other aspects of Aboriginal sexual relationships. Colonists had learned that amongst the Aboriginal people pubescent or young adult females were sometimes lent by husbands to other men, or there could be a temporary exchange of wives. The colonists did not recognise that amongst the Aboriginal people arrangement of sexual or marital partners was based on protocol[92] rather than exploitation and had a standard of morality. There was an understanding among individual Aboriginal adolescents and adults of the limitations regarding appropriate sexual partners. Incest was forbidden[93].

The colonists interpreted the Aboriginal practices of 'sharing women' and polygamy, together with their assumption that indigenous people were sub-human and ignorant of the teachings of Christ, as Aboriginal society not having a sense of morality. It was convenient therefore for male colonists to perceive that the behaviour of Aboriginal girls was immoral, and cohabitation[94] was no reflection of their own misconduct. They did not understand that an Aboriginal woman had to do as she was instructed by the elders who observed ancient tribal laws. Sexual cohabitation was exercised by women as a duty and to not obey was to put themselves under the threat of a beating or a spearing. The 'shame' came when they were judged by what the colonists considered 'moral' and 'immoral'[95].

There were some sympathetic colonists who attempted to understand the situation of the young Aboriginal women. This was reflected in a newspaper article of the period in which was included comment that it was 'the hard lot' of young Aboriginal women 'to have to barter themselves for food for their people'[96].

When Lallie reached puberty it was most likely that she would become a participant in the practice of cohabitation. She would be encouraged at times to follow such directions by the elders and to go with the older girls into miners' camps.

The traditional methods by which women were punished when they did not sleep with the man they were sent to sleep with, may provide some explanation for why the women appear to have never protested about this way of life. Until now there do not seem to be any records of Aboriginal girls complaining openly or protesting about their experiences of cohabitation with colonists. However, recent oral histories collected from the descendants of part-Aboriginal Wongai women who are now settled between Kalgoorlie and Leonora reveal that cohabitation was a real source of fear for Aboriginal females. They were often intimidated by the threat of violence to them, from both the colonists and from the elders who could send a spearman to deal their punishment. One form of violence executed on these girls by the colonists, impregnation by rape, would have disturbed them mentally and spiritually, as well as violated them physically. However, to resist being sent into the mining camps could result in, through the orders of the elders, being disciplined by the spearman or the 'medicine man'.

Many of the colonists who could juggle in their minds that it was not inhumane or immoral on their part to seek out Aboriginal females for company in their houses or camps may have known that cohabitation with these females was at least illegal. These men may have heard from the police who patrolled their area that it was an offence against a Section of the 1905 Aborigines Act for Caucasian men to have sexual intercourse with Aboriginal females[97]. Nevertheless, many miners, prospectors and itinerant labourers in the bush, and some settlers and pastoralists, took these girls for sex. 'Gin sprees', defined by a contemporary as 'drink and prostitution orgies', were conducted in and around settlements by colonists who had become intoxicated and who were seeking to top their fun with sexual pleasure. The outcomes of these sprees was multiple rape of

Aboriginal girls and their abandonment[98].

The sources that describe cohabitation with colonists from the experiences and feelings of Aboriginal women are rare still. The main sources reflecting the experiences of the women of Lallie's tribal group are recent interviews of Wongai female descendants around Kalgoorlie, Menzies and Leonora conducted by an Aboriginal academic woman, herself a daughter of these women. It was reported in these interviews that these men resorted to intimidation as a means of preventing the girls from naming the rapist or the father of their child to the police. It is alleged that the men told the girls that if they informed anyone of their names that those man would track them until they found them. Then the girl would be badly hurt or killed. In case the girls realised that they were being threatened with murder, and they or a sympathiser of theirs might want to go to the police to report this, the men emphasised to them the futility of them identifying them. They suggested to the girls that nobody would care if the 'white man' did try and kill them[99]. Nor could the girls complain or protest to the elders who had sanctioned their cohabitation.

It is not documented exactly how many miners were aware of Section 34 of the 1905 Aborigines Act which made it a regulation that when a local protector found out which miner was the father of which Aboriginal baby he could apply to a Justice of the Peace for a summons to be served on that European father for the purpose of obtaining a financial contribution to the support of the half-caste child.

However, there was a loophole within this Section of the Act which made it difficult to prove which man was the father of a part-Aboriginal child and so let many European fathers escape their paternal and financial responsibilities. To prove in court which man was the father required more than the word of the Aboriginal mother. One can imagine how hard that would have been to arrange. Also, two Justices of the Peace had to be convinced of the evidence given[100].

Infanticide, forced removal and institutionalisation of children, disintegration of families, single parenthood, dislocation and sexual exploitation and violence to Aboriginal females were aspects of the social circumstances in which Lallie grew up. The best protection Tjirrgulu could offer her daughter was to keep her away from settlements as much as possible, in the bush and close to her people. She was Lallie's true protector, keeping her as safe as was possible from death, destitution, police custody, exile, exploitation and physical violence. Tjirrgulu wanted them both to live by the ancient laws and beliefs of her tribal people. She may have hoped that in time the elders would find a tribal husband to whom Lallie could be promised. This in turn could increase her daughter's status amongst her people, as well as provide her with a hunter. As a married woman the police would be less likely to assess her circumstances as being those of neglect.

By the time Lallie reached marrying age the elders had chosen a tribal man for her. His name was Burtville Jack and he was a full blood[101]. It was a good choice. Burtville Jack would be a reliable and resourceful food provider, not only for Lallie but for her mother as well. The need for Lallie to practice cohabitation with its accompanying threats could be reduced.

Close to the time when Lallie was to be passed to her tribal husband, an event Tjirrgulu had waited for for some time, another man who was beyond the Linden mob announced his desire to have Lallie as his wife. Within the ancient logical framework of arranging marriage partners this man would not have been considered by the elders as a suitable or practical choice. The suitor was an Afghan, an itinerant camelman and hawker, and of the broader group labelled by the colonists as 'Asiatics'. He was not a stranger to Tjirrgulu and the Linden-Laverton Wongai people. Lallie's DCS file indicates that he became familiar to them because of his many trips throughout the bush in the eastern goldfields in the 1910s and 1920s. A number of the Wongai group regarded him as a friend to the Linden mob. The Afghan, named Jack Akbar, had apparently seen Lallie grow and mature to a marrying age. He had recently informed the elders that he was prepared to seek from the appropriate authorities permission to marry Tjirrgulu's daughter.

Jack Akbar was one of the few hundred immigrant Asiatic camelmen of Afghan descent or Indian residency who had been drawn to the Western Australian goldfields since the 1880s. In the 1890s a number of gold discoveries created a population boom. The population of the western colony lept from 82,014 in 1894 to 161,694 in 1897[102]. This in turn stimulated the demand in the more arid interior for extensive, durable transport and carting a great range of commodities including water, food, building supplies and equipment.

Many of the Afghans that came into Western Australia came across the border from the eastern states. By the late 1860s a substantial number of Afghan camelmen and camels were working in South Australia where pastoralism, more so than mining, was the main drive for development of an arid interior. By the 1880s in South Australia the

Afghan and Indian camelmen had established their own settlements which were located around ports, rail sidings or railhead towns. The main features of these 'Ghan' towns were the Asiatic man in traditional costume, their tin huts, camels, camel yards and a prayer house called a mosque. The most notable Ghan towns were at Port Augusta, the railhead town of Marree, which had the largest Afghan community and earned the nickname of 'little Asia', at Beltana, Farina and Oodnadatta. Members from these Ghan towns, and that of Broken Hill and Bourke in New South Wales, moved to the Western Australian goldfields in the 1890s to chase business for their camel strings in the booming mining communities. They crossed into Western Australia either through the far north of South Australia from Marree via Oodnadatta, or from Port Augusta across the Nullabor Plain via Eucla and Ooldea[103].

The other point of entry of Afghans into Western Australia was Fremantle, the port of Perth. From there they either branched out along the coastline to reach the remote north-west areas or moved into the more arid interior. One of the earliest records of camels disembarking in Western Australia was in August 1886 when a camel string travelled from a coastal port via Cossack to Derby and continued out to mining fields around that district[104].

During the 1890s more camels and Afghans and Indians were brought to the Western Australian goldfields by either European or Afghan camel proprietors. By the mid-1890s there were a number of Ghan towns established around coastal settlements far north of Perth and on the outskirts of various mining centres in the northern and eastern goldfields. The Ghan town at Fly's Flat on the outskirts of Coolgardie was the most significant one. Other notable Ghan towns in the eastern goldfields included those adjacent to Laverton, Leonora, Mount Morgans and Bummers Creek, and in the northern goldfields adjacent to Port Hedland, Marble Bar and Cue. According to one of the few sources that included the cultural group of the Afghans in a population census of Western Australia, by 1897 there were 'about 700 Afghans and Indians employed on the [gold]fields'[105]. Another source suggested that there were about 200 Afghans or Asiatics in the goldfields, about ninety per cent of whom were Afghans[106]. By 1903 there were estimated to be about 500 natives of India or Afghans resident in Western Australia[107].

The religion fundamental to the Afghan immigrants was named Mohammedism and its followers called Moslems or Muslims until its name change in the twentieth century to Islam[108]. The Afghan camelmen established the first Moslem community in Australia. The Afghans in Western Australia raised sufficient donations to finance the building in Perth of a major centre of worship and community support. In 1905 a mosque was erected near the city centre on the corner of William and Robinson Streets, Hyde Park[109]. In South Australia a large mosque had been built in Adelaide during the 1880s with funding donated by the South Australian, Northern Territory and New South Wales Moslem communities.

It is not possible to verify the date of Jack Akbar's arrival in Australia or his purpose for immigrating. Police investigations conducted later in his life into his background documented that Jack Akbar was a 'native of Punjab and India'[110]. He was a British born subject, as was his father, named in Lallie's DCS File as Dilber Khan, and his grandfather was a naturalised British subject[111]. These details indicate that Jack Akbar was an Afghan descendant living within the British Empire in the Punjab, a region of India[112]. It is not possible to determine whether Dilber Khan and his son Jack Akbar disembarked at Port Augusta in South Australia or at Fremantle in Western Australia.

Calculations using dates from Lallie's DCS file indicate that Jack Akbar had been in Australia at least since 1894[113]. Though the file did provide the name of Jack's father the details are not accurate enough to clarify whether or not Jack emigrated in the company of his father. Nor was it possible to discover the reason for the difference in their surnames. The file indicates that Jack was probably a teenager, about fourteen years old, when he migrated to the Australian colonies. It is possible that either Dilber Khan emigrated from India to one of the colonies, as many men did at that time, to find reliable work and brought his son with him as he was old enough to work, or Jack was contracted near Karachi to come out to the Australian colonies as a camel labourer. Before young Jack left India to come to Australia with his father it seems he had been to Kashmir where he learned the craft of basket weaving[114]. It was a skill that became very useful later in his life.

Nor was it possible to confirm the movements of Jack Akbar after his disembarkation and where he spent the remaining years of his adolescence and his early adult years. Jack Akbar's first recorded location was in the Western Australian goldfields in the 1910s, when it is estimated that he was in his thirties[115].

Jack's physical appearance as a young man has been recorded in a surviving photograph of him in an official pose [see p.18]. It shows him to be a handsome man. The composition of large, dark brown, almond-shaped eyes, even white teeth against ruggedly textured olive skin, a large aquiline nose bordered by high, pronounced cheek bones and well-formed lips appearing below a thick, black moustache, produced a handsome countenance[116]. A few other surviving photographs of Jack Akbar reveal that he was tall and fit looking, with well-toned, muscular torso, arms and legs. As was the practice of devout Moslem men, he kept his hair cut very short and regularly wore a turban with one end of the material hanging down to his shoulder. When he conducted business or worked as a hawker he donned a Western style suit consisting of jacket, trousers and vest. When he was dressed for prayers either at his residence or when he visited a mosque, he donned his white bloomers, long loosely hanging shirt and turban.

The timing of Jack Akbar's arrival in the Western Australia goldfields, in the 1910s if not earlier, could have meant that his experiences and choice of district would have been affected by the factors already existing in Western Australia which led to much antagonism against the Afghan community. The outcome of the concentration of several hundred Afghans in the Western Australian goldfields meant that the colonists faced competition for employment and economic survival by another 'inferior' group. The colonists tended to exaggerate certain attributes of the Moslem community, which made that race even more despised. These circumstances may have influenced the choices Jack Akbar made about where he lived, what range of jobs he took on, and what woman he would be happy with and with whom he one day might marry and establish his own family.

The many factors concerning the economic, social and political impact of the Afghans were the subject of bemused and critical articles in several newspapers in Western Australia, particularly from the 1890s to the 1910s, such as the *Sunday Times*, the *Western Australia Gold Fields Courier, Western Argus* and the *Morgans Courier*[117]. The articles that outlined cases or events involving Afghans often cited names of individuals. Neither Dilber Khan nor Jack Akbar are mentioned in the public literature of the day. There are at least three possible explanations for this. One is that Jack Akbar did not cross the border into Western Australia to find work in the goldfields until the turn of the century. Another is that for a while his preference in accomodation was in the Ghan towns and there never was an accurate account of occupiers of each abode in these places during any census count or annual postal directory recording of residents.

A third is that Jack, though remaining a devout Moslem, finally chose to live away from his compatriots and the Ghan towns and to take up rental accomodation in settlements. He would not be situated, then, to be caught up in the kinds of fracases, cases or events involving Afghans that triggered the interest of the journalists of the day. Jack may have chosen to limit his business and social interactions with Moslem communities, and to develop a business and reputation in the wider society. Reasons for this choice could include both his awareness of the perceptions of, either valid or invalid, and the antagonism held by, many sections of the wider community. The apparent limited association with his fellow countrymen may contribute to understanding the circumstances that led to Jack Akbar to choose an Aboriginal adolescent female, and Lallie in particular, as his wife.

One characteristic of some Moslem men that contributed to the public's perception, from the 1890s to the 1920s, that Afghans were undesirable, untrustworthy, treacherous, aggressive and a 'lesser race' was the nature of their relationships with European women. In the decade in which Jack chose to marry there were still sectors in the Australian community calling for prohibiting miscegenation between Afghans and European women. This concern was founded on a history of unfavourable stories about how some Afghans treated European women, either their wives, de factos or neighbours, and their daughters.

As Australian immigration regulations prohibited Afghans, Indians or any Asiatics from bringing or sending for their wives, the Afghans either remained bachelors or found a wife in this country. Some in Western Australia cohabited with 'white women'; fewer still married Aboriginal girls.

There were differences in South Australia and Western Australia regarding relationships of Afghans with European women. In South Australia during the 1890s to 1910s several Afghans married the daughters of European parents in far northern, remote settlements. Some of the Afghan camelmen had saved up enough money and owned enough camels to be considered established businessmen and potentially good providers. They were prepared to negotiate with European fathers who would be prepared to accept money and sell their daughters. This arrangement could be compared to the significance in their culture of the dowry. As the first generation of Afghans born in Australia grew up, the fathers, reflecting the tradition from their homeland, were prepared to sell their own part-European daughters[118]. Should an Afghan choose to marry an Aboriginal daughter there were no laws to forbid such a marriage. The Afghan communities of Marree and Port Augusta in South Australia and of Broken Hill in New South Wales included families originating from marriages with European and some Aboriginal women. The calibre and character of the wives of the Afghans in the eastern states on the whole tended to be unquestionable and reputable.

In Western Australia during the 1890s and into the 1910s the occasional newspaper articles on Afghans' relationships with European women were not complimentary. They reported that Afghan men tended to mistreat the European women with whom they had relationships. Their attitude to women may have been affected to some extent by them transferring customary behaviour towards women raised in Moslem society. The newspaper reports selected incidences of Afghans hitting women, threatening to shoot women and stealing money from them[119]. The matter of Afghans insulting and intimidating women alone in their homes when husbands were at work was addressed in the *Coolgardie Miner* in 1897. Some people were not willing to move into a house if their neighbours would be 'them black devils' because they might intimidate the wife[120]. In 1906 the Morgans newspaper commented that the 'smellful Asiatic' is here in great numbers and 'is, in many cases, living with or married to white women'. It suggested that 'any person who marries or lives with natives of a coloured country should be imprisoned for a number of years. The Unions should act to have an Act passed embodying such a clause'[121]. According to the details of the newspapers of the times, the calibre of European women who tended to associate with Western Australian Afghans were generally poor, destitute, abandoned by their husbands and left with children to provide for, apparently naive about Moslem customs and beliefs, and somewhat emotionally or mentally unstable.

The newspapers kept the issue of banning mixed marriages between Afghans and European daughters in the public's attention by relating incidents in which Afghans would take their daughters born of a European mother to northern India or Afghanistan, possibly to be sold into the slave trade. Police and parliamentarians were brought into this issue. In 1907 Nellie married Abraham Mahomet who was an unfaithful husband, a gambler and a wife beater. He took her and her children to India but she managed to leave him and get her children back to

Australia[122]. In 1908 Moab Khan took his step-daughter Leon Tene Adell aged nine or ten to Rawal Pindi on the north-west frontier of India and left her there. It was believed that the object of taking this girl there was that when she reached adolescence and was thus of a marrying age she would be desired by Indians of high caste with plenty of money[123]. Such occurrences implied a 'white slave trade'.

In 1909 the newspapers promoted the alarming concept of a 'white Australia' being replaced by a 'piebald Australia'. They proposed the need for a law to prohibit the marriage of white women with Asiatics or coloured men, or vice versa, and that the example be followed of the United States of America where racial inter-marriages were barred in many places[124]. 'Life as a Mahommedan wife will mean degradation and servitude...Among Mahommedans woman is regarded as a very inferior being...Slavery is a mild term to describe the life of the average Mahommedan woman'[125].

In 1911 a case reached the media which raised the issue again of prohibiting mixed marriages. The subject of this case was the supposedly numerous visits by 'sultan tourists', driven by their 'rampant lusts', who were seeking 'white beauties to build up their oriental harems'. More repugnant to white Australians than the degrading competition in the Australian labour market was the 'generative admixture of the white and Asiatic races' and the consequent 'mongrel parentage'[126].

Paranoia around the issue of Afghans marrying European women was brought to a head by a minister of the Congregational Church in Adelaide, South Australia. In April 1913 Mr J.C. Kirby sent a letter to the Federal Premier of the Department of External Affairs in Melbourne on the subject of 'Marriages of Afghans to Australian White Women'. He stated he was aware that Afghans who married white women took them to Afghanistan 'where they were reduced to slavery and worse'. Minister Kirby suggested to the Federal Premier that as a measure to minimise this evil the marriage of girls under 21 years old with Afghans should be prohibited: 'a Magistrate should be required to personally interview the female and tell her of the consequences...The woman should not be allowed to pass the boundaries of India into Afghanistan...I do believe Afghans make cruel husbands'[127].

In 1913 Indian authorities were still very concerned regarding the fate of white women who passed into Afghanistan with Afghan husbands, and that the Indian authorities also regarded this movement as 'one phase of the white slave traffic'[128].

The resurrecting by the newspapers and in government departments of the inappropriateness of marriages between Afghans and European women would have made many such women in Western Australia wary of associating with, let alone marrying, an Afghan. Jack Akbar was most likely aware of the anti-Afghan attitudes. However, it is not clear to what degree Akbar was aware of how the 1905 Aborigines Act directed the Chief Protector of Aborigines to control the relationships of Aboriginal women and their cohabitation or marriage with Aboriginal and non-Aboriginal (European and Asiatic) persons.

There is an absence of evidence from 1894 until the 1920s on where Jack Akbar resided. If he lived in Ghan camps the chance of him encountering a European woman who might become his wife was unlikely. It does seem that during the 1910s and 1920s he spent a lot of his time travelling on bush tracks doing business with mining settlements, mines, railyard and retail merchants in larger towns and visiting pastoral homesteads. This predisposed him to encounter bush Aboriginal groups. He was more likely therefore to encounter an eligible Aboriginal woman than an eligible European woman.

By the 1900s the relationship between the Afghans and the Aboriginal people, two minority groups in the newly formed Australian nation, would most likely have been amicable. Causes for them to have some empathy for each other could come from common cultural traits and social practices, experiences in both their histories of subjugation and usurpation, and geographical proximity. The turbaned camel labourers and proprietors came from a society based on tribal groupings, as did the Aborigines. In Australia the Afghans represented two larger tribal groups, the Pathans and the Belooch (also spelt 'Baluch'), in comparison to the Indian camelmen who came from the Punjab and Sind regions in north-west India[129]. The Afghans had some experience of British invasion of their homeland, with the aim of the invaders to rule. The first Anglo-Afghan War of 1838 to 1842 was followed by two others, but Afghanistan was never incorporated into the British Empire. The Afghans did not intend to compete with the Aborigines for their land, or to displace Aboriginal tribes from their land. Except in the rare experiences of Afghans who were attached to European exploration expeditions that no doubt transgressed tribal or sacred land, there were no individual or mass killings of one of these races by the other. Both races adapted to the desert and understood how to survive in it without wanting to destroy elements of it. Both races accepted living in nomadic, simple conditions, their tribal routes and camel pads sharing the deserts. Aboriginal women did not protest their lot, due to the way they were raised, which was in many ways similar to the expectations and duties placed on Moslem women. The Afghans would employ Aboriginal males and the Aborigines accepted the low wages paid to them by the Afghan camelmen. Colonial legislation excluded Aborigines and Afghans from gaining citizenship. The Afghans in general spoke well of the Aborigines[130].

Many Afghans believed that Aboriginal women made more suitable companions or wives than did European women. They were ammenable to working in the camel camps, to cooking, to looking after the houses of the Afghan camelmen when they were away for several days or weeks at a time carting along bush tracks, and to helping with the loading of the camels. They helped round up the camels which had been hobbled and let loose for foraging. The Aboriginal woman was accustomed to the basic, demanding life of the bush and suited to living in remote Ghan camps as a Moslem wife[131].

By perusing details in Lallie's DCS file that indicate where Jack worked during the 1910s and into the 1920s it can be understood how he would have repeatedly encountered Lallie, particularly in the eastern goldfields in the 1920s when she reached the marrying age. It seems that during the 1910s Jack worked more in the northern goldfields. During this time he had enough money by 11 November 1915 to purchase two male camels from a fellow countryman, Lal Mahomet, at a cost of eighty pounds. The receipt that records this sale is one from the business of Silbert and Sharp, on which Lal Mahomet has crossed out that business name and written his own in its place. This suggests that Lal Mahomet was in the vicinity of Leonora[132]. With two camels and a wagon Jack Akbar was now in a position to diversify his work and take on carting contracts for the wholesale fruit, produce, provision merchants and commission agents named 'Silbert and Sharp' in Leonora[133]. This is assumed to be the foundation of Jack's own carting and hawking business. He purchased the goods for his hawking business from the same company for which he carted. His carting contracts included transporting water. He eventually won the tender for a government contract to carry the mail that came up from Kalgoorlie between Leonora and Wiluna[134].

Jack may have had moments of uncertainty, hardship and danger in the frontier environment of the goldfields in the early part of the twentieth century. During one trip on the lonely Leonora-Wiluna mail run Jack Akbar had a very bad accident. One of the two bull camels that he had purchased was less manageable than the other and on one trip caused the camel team to bolt and the wagon to tip. Jack jumped to clear the wagon but it caught one of his legs and pinned him to the earth. A search party sent out by the Wiluna post office took Jack to the hospital in Leonora where he, motivated by 'religious beliefs'[135], forbad the doctors to amputate his severely damaged leg.

On resuming work full-time Jack Akbar took on carting contracts that drew him by the 1920s to the eastern goldfields. He held a job for a while at Murrin Murrin[136], a rail siding town on the Kalgoorlie to Laverton branch line. He most likely sought carting contracts occasionally at the railhead towns of Laverton, Comet Vale, Menzies, Kookynie and Morgans. There he could also either replenish his stores for his own hawking business, or obtain orders from forwarding agents or the office of the rail goods yards there for deliveries.

In 1922 Jack Akbar got work with the company of Clarke and Lamont in Laverton. That business combined a forwarding agent, auctioneers and contractors and had been there since 1915. When Jack came into Laverton that company was looking to employ an extra man to take on a contract to cart for sandalwood pullers. Sandalwood pulling was a very widely distributed and common alternative occupation for unemployed miners and unsuccessful and struggling pastoralists. Throughout the goldfields there was a constant demand for haulage contractors to cart pulled and cleaned sandalwood to local buyers who were wholesalers, and who in turn sold it to company buyers who would procur it for the market overseas.

Clarke and Lamont were very pleased with their employee Akbar's work performance. When Jack completed his contract with them and asked for a character reference the manager George T. Smart provided him with a good one. On 6 September 1924 Smart wrote that Jack Akbar had 'been carting sandalwood for us for three years. We have always found him most willing and obliging to the pullers and always keen on getting their wood in from the bush. He has always proved a good townsman paying his accounts promptly. We can with confidence recommend him to anyone requiring his services at the same class of work'[137].

With many mines closing down during or just after World War One Afghans also had to diversify in the work they were prepared to take on. In the early 1920s Jack Akbar delivered meat rations and timber to the mining site of Mount Morgans[138]. Many Afghans went to Linden in those days because it still had a degree of activity and prosperity as a mining centre and needed food and other material stores and water[139].

It is believed that Jack delivered building materials to Linden[140]. That town, Morgans and Burtville all had ration depots to which Wongai would come regularly, and Laverton and Linden had Afghan camps. There were numerous opportunities in these years for Jack Akbar to encounter Tjirrgulu's family and members of the Linden Wongai and come to know some of them personally. Jack would have been a familiar sight to quite a few of the surviving nomadic, indigenous groups who moved between the bush tracks and the mining settlements and depots. In the 1920s he saw more and more of the maturing Lallie.

His persistence and hard work earned him a status that may have made him an extraordinary Afghan. Jack Akbar earned the reputation throughout the eastern goldfields of being a trusted and reliable businessman and was respected by prominent members of the dominant European community. There were several citizens in the colonists' business sector in the goldfields, apart from George Smart of Laverton, who were prepared to write a good reference for Jack Akbar if he ever required one. These businessmen included Mr Beresford of the Westralia mine at Mount Morgans, the hotel keeper Mr Swanson in Linden, Mr Crampton of Field and Co store and storekeeper Mr Kidd, both of Leonora, and the solicitor Mr John Cook at F.W. Wright and Co.[141].

Though the Wongai apparently accepted and trusted Jack Akbar, the mothers of the children of non-tribal fathers would have maintained a cautious distance between them and the traveller. This could be because of another kind of person whom Jack Akbar encountered regularly in his travels throughout the district: the mounted constabulary. These men would make enquiries of Aboriginal people they were seeking while out on their patrols. As Jack's range of business required him to make numerous and regular trips into the bush the police might have considered him to be a most appropriate fellow to track, or to interview occasionally when they needed specific details about individual Aboriginal children they had been ordered to catch. The mothers of these children, in their ongoing effort to prevent any risk to their children, would keep them from being too familiar to the Afghan hawker. This would reduce the number of children's names he could come to know. Should the police ask him for details about specific children he would not be in the position to be an informant.

The mothers may have also anticipated that Jack Akbar might one day possibly take advantage of his accessibility to them and their children and would want to take away one of their girls for his convenience then eventually abandon her when he was finished with her. If he took one of their girls away to travel with him they realised he would also increase the risk of her exposure to the police. Against this background of fear and precaution which triggered the reactions of protective Aboriginal mothers, the Afghan hawker had sighted one Aboriginal girl whom he would not forget.

Circumstances may have been directing him to choose Lallie as a most suitable wife. He may have been considering an Aboriginal woman for a companion and wife because there were no Afghan daughters nearby for him to offer a price to the father for. Some unmarried camelmen had remained bachelors or took on Aboriginal women for a while, as other men did, to work around their camps. There would have been remnants of the attitude to prohibit miscegenation between white women and Afghans. However, he still did not want to marry just any girl. It had to be one whom he considered had finer qualities than others.

Lallie may have seemed out of the ordinary to Jack Akbar for a few reasons. Her personality was unusually attractive, despite hardships faced by her mother. She was pretty, light hearted, good natured and sensible. To Jack she seemed affable, sociable and approachable. She was not bitter, retiring, defeated, resentful or out for what she could get[142].

In 1924 Jack had accumulated enough finance from his enterprises to be able to open his own commercial premise. He obtained the registration for 'a shop or warehouse' and opened a general store in Burt Street, the main street of Morgans[143]. After Jack opened his store in Morgans the Wongai started to visit him there. Following her people, Lallie started coming into Jack's store[144]. With part-Aboriginal teenagers like Lallie amongst them the Wongai around Jack's shop would be frequently on the alert for the policeman always ready to drive them out of the town.

By 1924 Jack's age would be estimated to be in his mid-forties, Lallie would have been about fifteen, and by his own words to his solicitor he would have known her for about fourteen years[145]. Their age difference was probably not an issue for themselves or for Lallie's people. The Afghan and Aboriginal cultures functioned with marriages in which the husband was much older than the wife. In Moslem societies such as that of Afghanistan and the Punjab district of north-west India, it was traditional for a man to work and save some money over years until he had a substantial and regular income and could afford to support the young woman he would marry and the children they would have. A girl would be promised to him when she was a child and their arranged marriage would occur when she reached puberty and while she was still a virgin[146].

Akbar may have preferred to marry a virgin, a condition of the female highly valued in the teachings of his faith and the traditions of his society. However, over the fifteen years in which it is known he lived, worked and travelled in the goldfields, he would have come to understand much about the culture and customs of the Aboriginal people and the circumstances that affected their lives. He could have been aware that most young Aboriginal females whom he encountered would have practised some sexual cohabitation as a means to contributing to their people's survival. He may have appreciated that it would be very unlikely that his chosen Aboriginal woman would be a virgin.

Considering the circumstances in the Western Australian goldfields there may have been some aspects of Jack's religion that he would have had to prioritise, to make it acceptable to him to marry a non-Islamic woman who still held some virtues for him. There were aspects about the way people conducted themselves in the goldfields that he did not find morally acceptable. Moslem teachings, his personal beliefs and values could not allow him to accept the practice of cohabitation. He could not contemplate taking a woman just for his own pleasure then abandoning her, or possibly causing a teenage Aboriginal girl to become pregnant and then leaving her to find her own way back to her people. When he would have a woman as a companion it would have to be within the state of marriage, recognised by both his religion and the government of the land in which he lived. He would want any children he would father, and their mother, to have his name.

By 1924 Jack Akbar managed and owned a business as a storekeeper, a hawker and carrier. His business became well known throughout the Morgans-Laverton district[147]. Now that Lallie was aged about fifteen or sixteen, this was the time to approach the appropriate authorities in regard to seeking permission to marry Lallie. The woman who was his wife could keep him company in his new store and could be a support to him when his gammy leg made some tasks a bit awkward or difficult. It is most likely that because of the qualities he saw in Lallie, Jack decided that she was the woman he could trust and rely on, the woman he wanted as his wife and even assistant in his store.

Since Jack had learned much about Aboriginal customs and laws he appreciated that he would need the permission of the elders of the council of the Linden mob to have Lallie as his wife. It was during

1925, as was calculated from Lallie's DCS file, that Jack approached the Linden elders to request that they consider him as a suitable provider for Lallie. He may have understood that they would need some time to evaluate his case against their traditional arrangement.

It seems that this was one point in Lallie's life in which circumstances were in her favour. The elders had a choice of two providers for Lallie. One was a skilled hunter who would be a reliable provider for her and, when necessary, for her mother. The other was a businessman who in some ways could change Lallie's life so as to improve it. That same man had admired her for some time. The elders made a choice.

While Akbar waited for a response from the elders he was not aware that the action of giving Lallie as a wife was already in process. The elders had chosen to abide by their ancient tribal ways. They had no need to consult the Afghan about their choice of husband for one of their girls. The elders believed that their decision regarding the arrangement of Lallie's marriage was made in the best interest of herself and their people. During 1925 the Linden people's elders had passed Lallie to her promised husband, a full-blood man known by his Christian-given name, Burtville Jack[148]. Burtville Jack would have been pleased to receive a young wife who was so pleasing in appearance, so healthy and so sound in character. He took his young wife to live with him at Burtville.

While continuing his carting and hawking about the bush in the district the disappointed Akbar may have had the occasional sighting of Lallie. He remained very fond of her but did not attempt to disrupt her life. He would have understood that if he attempted to revolt against the decision of the Wongai and to throw off the shackles that the ancient laws put on Lallie's life it would not bring happiness to either of them. If Jack Akbar persisted with his case with the elders, when the tribal laws had declared that it was not the correct arrangement to give Lallie to the outsider, then the elders could view Lallie as being unfaithful to her husband, perhaps an adultress, or disobedient regarding her people's ways. Both Lallie and Jack could be punished with a spearing which would cause them injury, even death. If Jack made an effort to see her privately or asked her to travel with him in his truck while he made deliveries to mining camps or visited Aboriginal camps, the elders could decide that she should at least deserve a beating or a mutilation to prevent her from further association with the Afghan.

It was early in January 1926 that an unexpected and most irregular event took place which gave Jack Akbar legitimate reason to revive his hopes for a future with Lallie. One other event he did not yet know of was that the police had been asked to search for Lallie and to apprehend her once they found her.

CHAPTER TWO

The Akbar-Matbar case goes to the police

During January 1926 Burtville Jack returned the Linden girl to her people. The relinquishment of a young wife was an irregular thing to do. Some explanations of Burtville's Jack's extraordinary action were given by some female Wongai descendants around Kalgoorlie.

When the elders indicated it was time for Lallie to go to Burtville Jack, he already had a wife who was a 'full-blood' person. In the tradition of polygamy Lallie might have been given to Burtville Jack as the younger wife. After spending some time with the both wives, Burtville Jack may have decided that one of them was more suited than the other to his lifestyle.

Lallie may not have been suited to living a bush life with a tribal man. As a son of two Aboriginal parents Burtville Jack would have spent a lot of his time tracking game as a hunter in the bush, and not needing to migrate back towards fringe camps, as 'half-caste' people did. A tribal wife could participate in a traditional lifestyle more ammenably than a 'half-caste' wife. The former could more reliably supplement nourishment for herself and two others when living deeper in the bush or the spinifex country. It was most likely that Burtville Jack and his tribal wife would have to come back to settlements so that Lallie could obtain her rations[1].

One of the Wongai descendants suggested that another reason for returning Lallie was that Burtville Jack may have considered that the 'white' characteristics in her made her 'unreliable and untrustworthy'[2].

According to Lallie's DCS file at this time Lallie was pregnant and Burtville Jack was not the father[3]. This implies she had practised some cohabitation before she went to Burtville Jack. There was not the same pressure from the elders for the 'full-blood' wife to be exposed to the practice of cohabitation, and she would more likely be a sexual partner to him only. Burtville Jack decided not to be the provider for the part-Aboriginal child and the part-Aboriginal mother. With the diminishment in bush tucker it was difficult to find sufficient food for a family of a man, two wives and one child or more. Burtville Jack eventually returned Lallie to her people, and soon after he and his first wife left for the spinifex country[4].

In spite of Burtville Jack's intention of returning a wife without offending any customary laws, his action evoked anger amongst the Linden people that was to have long-term repercussions on Lallie's life. There was vigorous disagreement about whether or not a law had been broken, a punishment should be dealt, and whether or not Lallie was actually single again. A sympathetic faction believed that Lallie was not a rebel or an upstart, as it was not Lallie who had made the choice to leave her husband without his consent. Neither Lallie nor Burtville Jack had broken any ancient customs and no punishment of either party would be necessary[5]. A more staunchly traditional faction of the Linden mob did not accept this generous view of Burtville Jack's action. They believed Lallie retained her marital status and should be with her husband. An offense had been committed and there was a need for disciplinary action. If the punishment could not be meted to either Burtville Jack or Lallie, then the mother should receive it, as was the law.

As Jack Akbar's hawking, haulage and delivery routes took him through the scrub where he encountered Wongai, it was inevitable that within time he would learn of Lallie's return to her Linden people and probable single status. The news would have renewed his hope of marriage. There was a chance that the elders might now reconsider a proposal from another man to be Lallie's provider and protector. Lallie's pregnancy did not deter the Afghan from his most important goal in life.

Lallie needed a husband quickly. It would be a while before the elders could identify a suitable man from their people who could be her husband and who would be willing to provide sustenance for an additional three mouths. While she remained single, pregnant and under seventeen, she was in a vulnerable position. Her people would expect her to use what means she could to supplement food for her own family group, whether it be by gold specking, rations or cohabitation. The birth of her part-Aboriginal child would add to the increasing population of half castes who had to be supported by the Aboriginal people. Therefore there was a chance that Lallie's baby would be faced with either abortion or infanticide. An additional concern for Lallie's people was that should the police learn of Lallie's non-marital and pregnant condition it was likely that they would try harder to find and seize her. Lallie would be considered very fortunate if, within a short time, the elders could find another man to whom she could be given as a wife.

Though Jack Akbar was hoping the elders would consider his marriage proposal as convenient, the elders at this time may not have seen a marriage of Lallie to the Afghan as the most desirable solution. One possible fear was that if they permitted Jack to court Lallie regularly in her present condition and the police learned of this relationship, they could use the Afghan to track their way to Lallie and seize her. If Lallie started to keep company with the Afghan carrier their movements could take Lallie out of the bush and expose her location. The elders may have believed that Jack's earnest desire to be with her could result in Lallie going to the detested Moore River Native Settlement. Jack may not have realised at this time that, ironically, his desire to be with her and care for her would have been placing her at greater risk of exposure to the police.

There is no documentation of any meetings that may have occurred between Jack and Lallie in the first few months of 1926. It is not recorded how clear it was to Jack that from the time Lallie resumed a life of cohabitation, in early 1926, that she could be assaulted, could lose her baby or be forcibly removed from her district by the police. Lallie lost this pregnancy. There is no official statement in her DCS file of where or why it occurred, although it is known that very young mothers did often miscarry.

Circumstances determined that it took some time for discussion between Jack and the elders to progress and this left Jack powerless to prevent Lallie's return to cohabitation. As well as needing the elders' authority to marry Lallie, Jack Akbar sought information from the local government authorities on procedures regarding obtaining permission to marry an Aboriginal girl. It was not long before Lallie was pregnant again. This was calculated to be her third pregnancy[6].

The local authority who Jack approached for information about regulations of a civil marriage between an Afghan immigrant and an Aboriginal woman was the constable in charge of the police station at Morgans. Police Constable (P.C.) Samuel E. Perks had been transferred in 1923 from Wiluna in the northern goldfields to Morgans in the eastern goldfields. Wiluna was in the tribal area of the Darlot people who were seen to be a more aggressive, belligerent Aboriginal group than were the

Wongai. In earlier years the Darlot people would raid the Wongai people to take some of their women away. Because of his experience with the Darlot people Perks had become accustomed to perceiving the eastern goldfields Aboriginal population as wild, unpredictable and in need of constant surveillance[7]. Aborigines in the eastern goldfields were some of the last indigenous groups in Western Australia to still retain much of their tribal practices and customs.

Perks was a sound and reasonable officer. His intention was to do his job well while avoiding being cruel[8]. Perks was liked by the Europeans, pastoralists, town residents and missionaries. He was viewed as a gentle, civilised sort of man. However, the Morgans policeman did not share, either in his official capacity or personally, the respect and tolerance for Aborginal people of the Morgans Afghan storekeeper. Perks' experience of the Aboriginal people had involved confrontation, controlling, settling conflict, punishing those who had ignored the regulations of the 1905 Aborigines Act, or picking them up for minor theft or loitering. His views of the treatment and location of the Aboriginal people were in alignment with those of the wider community. Perks had a ration depot at Morgans to manage and accepted that the Wongai had to come into his town at least once, when it was the day for distributing the rations. He preferred that for the rest of the time they were out of sight and in the bush.

It was about six months after Lallie's return to her people when Jack Akbar went, on 21 July 1926[9], to Constable Perks to make some preliminary enquiries about his desire to get married. Most likely his perception of his own position was reasonable and so he expected cooperation from the local constable. Constable Perks may have had two views of Akbar's proposal, one official and perhaps one that was personal.

Officially, Perks's response to Akbar's enquiries would be restricted, as the issue concerned an Aboriginal person. An Act of parliament determined that the police had a dual role in dealing with the Aboriginal people. With the increasing number of part-Aboriginal people there was a need for the Chief Protector of Aborigines to seek the support of the police force in some Aboriginal matters, as the total number of his own staff, which included a Deputy Chief Protector of Aborigines, was very few. The Aboriginal Protection Board, set up in 1886, had five staff to deal with all affairs relevant to the Aboriginal population of that colony[10], and did not have inspectors to oversee the conditions of Aboriginal people throughout Western Australia. In that period 'indigenous population' did not include part-Aboriginal people. The Board had to co-opt the services of resident magistrates, police and government officials to be 'honorary' local protectors. The 1904 Roth Royal Commission found that the Chief Protector of Aborigines had no power to enforce the provisions of the Aborigines Protection Act of 1886, so it recommended that the Government establish and recognise in legislation a rudimentary field organisation by appointing in each magisterial district one existing official, preferably a resident magistrate or a policeman, or a senior police officer such as an Inspector of Police, who would be directly responsible to the Chief Protector of Aborigines. They would be a protector at the local level. One outcome of this was that the distribution of relief was to be entrusted to district police officers[11]. From 1915 Neville had to continue to depend on the system of honorary local protectors. With this additional role the load of duties of the local policeman in the outback areas expanded. He was responsible not only for keeping civil law and order, going out on patrols and keeping records, collecting statistics, supervising vermin destruction, issuing licenses for vehicles, firearms and dogs, and picking up offenders for placement in the local lock-up, but also protecting Aboriginal people, catching Aboriginal children and distributing rations. Police were the implementers of Section 12 of the 1905 Aborigines Act, which declared that any Aboriginal person could be removed to and kept within the boundaries of a reserve or removed from one reserve or district to another reserve or district. If an Aborigine refused to cooperate with removal, he or she was deemed to be guilty of an offence against the Act. Considering that all children sixteen and under were wards of the Chief Protector of Aborigines, this made children the majority of individuals who were forcibly removed from their families and districts of their birth[12].

It appears that the police were not pleased to have the dual roles. In the remoter areas a lone constable often was responsible for peace and order over hundreds of square kilometres of scrub and settlement. It is most likely that these police in particular were often caught between duties of policing on the one hand and 'protecting' on the other. As a protector he was a welfare giver, but as a policeman he had certain obligations. He was a long way from the Chief Protector's office and could not act in his protective capacity without first a reference to the Chief Protector in Perth. As a policeman he had more immediate authority. The oath of the police officer made the role of guardian of law and order and the enforcer of penal sanctions, prior responsibilities. It evolved that his role in 'welfare' and acting as an agent of the Chief

Protector of Aborigines was to the police officer a secondary function[13].

It has not been possible to verify how much Jack Akbar knew of the duality of the responsibilities of the police in regard to the Aboriginal people. In 1922 in Wiluna, and from 1923 in Morgans, Police Constable Perks was the local protector as well as policeman. He sent regular reports to the district police office in Kalgoorlie, and was the regular contact with the Chief Protector's office for the manager of the Mount Margaret mission which was in Perks's district, or for anyone who dealt in matters that concerned the Aboriginal population. When Jack Akbar came to speak to Constable Perks about his matrimonial intentions involving an Aboriginal female, he was dealing with an official who could be his ally or his foe.

Akbar and Constable Perks were most probably acquainted with each other at a distance and may have interacted through business matters. They would have exchanged paperwork or words occasionally as part of the administrative requirements of their individual occupations. Jack Akbar may not have anticipated to what degree he was about to antagonise Constable Perks when he approached him to make some simple enquiries about obtaining the authority for a civil marriage ceremony. As well as being influenced by official guidelines, Perks had developed a personal view regarding Akbar. The Morgans policeman was irritated intensely by Akbar's presence in his town. His deep seated resentment of the Afghan had accumulated over time but had fired up, particularly since 1924, when Akbar opened his store within Perks's town. The explanation for this resentment was complex and historical.

The 1905 Aborigines Act institutionalised the practice of keeping Aboriginal people out of settlements. The duty of the country and outback policemen to keep their municipalities quite free of the indigenous population was guided particularly by two regulations of that Act. Section 37 stated that, 'If at any time he thinks it necessary to do so, a protector may cause any Aborigines or half-castes who are camped or are about to camp within or near the limits of any town or municipal district to remove their camp, or proposed camp, at such distance from such town or municipality as he may direct... Any native neglecting or refusing to obey such an order shall be guilty of an offence against the Act.'

The second regulation Perks followed diligently was Section 38; 'Any Justice of the Peace or police officer may order any Aboriginal found loitering in any town or municipal district, or being therein and not decently clothed, forthwith to leave such town or municipal district'[14].

The usual time for curfew for the Aboriginal people was between 3.30 p.m. and sunset[15]. Some of the constabulary drove them out of the towns almost every day and became very proud of the record they established for keeping their town 'clean' of these indigenous people[16]. Perks was a policeman who did his job 'according to the book'. He had built up over the past few years in Wiluna and now in Morgans a good record of keeping Aboriginal people out of his town.

The Police and Aborigines Departments did not have the same sympathy or attitude towards the Aboriginal people as did the Afghan storekeeper in Morgans. Akbar's observations of the life of Aboriginal people helped him understand why the Wongai of the eastern goldfields were hungry, unhappy and cautious to the extent of being intimidated and fearful. Akbar's perceptions of the Wongai would have been affected by what he understood shaped their circumstances. His own Afghan tribal ancestors would have had a similar experience, as have most indigenous groups, of facing invaders considering themselves the superior race and the resulting damage to their culture, heritage, and relationship to the land that that invasion rendered. Persecution by a repressive legislation, subjugation, the loss of dignity and often of freedom, were common characteristics of such invasions. The damage thus done to the society and culture of the Aboriginal people was extensive and permanent.

However, the perception held by the police of the Wongai was different. They saw these hungry and displaced indigenous descendants as nuisances and wretches. This perception was reflected in some words uttered in the 1920s by Mr E. Copping, the Deputy Chief Protector of the Aborigines Department in 1921. Ernest E. Copping had joined the Aborigines Department in 1919 when he was transferred from the Metropolitan Water Supply, Sewerage and Drainage Board, where he had been an assessor and receiver. Before 1919 Copping had no experience in Aboriginal affairs[17]. At his commencement of employment in the Aborigines Department Copping travelled about the country and visited the goldfields to do inspections and represent the Chief Protector. In 1921 he proposed to Police Commissioner Connell that the way to solve the increasing menace of Aboriginal people around Laverton would be to have all the indigenous people sent out to the bush where they should find a plentiful supply of food. It would be even more effective if the police were instructed to 'drive the Aborigines well back into the open country', which was essentially the arid spinifex country[18]. Between 1921 and 1926 the police stationed in the eastern goldfields at Laverton and

Morgans believed that a great deal of their time in police duties was preoccupied with keeping the local indigenous population in order and in removing them from towns and mining settlements. The Police Department used to control the 'problem of the natives' by keeping them out of town and out of sight[19].

By the time Akbar took up a business in Morgans in 1924 Constable Perks had significant control over the Wongai's movements in his town, keeping them out most of the time. The aggravation by Akbar of Perks could have been compounded by the arrival out of Morgans of another sympathiser of the Aboriginal people. A missionary, Rodolphe Schenk, had started a mission settlement in 1921 about 11 kilometres (seven miles) from Morgans. He was attempting to draw the Wongai from all over the district and to teach them to give up their nomadic ways and settle there. Perks would have been concerned about the two attractions to Aboriginal people in his area. The combination of the proximity of the mission and of the Afghan's store to his town site would increase the presence of Wongai in his town. This could affect adversely his reputation for keeping his town 'clean' and in order. On 31 May 1923 Perks reported to his superior, District Inspector H.E. Spedding Smith based at Kalgoorlie police headquarters, that there were 'about 130 indigents' at Morgans and the nearby mission[20].

By March 1924 Constable Perks was particularly alarmed about the presence and activities of Aborigines in his district. He reported to the District Police Inspector in Kalgoorlie that 'tribes of Aboriginal natives have been migrating for the past five weeks to Morgans from the spinifex country, Laverton, Kurnalpi, Yarri, Edjudina, Linden, Burtville, Sandstone, Wiluna, Lake Darlot and Leonora and various other centres, even from the Commonwealth Trans Australian railway line. Three to four hundred more were at the mission station where they were holding corroborees.' Perks admitted that the main reason for so many Aborigines coming in from the spinifex country was because 'many of these were starving'. It concerned him that his town might be beseiged by many Aborigines begging for food[21]. Soon after Perks reported that the missionary Schenk had managed to convince between three hundred and four hundred Aborigines to collect around his mission, and was either encouraging them to stay, return or leave their children with him[22].

With so much energy and commitment given to keeping Aboriginal people out of his municipality Perks most probably viewed any newcomer who was a sympathiser of the local Wongai as undermining his achievements, or possibly a threat to civil peace and order. Such persons were difficult for Perks to tolerate.

When Jack Akbar approached Constable Perks on 21 July 1926 to raise with him quite genuinely the notion of marrying one of the Aboriginal girls this would most probably have aggravated the policeman. Knowing what he did of relationships in Aboriginal families, Perks would have anticipated that a marriage of an Aboriginal girl to the town's storekeeper would initiate regular visits by her relatives. The rest of the Wongai, with their high regard for family and communal relationships, would follow. This could set back what he had achieved in keeping Morgans quite free of Aboriginal people. The townspeople and pastoralists, who were intolerant of Aboriginal sympathisers, could become so irate as to make formal complaints to police district headquarters in Kalgoorlie. Constable Perks could be seen as ineffective in his job. The missionary and the Afghan storekeeper presented a threat to his reputation and excellent record.

Should Constable Perks ever decide to rally opposition to the presence around Morgans of either the Afghan or the missionary he would find support quite readily. The 1920s was a decade emerging out of a preceding century that yielded the Darwinian biological theory which proposed that full-blood indigenous people were not humans in the full sense of the word. It was taught in academic institutions in the Western world, and believed by the literate and educated, that indigenous people were not likely to reach adulthood intellectually[23]. They were limited in their mental capacity and their level of achievement. Many colonists did not think that Aborigines had human emotions[24]. The prevailing attitude was that Aborigines were considered to be a dying race and there was nothing anyone could do[25]. To be sympathetic for the Aboriginal people was wasted sentiment. It would not win many votes for a political party to have as an election issue the abuse of civil rights of, or discriminaion against, the Aboriginal people.

With the combination of the evolutionary theory and the fact that many Aboriginal groups in the eastern goldfields still retained much of their traditional practices and customs, the police and the pastoralists in the eastern goldfields considered the Wongai and the Darlot to be the 'wildest and laziest tribes' in Western Australia and that nobody was safe from them. Their behaviour was socially undesirable and they were untrustworthy[26]. Accordingly, there would be minimal compassion for an Afghan, though well established commercially and regarded by his peers with respect, wishing to marry an Aboriginal girl.

The pastoralists represented some of the State's established wealthy families and occupied most of its interior land. A Pastoralists Association of Western Australia had existed since 1907 and had some influence in Parliament[27]. The police and the Chief Protector of Aborigines were sensitive to this group when their roles in controlling the Aboriginal population were criticised.

Pastoral lessees had their own particluar reasons for being vexed by the Aboriginal population. In their search for water the displaced indigenous people would camp near windmills on the cattle runs of pastoral properties. When cattle approached the dam adjacent to the windmills they became nervous once they sensed the presence of humans. The cattle would not come in close enough to the dams so that they could drink, and this was particularly threatening to livestock in summer or drought time[28]. The situation was aggravated when some Aboriginal people threatened the cattle further with guns. The authorities had supplied some Aboriginal people with rifles and ammunition so as to shoot kangaroo and other bush game for food. However, the Aboriginal people would seek this game out around waterholes, windmills and troughs. To get their prey the Aborigines would come down after sundown in a group to the water site and by shooting at the game would frighten the cattle and horses from the water. So the pastoralist's livestock would miss out on their drink. Some Aboriginal people shot holes in the water tanks. The damage to property and loss of life of their livestock increased their resentment and intolerance of the Aboriginal people[29].

Consequently, the pastoralists were allies of the police and the townspeople in driving the local Aborigines deeper into the scrub. In turn Perks realised the pastoralists and Morgans residents would not look upon him favourably if he took an individual stance and supported the application by the Afghan resident in the town to marry an Aboriginal female. They all knew the implications of the girl's relatives coming into the town and district.

The announcement by Akbar to Perks of the name of his proposed fiancée sealed the issue for the policeman. He recognised it as being the name of a part-Aboriginal girl that the Chief Protector had included on one of his Department's lists distributed to the local protectors in police stations. Thc name the Afghan mentioned was written on one of those lists as 'Nilba, alias Lallie Matbar, daughter of Tjirrgulu (Polly)'[30]. The police as local protectors were required then to observe the movements of those people in anticipation of their apprehension.

Perks had spent many of his hours on patrol in the previous years seeking information from the local Wongai on Lallie Matbar. In a report he sent on 26 August 1926 to District Inspector Spedding Smith at the Police District Office in Kalgoorlie, he declared that since his arrival in Morgans on 29 March 1923, he had 'done his utmost to secure the half caste girl Lallie Matbar at Linden'[31]. Until now when Akbar came to speak with him about a marriage, Perks had never actually seen Lallie. He was not able to identify her and this had been one of the reasons why he had not been successful so far in seizing her.

Perks may have expected that informing the Morgans Afghan of the regulations and procedures pertinent to marriage with an Aboriginal girl would have dissuaded the Afghan from persuing his case any further. He explained that the policeman acting as a local protector could not give the authority for such a marriage to occur. That authority had to come from the Chief Protector of Aborigines who was located in Perth. Perks had in mind Section 42 of the 1905 Aborigines Act, which stated that the marriage of a man who was not an Aboriginal to a 'female Aboriginal' would be allowed only if the Chief Protector of Aborigines gave it his permission, and it had to come from him in writing[32].

Constable Perks would have realised also that Akbar was quite familiar with this girl who was wanted by the police. Akbar had the advantage over Perks in that the former knew her identity, had known her for some time and most likely knew how to locate her at any time. It must have raised some anger about Akbar in Perks to even think that this Asian foreigner was making effortless progress in the matter of knowing this girl and locating her at will, a matter in which Perks was expected by his superiors to show wit, cunning and intelligence and in which over time Perks had not made any progress. For both official and personal reasons Constable Perks could not consider rewarding this Afghan for his upper hand in a police matter by despatching to the Chief Protector a request to obtain permission for a marriage between a resented Afghan and a wanted Aboriginal girl.

While Jack Akbar was talking on the subject of his proposed marriage Perks used this opportunity to his advantage. He thought of a way in which this Afghan might be of some assistance to him in completing a task. He would utilise the Afghan to help him catch the Linden girl and thus maintain his impeccable reputation. Perks needed to be able to recognise the girl's face so that when he was out on patrol he could himself catch her. He would attempt to convince Jack Akbar to bring the girl out of the bush into Morgans and then he would have a good look at her. What the Linden people feared, the use by the police of Akbar to get to Lallie, was about to commence.

This ploy would have an additional benefit for Perks. The Morgans constable had also been wanting to find a means to discredit the reputation of the Afghan storekeeper with both the Police and Aborigines Departments. If he could demonstrate to these two government departments that Jack Akbar may have breached any regulations of the 1905 Aborigines Act then he may be able to convince his superiors to initiate the closure of Jack's business in the area, and thus accomplish the eviction of the Afghan storekeeper from the municipality. Once Jack had departed, a major factor influencing the presence of the local Aboriginal people in town would be removed.

One regulation of the 1905 Aborigines Act that Perks considered the Afghan may have breached was in Section 43, which made it illegal 'for any person who habitually lives with Aborigines, or any male person not his husband or wife, to cohabit if not married'. This section further declared that 'every male person, not being an Aboriginal, who travels accompanied by a female Aboriginal, shall be presumed to be cohabiting with her, and it shall be presumed she is not his wife'. Another regulation Perks hoped to catch Akbar offending was in Section 36: 'It shall not be lawful for any person without lawful excuse to enter or remain or be within or upon any place where Aborigines or female half-castes are camped'[33]. Perks had learned by his enquiries of other Aboriginal people in the district of Lallie's third pregnancy. At this stage his investigations had not revealed who the biological father of this baby was. If Perks could present a convincing case that Jack was most likely the father then he could persuade the Chief Protector and the Police Department to consider that the Afghan had committed one or two offences against the 1905 Act. Not only may have Jack, an Asiatic, practised cohabitation with a half-caste female, but it was specifically stated that Asiatics were forbidden to associate with them and they to travel with them and Perks may be able to prove that Jack and Lallie had committed these offences.

Perks deduced that there could be another offence that Jack may have committed. If Perks could verify that Akbar knew where to find Lallie Matbar, and he had not informed the police of his knowledge, then that could be construed to be 'harbouring a half caste sought by the law'[34].

If Perks could present a solid case that unlawful behaviour had been committed by both Jack Akbar and Lallie Matbar, then it would be possible that an order would be made out to have both the Afghan hawker and the Linden girl taken into custody and removed from the district. At this stage the case against Akbar and Lallie was all mere conjecture. The Constable needed more proof of the condition of the girl and the behaviour of both. He needed to see Lallie.

Jack Akbar also needed the cooperation of the Morgans policeman. He wanted the policeman to believe his proposal was genuine and to consider his case seriously enough to write the application on his behalf to the Chief Protector of Aborigines in Perth, and to include the request for an exemption to Section 42. He suggested to the Constable that the girl's pregnancy and consequent health deserved some special consideration. Akbar hoped that the constable would persuade Mr Neville in Perth to comprehend how exceptional was the situation of Jack Akbar and Lallie Matbar, and the need for promptness in permitting their marriage. The Morgans officer informed Jack Akbar that he could give him more specific advice if the girl was brought to him so that he could assess the state of her health.

Perks provided further reason to convince Akbar of the expediency of bringing Lallie to him. The Constable reiterated how difficult it would be for Akbar as a non-tribal man to get permission to marry an Aboriginal girl. However, with Lallie present before him he could assess the girl's pregnant condition and determine the degree of urgency of Jack and Lallie's overall situation. It would be easier for Perks to attach an appeal for special consideration to Akbar's request for permission to marry an Aboriginal girl.

This suggestion would have stirred some anxiety and alarm in Jack's heart. He knew that the Wongai were afraid of police coming too close to their people and, in particular, of removing pregnant, unmarried, part-Aboriginal girls. Jack would have known of their concern about police taking the opportunity to track him in his truck into the bush to find their way to Lallie. Constable Perks was not offering any guarantee that if Lallie was brought into Morgans she would not be seized and locked up in readiness for removal. The Morgans policeman was now putting Akbar in the situation of being the one who could possibly put Lallie at serious risk.

Jack Akbar acknowledged all sources of authority. With Constable Perks making clear to him the regulations of the 1905 Aborigines Act, Jack comprehended how dependent he was on the government's leniency in granting him an exemption. Understanding the conditions attached to Perks sending the written application off to Perth, and understanding the need to cajole the government to develop a sympathy for his case, there was little left for Jack to do but to cooperate with Perks's suggestion of convincing Lallie to come into town and out into the open.

After his conversation with Perks Jack had two significant matters to raise with the elders of Lallie's people. He had to maintain their interest in considering his proposal to marry Lallie. He had also to obtain their agreement to bring one of their unmarried, pregnant girls out of the seclusion of the bush into a town to face a policeman. The first proposal the elders might consider acceptable and for the benefit of their girl. They would undoubtedly perceive Akbar's second proposal as tinted with risk and against their better judgement. Akbar could understand that the elders would need some time to consider these two proposals before they could give him their decisions. The granting of permission by the elders was not a simple matter. For himself, Akbar must have felt that for every step forward, for every little bit of hope he was given in his quest for marriage to Lallie a challenge or frustration immediately arose. However, he would not be deterred from the decision he had made about who was the woman he wanted as his legal wife.

It was still complex for the Linden elders to assess Lallie's single status, and to find an appropriate husband for her. In regard to their culture and the consequences for their people, they had a number of issues to take into account. One issue was that the elders would have to refer to the traditional customs and laws that set out who should be promised to whom, and who were in the appropriate group for partnership. If they could find another man amongst their own people to whom Lallie could be promised, they would be bound to give priority to that arrangement. The Afghan's offer to be Lallie's provider had to wait its turn to be given due consideration.

Another issue the elders had to consider was the safety of the children in their group, as well as the safety of individuals. The elders were aware that the police knew now that Jack intended to marry Lallie and that he had been seeing her. They were most likely to intensify their efforts to catch Lallie, and track Jack to her and her people. The least attention the Linden group could draw to the members or the whereabouts of their group, the greater their degree of safety and the safety of their children.

The time came when the council of elders reconsidered the marriage of Lallie to the Afghan from Morgans. One factor they may have taken in to account was that Jack Akbar had been a friend and a good person to these people for a long time. As it had been difficult for them to find a suitable tribal man who was prepared to be a provider for her, her expected child and perhaps her mother, they were prepared to accept Jack Akbar into their people. The elders finally consented to the marriage of Jack and Lallie.

Jack would have conveyed to the elders how pleased their decision would have made him. However, his personal business with the elders was not complete. He had yet to convince them of another proposal. They had to see reason to giving him permission to take Lallie out from the cover of the bush into Morgans where a policeman would be waiting to see her. The earnest suitor was eventually given an answer regarding taking Lallie into Morgans. They would allow Lallie to leave the protection of her people and go to Morgans with Jack. The condition to this arrangement was that some of the elders would accompany Tjirrgulu's daughter. The policeman had not guaranteed the girl's safety[35].

Akbar was probably not aware of what the name 'Lallie' meant to Constable Perks and the Aborigines Department. He may not have known of recent developments. As the police had made little headway over a period of time in trying to locate then catch Lallie Matbar the Chief Protector of Aborigines himself had ordered a senior representative of his department to go out to the eastern goldfields to investigate the situation concerning this case. In July 1926 Deputy Chief Protector Copping visited Constable Perks of Morgans police station. Copping raised his department's concern about the lack of progress by this policeman in catching and removing this same girl. During their discussion Copping strongly advised Constable Perks to maintain his attempts to secure the Linden girl. The Constable was encouraged by Copping to anticipate that when Lallie was caught an order would be made out for her removal[36]. It was about ten days after Copping met with Perks that Akbar first announced that he wished to marry the same girl that Copping had admonished Constable Perks for not yet catching!

The day came when Jack Akbar drove Lallie into Perks's town. One can imagine the feeling of satisfaction which would have surged through the Constable's body. Jack introduced the pregnant girl as Lallie and their companions as some of the elders of the Linden mob. It would have been very likely that the interaction between all was determined by the questions the policeman asked.

The elders conveyed to the Morgans policeman that they were agreeable to the marriage of Lallie and Jack. They added that they believed their girl 'wished to change her mode of living' and that she was agreeable to the marriage also[37].

Perks would not have been very interested in the words of the elders or what Lallie's needs or wishes were. He had an ulterior motive for them all being together and was mindful of expectations placed on him by Deputy Chief Protector Copping. The focus of his attention was on the physical appearance and state of health of the girl. While she was in his field of vision Constable Perks would memorise her physical details, assess the state of her health and the stage of her pregnancy. He needed to be able to identify her from other girls her age, given that he may be in receipt soon of an order that would require her seizure. He could have surmised privately why she was in that condition and whether or not she indicated she was experiencing neglect.

Perks's ulterior motive was satisfied. He could now identify Lallie Matbar when the time came to apprehend her. By witnessing her pregnant condition he assumed that he had sufficient evidence on which to build his case that the Moslem Asiatic and the Wongai girl had offended sections of the 1905 Aborigines Act. The knowledge that Jack had been keeping company with Lallie together with her pregnancy implied to Perks that Jack Akbar had breached Section 43 of the 1905 Act. According to the information Perks elicited from the elders, Lallie Matbar currently had no reliable provider for herself and her expected child. This made it more of a priority for her to be removed from her people and transported to an instituion where she and the child could be given a better kind of care, moral environment and discipline; a 'native institution' like the Moore River Native Settlement to the north of Perth.

It is most likely that Perks did not perceive any positive attributes in the three parties petitioning him. The Constable's view of the situation was most probably that an Afghan was enticing local Aboriginal people to come into the town from which they were barred. To Perks the Afghan's pursuit of a matter that he had been expressly told was prohibited demonstrated a lack of cooperation with the law. Perks did not regard the Aboriginal girl as being of strong character for taking a comparatively brave stand by coming out of the bush into his proximity. Nor did the policeman respect the quality of the proposal Jack was making. Many men of British, European and even Asiatic ancestry got an Aboriginal girl pregnant, or used her company for the night, but rarely did any of Perks's own race come forward, as did this Afghan, with such dignity, pride and demonstration of responsibility and offer to permanently provide for an Aboriginal woman with or without a child.

The Constable of Morgans did not make his move to seize Lallie on this occasion. He used the opportunity to remind them all about the regulations of the 1905 Act such as Section 36, 42 and 43 concerning relationships with and marriage of part-Aboriginal females. He reiterated that the marriage of Lallie and the Afghan was illegal and an impossible partnership. He insisted there was no future for their relationship[38].

The elders realised that the policeman did not consent to Lallie's marriage to Jack Akbar and his words were sounding alarm in their hearts. They wanted to leave Morgans and take Lallie back to the bush where she would be given genuine protection. Before departing with his Aboriginal companions, Akbar wanted to confirm Perks's intentions. He had cooperated with the policeman and wanted to know if the policeman would be reciprocating by writing to the Chief Protector in Perth to request an exemption to Section 42, and attach an appeal for special consideration. Perks worded his reply so that the Afghan suitor was left believing there was no need to doubt that the request with its appeal would be written and sent to Perth.

Perks watched Jack's truck as it drove out of town to take Lallie and the Wongai men back to Linden. The Constable felt that he had given Jack Akbar all the courtesy and information he was bound by duty to give. However, he was not about to bow to the extraordinary expectations of this seemingly arrogant, ignorant, even insolent Afghan who would not take the Constable's advice and end the subject of his marriage to the bush girl. Looking at the markings the tyres of Jack's truck were making in the dust Perks must have been amused by how easy they would make the future search for Lallie.

While waiting to hear word from Perks that a response to his application had come from the Chief Protector's office in Perth, Jack Akbar continued to cart goods or make deliveries under contracts and to manage his store, and Lallie continued to live with her people. After a few weeks Akbar went to speak with Perks to enquire if he had received any response from the Chief Protector's office[39]. One can imagine how the raising of this matter by Akbar would have annoyed the policeman. Perks would have perceived this as the Afghan having not been intimidated enough by his authority to withdraw his request.

Perks's irritation would have been compounded by some new information he gained about the Morgans Afghan. He learned that Akbar was maintaining his relationship with the Wongai girl. He was in the weekly habit of selling foodstuffs in and camping at the Aboriginal camps at Linden, and that he invited Aboriginal persons to travel in his truck with him when he went from one centre in the bush to another[40]. There was also an increase in the number of visits by the local Aborigines to Jack's shop in Morgans. The local residents reported to Perks that when he was absent from town on patrol or pursuing inquiries, Morgans would be full of 'natives' whose behaviour they summed up as 'loitering' around Akbar's shop and being 'a source of annoyance to the public'[41].

What Perks had decided to tell Akbar now was in line with both of his dual roles, policeman and protector, in enforcing the regulations of the Act. The Constable informed the Moslem storekeeper that he had never written the request for exemption for one of the Chief Protector's young wards to marry an elderly Afghan. He then added directive to disappointment by reinforcing to the Afghan the absolute prohibition of his marriage with an Aborigine[42].

The Constable may have expected that his announcement of not writing the request would have made a final devastating, convincing impact on Akbar. The Afghan would feel both such depth of frustration and the weight and persuasion of the policeman's authority that he would accept defeat finally and totally. The matter of the Afghan's marriage to a half-caste girl should end there.

The Afghan may have been caught by surprise by the policeman's announcement. He may not have expected such deception. Nevertheless, he was not to be dissuaded from his quest and apparently was quick to collect his thoughts.

Akbar's reaction would not at all have been anticipated by the policeman. The unflappable and resolute Afghan announced that he would seek consultation beyond Morgans with an alternative authority on the law. He would refer his case to a solicitor in Kalgoorlie[43].

The resourcefulness of the storekeeper may have both startled and vexed Perks. Akbar's announcement was akin to defiance. The Moslem's persistence with his cause could have ramifications for Perks personally and professionally around the community. Akbar was creating the potential to undermine Perks's position and credibility in his own district. With Akbar not prepared to dismiss the marriage to the girl Perks would not be able to cease the problem of the swelling presence of Aborigines in his town and municipality.

After the unpleasant business with Perks Jack Akbar remained single-minded in achieving his goal, rather than feeling the dejection anticipated by Perks. Most likely, the man to have felt anger, frustration, defeat and ineffectiveness was Constable Perks of Morgans.

Perks was not to be deterred, either, from the pursuit of his own duties. His department had a channel of communication to which he could resort, though he may not use it as honestly and as openly as Akbar was to use his. The Constable would use the procedure of regular reporting to the district head office in Kalgoorlie to campaign for the discrediting of Jack's reputation, and possibly align enough opposition so that action would be initiated for Akbar's removal from Morgans. In the last few days of July 1926 Perks's reports included two letters addressed to two different departments, that of the Aborigines and of the Police, which included comments designed to discredit Akbar's character and to justify the need to compile a case against him.

One of the letters was addressed to Perks's superior in Kalgoorlie, the District Inspector of Police (D.I.P.) Spedding Smith. In that letter Perks declared that he had very good reason to believe that the Afghan named Jack Akbar, who had a store in Morgans, was not cooperating with the police or the law. He related to Spedding Smith that the Afghan suitor intended to ignore the advice of the local protector and go beyond Section 42 of the 1905 Aborigines Act by seeking the advice of a solicitor.

Perks raised the added suspicion that Perks had caught a venereal disease from Lallie. Since his meeting with Lallie, Perks had been informed that the Linden girl was suspected of suffering from venereal disease. The Constable knew his superior would take note of this detail. Venereal disease was a widespread problem amongst certain populations of Aboriginal people, and the Aborigines Department had spent much time in the past several years attempting to contain it[44]. As Akbar was known to keep company with Lallie it was quite likely that he had caught the complaint from her. This in turn inferred illegal cohabitation between a non-tribal man and a half-caste girl. If Lallie and Jack were keeping company it could be considered that Jack Akbar was harbouring her. The Morgans Constable may have hoped that the district office would see enough cause here to take action against the Morgans storekeeper.

Though Perks had not himself seen Jack displaying symptoms of a veneral disease, such information could be used by Perks to add to the case against the Afghan. Perks could infer to his Inspector that Akbar's relationship with the Aboriginal people was sordid, thus further discrediting the Afghan's character. His senior officer would be more likely to consider a case for having Akbar dismissed from the town altogether. Perks also recommended to his superior that Akbar should not be allowed to sell foodstuffs if he was suffering from any disease. The Constable had learned from informants that Akbar was telling the 'natives' that 'he is their brother', so Perks implied that Akbar may have caught the disease from one of them if not from Lallie. His deduction was that Akbar's association with the Wongai was unhealthy and could in turn, through his business, introduce unhealthy standards which could affect the local residents who purchased his foodstuffs[45].

The second letter completed by Constable Perks was directed to Deputy Chief Protector Copping. Details contained in the correspondence discredited the character of Lallie and Jack, and referred to the suspicion that both individuals may have contracted a veneral disease. He added that any person who was suffering from such a disease had no right to handle foodstuffs and sell them to the public, and consequently should be stopped by an appropriate health authority. By providing Copping with current details on the Akbar-Matbar case Perks hoped that the Deputy Chief Protector of Aborigines would consider that this case had become serious enough to recommend to the Chief Protector of Aborigines that action be taken. The apprehension and removal of the girl from the district could be followed by the closing down of Akbar's business and his dismissal from Morgans. At the bottom of the letter addressed to Copping Perks added that he did not want Akbar to know that he was the one who mentioned this matter about Akbar's dubious behaviour to Copping[46].

Inspector Spedding Smith did take some notice of Constable Perks's recent report regarding the Akbar-Matbar case. He passed it on, with an additional note of concern, to the Police Commissioner in Perth. Spedding Smith then quite promptly sent a reply to the Morgans policeman. He instructed Constable Perks to observe Jack Akbar regularly and to continue to furnish head office with full particulars on the Linden girl and on Akbar[47]. There was no mention of any forthcoming action.

A reaction from Copping or the Chief Protector of Aborigines took longer in coming to Perks. The overall achievement of the two letters sent by Perks to the senior levels of two departments was not as he anticipated. He had merely raised their interest in the Akbar-Matbar case, and in turn they had advised Perks to continue to watch for a girl he found difficult to locate and take into custody.

By early August 1926, Lallie's pregnancy was in its seventh month. Jack wanted written permission for their marriage to be in his possession before the child was born. He wanted to give the child his surname when it was born. It was while the response from the District Inspector of Police was on its way to Constable Perks that Jack Akbar left Morgans for Kalgoorlie to seek the services of a solicitor.

While Jack Akbar was seeking an exemption from a regulation, he did not want to go beyond the law. When Jack arrived in Kalgoorlie he made another attempt to comply with the Sections of the 1905 Aborigines Act. He went to police headquarters where he sought the assistance of the duty officer on the matter of his marriage to an Aboriginal girl. Jack

Akbar informed Sergeant W. McGuiniss where he had come from and why he had come to Kalgoorlie. The Sergeant would have understood that the Afghan's business was most irregular and would have suspected that the Afghan may have breached one, if not more, of the regulations of the 1905 Aborigines Act. In Lallie's DCS file it reports that Sergeant McGuiniss excused himself from Akbar's company so that he could check police files for what details they may have so far accumulated on Lallie Matbar or the Afghan.

When the Sergeant returned he told Jack Akbar that he had noticed in some reports that there were some references that implicated Lallie and the Afghan in illegal activities. Jack declared that neither he nor Lallie had committed any offences against the 1905 Act. However, McGuiniss was not prepared to offer Akbar any more help than that offered by Constable Perks[48]. To obtain the exemption so that he could marry Lallie Jack Akbar was left with no choice now but to approach a solicitor's office.

By 4 August 1926 Akbar had made the acquaintance of Mr Reg F. Cook, a solicitor of the Palace Chambers, Maritana Street, Kalgoorlie. Once Cook heard the full details of Jack Akbar's proposed business with him he would have realised that the appeal that the Afghan storekeeper wanted to put to the Chief Protector of Aborigines involved stepping beyond the law as stated in a government regulation and thus was quite irregular. Perhaps Cook was impressed by the sincerity and the calibre of the Afghan storekeeper, who wanted to be married legally to an Aborigine rather than participate in the widespread practice of cohabitation. Akbar had found his solicitor.

The two men attempted to identify and consolidate arguments that could be used in seeking an exemption from a regulation and being provided with written permission for a prohibited marriage between an Asian and a part-Aborigine. The contents in Lallie's DCS file indicate that in their conversation that day Cook suggested to Jack that the main assets in their case to demonstrate to the government Jack's genuine concern for Lallie would be: the credibility of Jack as a hard worker; his success as a businessman with a good and reliable reputation; the quality of his character, and that he was able to care for Lallie financially and morally. The solicitor then composed his first petition to the Chief Protector of Aborigines in Perth, Auber Octavius Neville, for an exemption to a marriage involving an Aboriginal girl[49].

To add weight to persuasion, the solicitor further informed the Chief Protector of Aborigines that Akbar would not be setting a precedent in being legally married to an Aboriginal girl. A local Afghan Habebullah, who lived around Kalgoorlie and who had been making some enquiries on behalf of his friend, had found out that 'a pastoralist named Beydullah in the Murchison district' was married to a part-Aboriginal woman[50]. Cook's letter was sent to Perth a week after Perks had sent the second of his two letters.

By August 1926 two main streams of communication had been established in regard to this extraordinary case. The sources of the two streams were common, being based in the eastern goldfields, but they flowed against each other to a common destination, the Chief Protector of Aborigines. One stream originated with the police constables in the goldfields in close proximity to Lallie, the Wongai and Jack Akbar, passing through their Inspector in the District Police Headquarters at Kalgoorlie, and finishing with the Police Commissioner in Perth, Mr Connell. He communicated with the Chief Protector of the Aborigines on police matters relevant to enforcing the regulations of the 1905 Aborigines Act. The second stream of correspondence was initiated by Jack Akbar in cooperation with his solicitor in Kalgoorlie and was directed to the Chief Protector of Aborgines.

After Perks received the letter from Inspector Spedding Smith which advised him to continue to monitor the movements and behaviour of the Afghan and the Linden Wongai girl, he may have felt initially that he was making progress in evoking support from his superiors. His department would be more likely from now on to pay more attention to any evidence, whether factual or conjectured, that he may raise with them. This would all contribute to defaming Akbar. Perks would be able to prompt the issuing of the order to remove either Lallie or Jack from the district.

Throughout August Perks attempted to monitor the movements of Akbar and to collect what details he could from informants on the whereabouts and state of health of Lallie. In his regular reports to Kalgoorlie Perks continued to remind the authorities that there was a case of the Afghan breaching a regulation of the Aborigines Act. His informants reported that Jack was regularly having Lallie sit beside him in his truck when he was making deliveries out in the bush. Some of the informants were accusing Lallie of lodging with Jack. When Akbar called into 'the whites camp' he would not allow any male person to speak to Lallie, but the girl was allowed to speak to any white woman[51]. This was probably in keeping with the Moslem tradition that girls promised to or wives of Moslem men could not speak with other men without their husbands being present. Perks attempted to incorporate the collaboration of the officer-in-charge at Leonora, requesting him to make what observations and notes he could on Akbar and Lallie. He was not to capture that girl until he received instructions to do so. Perks hoped that by collecting information from enquiries amongst the public that the police could gather enough incriminating, or direct, evidence to be able to prosecute Jack Akbar for lodging with Lallie[52].

Though the continued reporting on Lallie and Jack Akbar set off a ripple of concern in police headquarters in Kalgoorlie and in Perth, it did not evoke a decision from the senior administration level of the Police or the Aborigines Departments to take action against the two suspected offenders. It was still up to the Constable in Morgans to maintain their interest in the Akbar-Matbar case. District Inspector Spedding Smith in Kalgoorlie advised Perks in Morgans to adhere to the instructions of the Deputy Chief Protector of Aborigines and to still try and get hold of the Linden girl, as well as obtain proof that the Afghan trader was cohabiting with the Linden girl and could justifiably be accused by the police of breaching a regulation. Spedding Smith suggested to Perks that if he was sure that Akbar was dealing in and handling foodstuffs while he was suffering from a venereal disease, then he should collect more details to confirm this and send them in a separate report to his office in Kalgoorlie[53].

It had not been an easy exercise in the past few years for Perks to locate, let alone catch, Lallie. Even though now he could identify her, the task of actually coming face to face with her had not become any easier. Even though Perks could track the tyres of Jack's truck in the bush, the Afghan continued to outpace and outwit him. Constable Perks would need to lean more heavily on the collaboration of his network of spies and informants. These persons were either town residents or pastoralists who were in the position to observe the movements of individuals or groups of Wongai. They were supporters of the police policy of keeping Aboriginal people out of settlements and off pastoral properties. One pastoralist who agreed to cooperate with the police in attempting to catch Lallie was Mrs Lynch of Mount Celia station. She and Perks agreed that, should Lallie come onto her station, she would retain the girl by offering her work in household duties. Lynch would then send for Perks at the first opportunity. Perks made a similar plan with the residents of Yundamundra station[54].

The Constable's network of 'traps', places where people had agreed to be police collaborators, included both non-Aboriginal and Aboriginal people. In his setting up of traps about the countryside to catch Lallie

Perks was able to gain the apparently willing assistance of two Wongai. They arranged with Constable Perks to attempt to secure Lallie if she returned to Linden. As soon as they had done that they would ask Mr Swanson, manager of the Linden hotel, to telephone Perks so that he could come and get her. Perks was able to assure Inspector Spedding Smith that these two particular male Aboriginals would secure Lallie if they got the chance[55].

Though the genuine Afghan's case to marry an Aborigine did not develop any sympathy from the police or the Aborigines Department, his cause was apparently gaining sympathy amongst some individuals of his district. They believed that a man of Akbar's fine character, personal integrity, good business reputation and potential to be a good provider should be allowed to marry the woman he wanted as his wife. His persistence with his marriage proposal demonstrated to these people how genuine he was in his desire to marry and care for this girl. These people were less reluctant to cooperate with the police and when questioned by them did not give exactly accurate answers. This indirect support for Akbar's cause was one reason why, by the end of August, Perks had not been successful on his patrols in even getting close to seizing Lallie, in spite of his network of informants. His progress was obstructed by the dishonest or unproductive answers he received from a range of Aboriginal and European people when he made enquiries about the whereabouts of Lallie, and the movements and behaviours of Jack Akbar. Some of the Wongai who were sympathetic to Lallie 'marrying' informed Perks it seemed that Jack Akbar had taken her away from their camp. Other Wongai added to Perks's confusion about where he might go to find Lallie. Some commented that Akbar had Lallie secluded at Kanowna while he was conducting his business with a solicitor in Kalgoorlie. Others told Perks that when Akbar returned from Kalgoorlie he advised Lallie to go deeper into the bush with other Wongai who were heading out into the spinifex country. If the latter version was the correct one Perks knew he had no chance of catching Lallie. It was very far beyond his district and she could be out there for a long time. A fourth response Perks got from some Wongai was that Lallie could have gone out to Karonie, a rail siding settlement along the Transcontinental Rail Line towards the Nullabor Plain which was also a significant meeting place for eastern goldfields Aborigines[56]. Perks was left undecided about what would be the most effective action for him to take so as to get the best results for his efforts, given that her possible location extended over hundreds of square kilometres.

Perks became aware that those members of the community who were sympathetic to Akbar and Lallie's cause were observing his movements. It became difficult for him to approach anyone without them knowing already of or being prepared for his approach. It was obvious that people were being warned about his arrival and what it was that he wanted to know. Perks reported to Inspector Spedding Smith that when he was out looking for Lallie it was difficult for him to travel from Morgans to Linden 'without the whites or the aboriginals' knowing his movements. Perks suspected that one of those who warned the Wongai at Linden of the policeman's approach was Jack Akbar himself. Perks noted that the Afghan carter tended to arrive at Linden with his motor truck selling foodstuffs the day before Perks visited[57].

Perks was vexed by Akbar in a number of ways. In spite of Akbar being instructed by Perks to stay away from the Linden girl the Afghan continued to give food and clothes to Lallie, her mother and some of her people. The assistance, both in food and information, that Jack Akbar was giving to the Linden mob was a significant obstruction to the Constable's job. No doubt the Afghan and the Linden mob would discuss the policeman of Morgans. Perks presumed that because of his association with Lallie Jack knew almost all the time where Lallie would be. However, the Constable could not outwit the Wongai or track Jack to the girl. Because of his motor truck Akbar was always ahead of Perks, and because he camped anywhere in the bush he was not always placed conveniently for Perks to find him so that he could track him[58].

As Perks could not find direct evidence to charge Jack or Lallie with breaching any regulations he would be depending on Akbar's state of health to provoke the Police Department into effective action. Recent information could prompt a response. One informant was told that Akbar had broken out in running sores about his arms and body 'six weeks ago'. The Afghan had received daily medical treatment for a while at the Mount Morgans General Hospital, which was situated just over one kilometre out of Morgans[59]. Some medicines and ointments had been prescribed for Akbar by the matron, who in 1926 was Emily Hart[60]. However, by the time the informant actually conveyed this information to Perks the informant believed that Akbar was rid of this complaint.

Reports like this compromised the effectiveness of the evidence Perks was accumulating to prove that there were grounds for closing down Akbar's business. He hoped that there might be more evidence yet about this aspect of Akbar's health that could still be collected and used against him. He asked the informant to report immediately to the police if the sores reappeared on Akbar. Perks did consider personally calling on the matron at the Morgans hospital to make enquiries about her patient Akbar. However, he allowed himself to be intimidated by the possibility that she would tell him to 'mind his own business'[61].

While Perks was collaborating with his informants and senior officers to either trap the Linden girl or to find evidence that would justify closing down Akbar's business, the second stream of correspondence to A.O. Neville, produced by the partnership of Jack Akbar and Cook, his Kalgoorlie solicitor, was to increase in volume.

CHAPTER THREE

The Chief Protector of Aborigines

When the Chief Protector of Aborigines, Auber Neville, received the first letter from the Kalgoorlie solicitor in early August 1926, it was the third item of correspondence to reach him within a matter of days which referred to the case of a prohibited marriage between an Asiatic, Jack Akbar, of Morgans and a part-Aboriginal girl, Lallie, of the Laverton-Linden area. The two reports sent by Constable Perks, one to Police Inspector Spedding Smith and the other to the Aborigines Department's Deputy Chief Protector Copping, had already been received by Neville for his attention.

The three letters concerning the Akbar-Matbar case may have evoked annoyance and agitation from this senior administrator for a number of reasons peculiar to his official and personal circumstances. To respond officially to the request for an exemption to the regulations governing the marriage of his female wards would have been at the simplest level.

However, the rationale behind Neville's response to Jack Akbar's request for an exemption was much more complex. There were personal as well as official issues at stake. The timing of the arrival of these letters made it unacceptable for Neville to even consider this once making an exception to his own or an Act's rules. They came at a time in Neville's career when he was attempting to consolidate his department, improve its status and expand its control over the Aboriginal population. His rationale would have been based on several factors. The content of the letters would have conflicted with some of Neville's political and philosophical beliefs. The three letters brought all these into the foreground.

Auber Octavius Neville was born in 1875 to a clergyman's wife in

Northumberland, England. He was the youngest of eight sons and lived amongst the privileged landed gentry. Duty, authority, financial security, status, the adornments of a successful career, and the expansion of the British Empire were valued in the society of Auber's growing years. When he was twenty years old his mother died and the cohesion of the family was further fractured by some of Auber's brothers emigrating to the colonies to start new lives and establish careers. Auber and two of his brothers decided to emigrate to Western Australia.

In 1897 Auber found employment in Perth in the Public Service as a clerk in the Department of Works. He and his two brothers mixed with Perth's ruling elite families who maintained the codes of behaviour of the upper classes of British society. His two brothers married into families who had significant positions in administration and government. Auber was soon to gain promotion and by 1908 was Secretary for Immigration. In 1910 he took leave to visit England, where he was visited in turn by a Perth socialite, his friend Gypsy Sutherland Low, whom he married there. While in England a good position was found for Auber in the Public Service in Perth. He was selected to manage the new government department in Western Australia of Immigration, Tourism and General Information.

In 1912, Auber aged thirty-seven years and Gypsy aged thirty-one years became parents of a son, John. Within the next few years a shuffling of personnel within the public service improved Neville's job status once again. In 1915, the current Chief Protector of Aborigines C.F. Gale was dismissed from his office by the Minister for Aborigines R. H. Underwood, and Neville, who did not apply for that job, was given the position[1].

Though the attainment of this new position flattered Neville, it also brought criticism into his public life. His only experience for the job of Chief Protector was eighteen years as a civil servant in a city office, skills in the procedures of bureaucracy, and a background in duty[2]. Civil servants who questioned the way the previous Chief Protector Gale was dismissed wanted an enquiry into the change of personnel in that office. Because of the way in which Neville was appointed to the position his popularity was compromised from the beginning of his term in office. He was considered to be an interloper[3].

In his new office Neville had to be firm and decisive. Minister Underwood had an abrasive manner and wanted results from his staff. He was not interested in appeals for consideration or explanations for delays. From the beginning of his term as Chief Protector of Aborigines

Neville was under some pressure to perform. He attempted to demonstrate leadership and productivity by a reorganisation of the Aborigines Department, a cut back in expenditure and by aiming to produce results. So as to avoid visible failure Neville in turn could not show sympathy, nor condone exemptions to regulations. He did not receive any professional advice or support from Gale. It may not have been the most satisfying start for Neville. It had attracted a nucleus of critics who were to continue observing his career. Their existence contributed to his alienation from a faction of the conservative establishment.

Nevertheless, Auber Neville, now aged forty, wanted to be successful in this position and would exercise the power and authority to which he was entitled. In late September 1915 he travelled south on his first tour of inspection of his new wards. In April 1916 he toured with the Minister for Aborigines, Underwood, to the Kimberleys. Aboriginal affairs were to enter a new phase under A.O. Neville.

When Auber Octavius Neville took up his appointment on 16 March 1915 as Chief Protector of Aborigines his office was located in a rather obscure set of rooms at the rear of the Colonial Secretary's building at 57 Murray Street Perth[4]. Though Neville was given a position as head of a government department the department in which he was put in charge was small and politically insignificant. The Aborigines Department came into existence on 1 April 1898, replacing the Aborigines Protection Board as the agency responsible for the administration of Aboriginal affairs. It was allocated a small annual budget which could only support a small staff. This kept it near the bottom of the colonial administrative structure. Because of his department's insignificance, it had been assigned to the Colonial Secretary's Office. Though Neville was the sole proprietor of the Aboriginal people of Western Australia, there was no growth of funds and staff[5]. Because of the popular evolutionary theories of the times the Government probably did not consider the indigenous population significant enough for this department to be independent. Between 1909 and 1920 the Aborigines Department was amalgamated with the Department of Fisheries, and between 1915, the year of Neville's appointment, and 1920 it was combined with the Department of Fisheries and Immigration. The union with the Department of Fisheries emerged because the interests of both agencies lay in the north of the state. Before 1920 the administrative staff of the Department of Aborigines, Fisheries and Immigration consisted of a secretary and seven clerks. The Fisheries Department had seven inspectors compared to none for the Aborigines Department[6].

The 1904 Roth Royal Commission produced the 1905 Aborigines Act which has been described as esentially the 'first piece of anti-Aboriginal legislation'. Neville became the Chief Protector of Aborigines under an Act which had placed more Aboriginal people than ever before under the control of his office. The Commission had recommended that the definition of 'native', which referred to 'full-blood' Aboriginal people only, be revised so that it included the increasing number of 'half-castes', and that was the definition incorporated in the 1905 Aborigines Act. It was to be some years later that the definition of 'native' was revised again. During his career Neville wanted control over as many Aboriginal people as possible, particularly part-white Aboriginal people. This was motivated by his ideal of achieving assimilation. By the late 1920s Neville was proposing amendments to the 1905 Aborigines Act to Parliament. By 1936 the definition of 'native' was altered so as to include 'quadroons'[7]. In his ambition to gain as much control over as many people of Aboriginal descent as he could, combined with the terms under which Underwood expected him to manage his work, Neville would not have looked favourably on the subject of an Afghan seeking to marry a 'half-caste' girl. As well as this marriage interrupting the process of assimilation of part-Aboriginal people, one of his wards would be removed from his control.

If the Akbar-Matbar case had come to the Aborigines Department before 1905 there may have been a chance that consent to their marriage would have been granted more readily. The grouping in 1905 of 'half-castes' with 'full bloods', under the definition of 'native', significantly deprived the part-Aboriginal people of many legal rights they had previously enjoyed[8]. Before 1905, particularly in south-western Western Australia, many 'half-caste' children went to state schools and many European men married the Aboriginal mothers of their half-caste children. The 1905 Aborigines Act led to half-caste children being removed from state schools. They were forbidden, as were full bloods, to have a proper education. The children selected for forced removal from their Aboriginal people were less often 'full-blood' and increasingly 'half-caste'. Very few Europeans from now on married their Aboriginal partners because the 1905 Act controlled miscegenation and marriage of 'half-castes' more so than of 'full bloods'. The regulations of 1905 committed Neville to more control over more aspects of the lives of Aboriginal people.

From 1915 A. O. Neville tried to make his job more important in the eyes of his superiors and other government departments[9]. On taking office Neville had moved quickly to reorganise his department so as to improve its effectiveness. Methods of departmental record-keeping were reviewed and a more comprehensive system established. A cards system was to be maintained to show particulars of relief, blankets and clothing issued, marriages, crimes, breaches of the Act and personal records of individual matters[10]. Neville documented these initiatives in his first Annual Report, June 1915 to June 1916[11]. A new era in the management of the Aboriginal race in Western Australia had commenced[12].

Neville must have been personally disappointed by the decision in 1920 to divide the administration of Aboriginal affairs into two sections. Aboriginal affairs north of the 25th parallel was to be the responsibility of the newly created Department of the North-West, and the office of the Chief Protector of Aborigines was attached to that department. A.O. Neville, as Secretary for Immigration and as Chief Protector of Aborigines would have the responsibility for the Aboriginal population north of the 25th parallel. Aboriginal administration south of the 25th parallel was attached to the Fisheries Department. Fred Aldrich who was Chief Inspector of Fisheries was appointed Deputy Chief Protector of Aborigines. This division of the Aborigines Department may have impeded any ambitions Neville had to enhance his influence.

During these years Neville made several visits in the state to inspect the 'native reserves' and missions to assess how effective the 1905 Aborigines Act was in 'protecting' the Aboriginal population. He became quite familiar with their range of traditional practices and beliefs and saw many 'half-caste' children growing up alongside their 'full - blood' peers. These observations influenced his determination to segregate the part-Aboriginal children from their bush life so that their British side would be prepared for assimilation.

When the Department of the North-West was abolished on 4 July 1926, the Aborigines Department was reconstituted. Neville was once again in total control of all the Aboriginal people of Western Australia covered by the definition in the Aborigines Act. This must have been personally a very satisfying time for him. He was galvanised by energy and determination to recover lost ground.

Neville adhered to the scientific, evolutionary theories of his time. When the Darwinian theory of evolution was taken to its ultimate conclusion, it suggested that, in keeping with the premise of the survival of the fittest, the indigenous races seen as the inferior ones could ultimately evolve out of existence. They were a 'dying' race. Though Neville may have inherited to some extent the 'breed-out' and 'die-out' policy he became preoccupied with it. Between 1915 and 1925, judging by what he had seen, he may have decided that it was not working. From July 1926 he had the influence and authority to tighten this policy more and over time became dogmatic about it. He was determined to make it work[13].

The return to full control for A.O. Neville was accompanied by some criticism and opposition regarding Neville's approach in dealing with Aboriginal affairs in Western Australia and how he interpreted the protection of the indigenous race. The reconstitution of the Aborigines Department coincided with a significant revival of public interest in Aboriginal affairs in eastern Australia. This was due largely to the persistent efforts of the churches, missionary societies and the rising generation of Australian trained anthropologists[14]. Anthropologists such as Mr R.M. and Mrs C.H. Berndt, Mr A. P. Elkin and Miss P. Kaberry travelled amongst the Aboriginal people in various parts of Australia and produced copious amounts of work that were published and widely read. With their argument that aspects of the indigenous people's culture and society should be appreciated and preserved, they conflicted with missionaries who wanted to annihilate tribal society and culture and replace these with Christian, European ways.

The Akbar-Matbar case was put to Neville four weeks after the Aborigines Department was reunited. This case came at a time when Neville was intending to extend his control, to make sure that the Act's regulations would be adherred to verbatim, and simultaneously dealing with some public criticism of his administration. The Chief Protector expected his regulations to be taken literally, dogmatically defended and rigorously enforced. This was not the moment to authorise exemptions or allow wards, particularly 'half-caste' females, to be freed of his guardianship. There were also several other factors that had been a part of Neville's experience that perhaps shaped how he perceived the appropriateness of this marriage.

Neville may have been aware of his department's earlier dealings with the abuse and maltreatment of Aboriginal females, particularly part-Aboriginal females, and by Asiatic men in particular. The pearling industry in the north-west which commenced in the 1880s and which was located from La Grange Bay to Broome and north along the coastline near the mouth of the Gascoyne River, was run by Asiatics. The Asiatics included Malays, Manilamen, Chinese and Japanese. Aboriginal men who worked and camped at their shore bases also dived for them. During the lay-up season hundreds of the Asiatics converged on Broome where they supplied the Aboriginal people with alcohol in exchange for the favours of the Aboriginal women. As late as 1904 Aboriginal women were taken on boats and along the coastline and bartered for gin, tobacco and rations. Pearlers got rid of their surplus supplies of opium and liquor as payment for prostitution[15]. Venereal disease became rife amongst the Aboriginal people as a consequence of their interaction with the pearling crews. The Asiatic pearlers were thought to be responsible for prostitution and consequent venereal disease in the Aboriginal population from La Grange Bay to Broome[16]. During the Royal Commission in 1904 Dr Roth raised the concern about the absence of administrative powers to prevent European and Asiatic men from cohabiting with Aboriginal women[17]. The Government became concerned about the rising numbers of a 'mongrel race'[18].

Because of sexual exploitation of Aboriginal women, particularly in the north of Western Australia during the late nineteenth century, miscegenation and intermarriage became extremely undesirable and morally deplorable. Attempts to prevent sexual relations between Asiatics and 'half-caste' females, so as to protect Aboriginal women from sexual and physial abuse, were specifically catered for in the 1905 Aborigines Act by the inclusion of Sections 19, 20, 21 and 40. The first three sections banned Aboriginal males or female 'half-castes' from boarding any ship or boat, whether for a visit or for employment, and Section 40 specifically declared that no female, between sunset and sunrise, could be present within two miles of any creek or inlet used by the boats of pearlers. Any Aboriginal people ignoring these regulations would be guilty of an offence against the 1905 Aborigines Act[19]. By the 1905 Aborigines Act making cohabitation a punishable offence, it followed that applications by Asiatics to marry Aboriginal women were always refused[20]. Neville wrote on one occasion that 'there has been the marriage of indentured Asiatics to native women, resulting in their desertion, destitution and prostitution. Afghan and Aboriginal marriages have led to similar ends'[21].

In 1917 Neville was still dealing with the interactions of Asiatic members of the pearling community exploiting Aboriginal women. He conflicted with Father Creagh of Broome over marriages between Manilamen and part-Aboriginal women. Though Neville had issued instructions that these were expressly forbidden, the Catholic priest persisted in writing on behalf of couples wishing to get married. The Father, representing a humanist brand of Catholicism, was engaged in conflict with a government which had 'xenophobic anxieties about Asian-Aboriginal unions'[22].

Maintaining his department's efforts to control the spread of venereal disease amongst Aboriginal people, in 1920 Neville suggested an amendment to the regulations of the 1905 Aborigines Act that dealt particularly with the safe-guarding of 'half-caste' women. He proposed that it should be the right of a local protector to remove any 'native' suspected of being afflicted with a veneral disease to a place to conduct an examination, and to give medical treatment to 'natives' and 'half-castes' suffering from disease. If the native refused to submit to an examination by anyone acting under authority, then they would be committing an offence against the 1905 Aborigines Act[23]. This proposed amendment was not passed until its inclusion as Section 16 (a), (b) and (c) of the 1937 Native Administration Act[24].

As the Chief Protector of Aborigines, Neville executed his job according to a number of factors. Amongst his colleagues both back home in England and in Western Australia he discussed the popular doctrines on evolution promulgated by the book, *The Origin of the Species*, written by Charles Darwin and published in England in 1859. According to the Darwinian theory of evolution humans evolved millions of years ago from a simpler, less intelligent form of life. Over millenium some human races did not evolve as far away from their animal ancestors as did others. The Negro in Africa and the United States of America, and the Aborigine in the Australian colonies were considered to be closer to the end of the evolutionary scale where the apes were positioned. They were viewed as less advanced in their intelligence and emotions than the Caucasian or European[25], who were positioned at the top end of the evolutionary scale. There, intelligence had evolved to its highest level, and it followed that the associated civilisations were the superior. It was also popularly believed that the more inferior, indigenous populations like the Aborigines were due, by the dynamic process of evolution and the premise of the survival of the fittest, to eventually die out. Darwin's theory became so fundamental to British society that it significantly influenced the intellectual framework for formulating legislation and energised the period of colonial expansion during which the 'superior' European races built up empires around the world founded on conquering and eliminating 'primitive' races.

In Australia it provided a philosophical and intellectual framework for the colonisers' attitude towards the Aborigines and for the Western Australian Government's Aboriginal policies in the nineteenth and early twentieth centuries. It led to the creation in the 1890s of the Aborigines Protection Board, which was retitled in 1905 as the Aborigines

Department. It influenced the terminology of the 1905 Aborigines Act. As it was considered logical that 'full-blood' Aborigines were less likely to reach intellectual maturity, and then due to the combination of evolution and some of their traditional tribal practices to die out, Darwinism affected European attitudes regarding the education of Aboriginal people. As there was little point in sending 'full-blood' children to schools[26], the 1905 Aborigines Act prevented such children from being enrolled in schools. It was not logically a 'right' that Aboriginal people should have a complete education, become academics, have skilled jobs and professions, hold prestigious positions in society, or that their human rights be a political and civil issue. It was socially, even morally acceptable, that coloured races be prepared to fit into white society either as slaves or as cheap labour. As Caucasians, who included Anglo-Saxons and Europeans, were considered to have the superior intelligence and civilisation, educational, economic and political opportunities and high ranking positions should be given to them and, according to Darwinism, government officials working in Aboriginal affairs would know what was the best for the Aboriginal people. This also explains why increasingly 'half-caste' children were preferred to 'full-blood' children in forced removal from their Aboriginal families.

Neville's interpretation of what the term 'protection' of the Aborigines meant, and how it should be implemented, was shaped by the premises of these contemporary scientific beliefs. In letters he wrote in the capacity of his position as Chief Protector of Aborigines, and in writings and essays he wrote and published in later years, it was apparent that his ultimate ambition was for control over most aspects of the lives of the entire Aboriginal population so as to accomodate their eventual annihilation. His academic writings which discuss the 'die-out' policy reveal how he could see this being achieved.

Another scientific doctrine well canvassed internationally at this time and related to biological inheritance was 'atavism'. It held that intermarriage between certain coloured races and Caucasians produced babies who 'threw back' in colour. This teaching was debated vigorously in the United States of America where many children were being born as an outcome of sexual intercourse between Negroes and Caucasians. Family lines showed that a darker skinned child could be born of fairer skinned part-Negro parents two or three generations after the initial act of sex between a Negro and a Caucasian. In the Australian colonies it had been observed that babies born of a Caucasian and an Aboriginal parent would not 'throw back' in colour. It was believed that the skin colour of part-Aboriginal children would get fairer each generation[26].

According to the scientific teachings popular in the 1920s it may have been preferable for an Aboriginal girl to become pregnant by a European man then abandoned as a single mother, than for a marriage between a successful and established Afghan businessman and a bush native. Neville himself at one time did state that he could condone an unwed Aboriginal girl having illegitimate children to white men, even though she might be deserted, as this at least contributed to the breeding out of colour - a situation he viewed as more desirable than that of an Aboriginal girl legally marrying a non-European man who would look after her children[28].

The doctrine of atavism did not provide a scientific explanation about the possible degree of physical and mental abnormality of children conceived in a marriage between a part-Aboriginal woman and an Afghan, Indian, Chinese or Malay. It was Neville's view that such marriages and their consequent generations of children would interfere in the utopian plan to assimilate all fairer skinned children into the wider Anglo-Saxon community. Some years later Neville summed up his views on why Asiatic-Aboriginal marriages should be opposed. 'If a white man married a coloured woman of Aboriginal descent, possessing some Negro, Asiatic, Indian or other coloured ancestry, then there is a greater risk of atavism in any children of the union. If assimilation is the desired end the question of marriage is of paramount importance'[29].

The advocation of the breeding out of the indigenous populations directly influenced the Western Australian Government to anticipate their gradual elimination. There were two processes that facilitated this end and both were complex in nature. One of the processes was to achieve the gradual assimilation of the part-Aboriginal people into the wider colonial society. The 1904 Roth Royal Commission had concluded that it was absolutely necessary for the Chief Protector of Aborigines to maintain the right to decide where to place any children born of one Aboriginal parent. Section 12 of the 1905 Aborigines Act secured that authority for the Chief Protector. As official guardian of Aboriginal children up to the age of sixteen, he could remove them from any place and allocate them to another residence. The logic was that where 'half-castes' were found in 'communities whose influence is towards laziness and vice' these children would grow up as 'vagrants and outcasts'. The government's duty was 'to make good citizens of those whose blood is half British, by every means in our power'[30]. He believed that a part-Aboriginal child growing up in an Aboriginal bush camp was likely to possess few of the virtues of British society and nearly all the vices of either their indigenous relatives or those colonists who lived in the primitive conditions of the frontier settlements of the arid interior. The children with British ancestry had to be saved from,

> lives of prostitution due to cohabitation, ignorance due to no schooling opportunities, and quasi-slavery due to the customs of their tribal people...The destiny of the [part-Aboriginal not full-blood] natives...lies in their ultimate absorption by the people of the Commonwealth. All efforts should be directed towards this end[31].

In 1905 a statement made by the Colonial Secretary George Taylor reflected the contemporary fashion of intermingling scientific theories with social patterns and government practices;

> A half caste who possesses few of the virtues and nearly all of the vices of whites grows up to be a mischievous and very immoral subject...It may appear to be a cruel thing to tear an aboriginal child from its mother, but it is necessary in some cases to be cruel to be kind[32].

The administration of the Aborigines Department was convinced that the harsh measure of the separation of children from parents was absolutely necessary if the young generation was to be 'uplifted' from its Aboriginal background[33].

In the management of the exercise of the absorption of part-Aboriginal children into the Europeans' society, Neville had a concept of a time line: 'We could assimilate the coloured folk, the half-castes, in two or three generations. The coloured people must be lifted out of the rut of despairing futility, the utter purposelessness of their lives'[34].

With the increasing number of births of part-Aboriginal children an increasing number of these children were selected for forced removal from their bush families. Neville had to contemplate the capacity of existing native reserves, settlements and institutions to contain them. Within the first year of his appointment as Chief Protector of Aborigines A.O. Neville planned to open up a new Aboriginal institution which would house the re-allocated part-Aborginal children. One, Carrolup Native Settlement, already existed in the south-west of the state, but did not have the capacity to cope with the number of children removed by the government. As Aboriginal children who were considered neglected were 'in places north of Geraldton, along the Northern railway line and in the Murchison region, and in the bush in the eastern goldfields'[35], it was anticipated that more children would be brought in from the goldfields and the far north.

Another site geographically more central and closer to those areas would need to be developed. In January 1916 Neville took another step towards his long-term scheme to have all part-Aborigines living on reserves and mission areas, to be responsible to him[36]. He initiated the project of establishing a new Aboriginal settlement on a site to be selected somewhere in the Midlands. He was considering two locations in that district. One was 3,000 acres of wheat country. The other was ten thousand acres of sheep country around Moore River near the railway siding named Mogumber. He had estimated that about four or five hundred 'natives' and 'half-castes', would come within the influence of such a settlement in that vicinity. About one hundred and fifty of these were usually in receipt of 'indigent relief' from the Aborigines Department[37].

Neville preferred the second of the two locations. The bureaucracy moved slowly towards accepting Neville's proposal. He did not let the lack of decision-making and the disagreement with any of his recommendations interfere with his ambition for a native settlement at Moore River. By 1918 9,600 acres in remote farmland with a thinly dispersed population and limited travellers or visitors was selected. The nearest public transport stop was the Mogumber rail siding. By March 1918 the institution was functioning. The settlement was constructed to accommodate about two hundred 'inmates', the term used for its residents by the Aborigines Department. From 1918 the Aborigines Department had that site and Carrolup settlement. Moore River Native Settlement was north of the 25th parallel and Carrolup Native Settlement was south of the 25th parallel. In September 1919 Neville informed the Under Secretary of the Colonial Secretary's Department that the policy of his department was to now confine 'indigent natives' and 'half-castes' within settlements controlled by the Aborigines Department[38]. In June 1922 Neville arranged, with the cooperation of his Deputy Chief Protector Aldrich, to have Carrolup's inmates transferred to Moore River Native Settlement. The rationale was most likely to economise on resources, but it also placed more Aboriginal people under Neville's control. The total number of inmates of Moore River Native Settlement increased to 306, many more than the settlement was intended to cater for. At times the residents numbered as many as 500[39]. Neville was very enthusiastic to remove 'half-caste children' from their indigenous people. He viewed the 'half-castes' as 'poor whites'.

> The coloured people must be thoroughly fit and educated...As long as they can read, write and count, know what wages they should get, that is all that should be necessary. To achieve this...we establish settlements to undertake the training and education of these children so that they may become absorbed into the general community[40].

The forced removal of Aboriginal children from their homes was consolidated in March 1919 when Neville proposed an additional regulation be made 'pursuant to Section 12 of the 1905 Aborigines Act'. The new regulation would enable the Chief Protector to issue a warrant directing the removal of any Aborigine from any part of the state, and intern him or her within any reserve or district[41]. The actions of police like Constable Perks of Morgans and Sergeant Thompson and Constable Hunter at Laverton to seize part-Aboriginal children particularly and arrange for their forced removal from their mother's people and district was required by and in keeping with the 1905 Aborigines Act and facilitated the Chief Protector's overall program of 'protecting' these children through his Department's policy of assimilation. A measure of how successful Perks was in his control of the indigenous population in his district was the quantity of children he could claim he had caught and removed from his district. Jack Akbar's proposal to be given an exemption from a Section of the 1905 Aborigines Act, to be given permission as an Asiatic to marry a part-Aboriginal girl who was still a ward of the Chief Protector of Aborigines, was in total opposition to the whole, complex scheme of things as Neville perceived it and as legislation provided for. In 1926 when Neville had resumed total control of his office, circumstances discouraged setting any precedent that might encourage other Aboriginal people, particularly 'half-castes', to find the means by which to escape his influence or hold.

The second process that enhanced the gradual elimination of the Aboriginal population was to allow the 'full-blood' indigenous population to breed itself out. The attitudes of the times, and the colonists' shallow understanding of the ways of the Aboriginal people, were conducive to this. Neville had assessed that as 'full-blood' Aboriginals were of limited intelligence and educability, they would eternally be a drain on his department's limited resources. It was a popular view of the colonists that as full bloods were efficient at finding food for themselves through their traditional means of hunting wild game, the bush was where they ought to be. When they were hungry and ran out of rations they would find food there, and this would reduce their pilfering and begging. If the local protectors could maintain their occupation of the bush it would take pressure off his resources.

Auber Neville believed that full-blood Aborigines retained their traditional beliefs, customs and laws by living in the bush, and were themselves contributing to their inevitable annihilation. One of the traditional practices they maintained was the custom of polygamy. An older tribal man who was getting too old to hunt successfully for food needed younger eyes and feet to help him acquire food for himself, for his older wives and any of his children. More than one younger woman would be given to an older hunter. These younger wives rarely became pregnant to the elderly men. So it was calculated that over time there would be fewer full-blood children.

The other practice considered in these times to be contributing to the fall in number of full-blood children was the roughly-performed ritual of circumcision. It was performed when tribal boys reached puberty to initiate them into manhood. Occasionally, the damage done to the penis affected the fertility of some full-blood men. The contemporary perception was that full-blood Aboriginal people staying in the bush retained this practice and by doing so would produce fewer full-blood children in each generation.

The Aboriginal practice of infanticide, the frequency of which increased in proportion to the expansion of the colonial settlement, contributed to the death of full-blood as well as part-Aboriginal babies. The Chief Protector of Aborigines had little doubt that what his department and the police were doing with the Aboriginal population was appropriate. He was aware that he and his office could still receive criticism from the townspeople and pastoralists of the interior of Western Australia if they found the indigenous population had too much of a presence in their areas. He already received some criticism just after his department was reunited in July 1926 and did not want any further criticism to cause a further reduction in its size and power. Neville was more likely to take note of publicly-expressed opinions of townspeople and pastoralists about his Aboriginal wards than of an Afghan's request for permission to legally marry one.

Another way Neville tightened his control over Aboriginal people, particularly from July 1926, was to tighten up his department's policy on marriages of part-Aboriginal women. The continued mating between half-caste females and full-blood males would produce still darker skinned people, which in turn would prolong the rate of absorption of half-caste children into the colonists' society[42]. The regulations of the 1905 Aborigines Act included the prohibition of marriage between half-caste women and full-blood men. It was believed that such partnerships would lead to the 'return of paling half-castes to the black'. The implementing of this policy of the Aborigines Department was interfered with by the missionaries who would let either full-blood or half-caste Aboriginal people marry the Aboriginal person of their choice:

> In the past much carelessness has been exhibited by missionaries [who let full-bloods continue to mate with Aboriginal females] and clergy [who supported the marriage of Asiatics and part-Aboriginal women] in linking up people against tribal laws. There has been ignoring of tribal custom and culture, leading to quarrelling, murder and consequent punishment[43].

Neville interpreted this as interfering with the rate of assimilation.

Also, it had been observed by Neville and other colonists that when 'part-Aboriginal' women lived with 'full-blood' or 'part-Aboriginal' tribal men, those men had been known to ill-treat those women. Neville compared these wives' situations to being 'kept as chattels or a slave to the men. At times these ill-treated women were even beaten by their husbands'[44].

A.O. Neville supported the regulations which determined that his part-Aboriginal female wards should marry 'white men'. Such interbreeding was seen to hasten the process of biological absorption, social assimilation and total integration of the Aborigines into the wider community of the Commonwealth. In essence this preferred marital arrangement condoned the lifestyle of the goldfields at this time, where many colonists exploited Aboriginal girls sexually. The theory made it somewhat preferable that an Aboriginal girl should fall pregnant to a Caucasian and then be abandoned single and destitute than go with a 'full blood' man, even though the latter would be less likely to desert her.

In addition to the several factors and issues that impacted on Neville while he considered the contents of the three letters regarding marriage between Lallie Matbar and Jack Akbar, the Chief Protector's attention was also attracted to the controversial circumstances in the lives of these two people. It was very likely that by some of their past personal behaviours and practices these two individuals were already breaching a number of the Sections of the 1905 Act. One type of offensive behaviour attributed to Lallie in the correspondence was that she had been cohabiting illegally. Police investigations out in the field revealed that this unmarried teenage bush girl had been pregnant at least twice before her

A.O.Neville, Commissioner for Native Affairs, 1940, on retirement. Photo 5000b, Battye Library, Perth.

current pregnancy. Further police enquiries around the goldfields revealed that Lallie's first known pregnancy was in 1922, when she was about 12 or 13. The man suspected of being the father was William Taylor an employee of the Devon Gold Mine near Linden. Her second known pregnancy was early in 1925 and David Heppingstone, manager of Mount Celia cattle station was suspected as being the father[45]. The police did not seem to be aware of the pregnancy of Lallie when she was with Burtville Jack for a short time. Her current pregnancy was in reality her fourth, but the police files, going on what knowledge they had, stated it to be her third. The identity of the father of this child was not confirmed. The evidence before Neville suggested that Lallie was now consorting with an Asiatic.

The police details further proposed that the immoral and illegal behaviour of these two people had resulted in the passing of a venereal disease between them and this had its own implications. Though venereal disease was not proven yet by means of medical testing of both persons concerned, the Aborigines and the Police Departments were quick to take the opportunity to use that information to create further doubt about the morality of the petitioners and to provide a reason to the police for taking Lallie into custody. In 1926 Neville's amendment regarding bringing Aboriginal people forcibly in for a medical examination had not yet been passed; therefore, the police had no power, by the 1905 Aborigines Act, to arrest people for being suspected of having a venereal disease.

It seems that until 1926 A.O. Neville had not been aware of Lallie the Wongai bush girl from Linden. The proposal by the Morgans Afghan to marry one of his wards, which implied his taking her from Neville's influence brought much attention to her. It was in this year that the compilation of a file on Lallie was commenced by the Police and Aborigines Departments.

In mid-August, Neville reacted to the information he had been provided on the case of Lallie Matbar and Jack Akbar. He suggested to Inspector Spedding Smith in Kalgoorlie that it would be a wise move at this time to have the constabulary catch Lallie and when she was in custody to conduct a medical examination of her. If the results showed that she was a carrier of venereal disease then that would be another reason to have her removed for internment in Moore River Native Settlement. Perhaps then it could be proven that Jack Akbar was committing a number of offences, and it would be appropriate to order the arrest of both persons.

This advice however did not produce any results. The police were not able to catch Lallie, so she was not given a medical examination. Jack's sores had disappeared and the records kept on the patient Akbar by the Matron at the Morgans hospital were not consulted by the police.

Against the accumulative obstruction to Jack and Lallie's union Jack adhered singlemindedly to his goal. During August and September of 1926 Jack Akbar and his solicitor produced a number of letters in which Akbar resorted to a series of angles of appeal so as to persuade the Chief Protector to grant him an exemption. An early approach was to arrange with Cook to declare to the Chief Protector that it was not Lallie in particular whom Akbar wished to marry. In a letter dated 19 August Cook enquired of the Chief Protector if he would be agreeable to giving Akbar permission to marry any mission girl[46].

Jack and the solicitor may have thought that this approach might have been a more workable concept to the Chief Protector. The impression Akbar may have been attempting to convey to Mr Neville was that he was considering marriage with an Aboriginal missionary girl, perceived as a Christianised, civilised lady with some education and understanding of morality, as opposed to a bush native seen to be an immoral heathen who had a background of going with white men for a bottle of beer or a shilling. By 1926 a mission had been built about 11 kilometres (seven miles) from Morgans and Jack Akbar had a contract to cart food supplies weekly from the Morgans railway station out to the mission. It was possible that Neville might accept the notion that Jack Akbar realised that a girl raised by the missionaries would make a more fitting wife. If Jack could obtain the Chief Protector's written consent to his marriage proposal, perhaps he could manipulate the situation so as to use Lallie's name.

A second, indirect benefit of not committing Lallie's name might be in diverting police interest in Lallie's whereabouts and activities. The Chief Protector's response to Akbar's legal counsel was simple. There was no possibility whatever of Jack Akbar being permitted to marry a girl from any mission station or native settlement in any part of Western Australia. He reminded solicitor Cook that the issue was not which kind of Aboriginal girl Akbar could be permitted to marry. The issue was that any intercourse or marriage between Asiatics and Aboriginals was absolutely prohibited[47].

Neville also took the opportunity to twist Akbar's rationale so as to use it against the Afghan. He proposed to the solicitor that it was all the same to Jack Akbar whether he married Lallie Matbar or any other half-caste girl. He obviously did not care especially for the Linden girl and so there could not be any genuine substance behind his desire to marry her[48].

Akbar's concern to do the best for Lallie Matbar included marrying her before the birth of her child. When he next sought the services of Cook Akbar incorporated this point of concern in their next letter to the Chief Protector so as to add a sense of urgency about his proposed marriage. The baby Lallie was expecting was due within two months. He put the confession to the Chief Protector that he was the father and was prepared to act responsibly, when many others would not, and to marry the girl promptly so as to give his name to their child before it was born. Another statement Akbar included for Neville was that Lallie was refusing to leave him, and he could not get rid of her even when he tried. Jack claimed that he had been with Lallie for eighteen months. The Afghan hoped that the weight of the three claims he provided in this letter would make it seem logical that, since Jack and Lallie were in regular company and their child was expected, it would be a humane conclusion that their marriage be permitted[49].

While the Afghan and the solicitor in the goldfields waited for a response to their latest petition for an exemption, the Chief Protector and the Police Department in Perth were evaluating the amount of evidence collected so far on the Akbar-Matbar case. The persistence of the Afghan storekeeper at Morgans in wanting to marry, not just cohabit with, the pregnant part-Aboriginal Linden girl had manifested itself in a volume of correspondence which was amassing a reaction to the reverse of what Akbar hoped for. Neville believed that the circumstances around the case of this particular female ward were becoming too complex and were exhibiting defiance and ignorance of the law. The Afghan's persistence in not conducting his personal affairs according to the sections of the 1905 Aborigines Act was likely to manifest in undesirable consequences out in the community.

A fresh report that arrived from Perks caused Neville to consider seriously the potential this case had for causing disorder, even for violence, in the goldfields. From further enquiries on patrols in the Linden-Laverton area, the Morgans policeman learned that Lallie's situation and story were breeding a great deal of sympathy and support amongst the local Aborigines and there were still many Wongai about[50]. The authorities, who managed the Aborigines by fear and intimidation, did not want a cause around which or who the Aborigines could rally and become insurgent. Perks had conveyed these findings and concerns in his reports.

With both his ambitions for his department and attempting to avoid provoking criticism from the media or public, it was imperative that Neville not be seen to be failing in his job or weakening in his administration. He had to demonstrate to the community that the policy of his department in protecting Aborigines was foremost and that there was power behind his regulations. The community should know that the girl had been caught and removed in police custody from her people and the district, and that the Afghan had realised the futility of his proposal and ceased his pursuit of his marriage to the Linden girl.

While Neville and other officers in Perth were assessing what was the most effective strategy to employ for the welfare of his Linden ward, so were Lallie's people out in the bush. Some had accepted for some time that Jack's desire to marry their girl would be a good thing in her life. However, it was evoking an unexpected twist, too much attention from the police who through Akbar had a means of getting to her. It seemed that his commitment to the girl, rather than bringing the care, safety and security he had promised it would bring, was attracting danger to her, to her baby and to other children of her people. Lallie had survived infanticide and police raids into her camps and now Jack was a possible threat to her safety. While Jack worked to obtain official permission to marry her, Lallie's people had to keep trying to protect her and keep her safe and free. They were hiding her constantly, in her advancing pregnancy. She was moved about under seclusion so that no police informants or sympathisers could ever be sure they saw her or could be specific about her whereabouts. She was living the life of a hunted animal and a criminal and yet she had not broken any laws or been offensive to humanity. As her pregnancy advanced Lallie would have anticipated that while she lived this lifestyle the same kind of fate would fall on her child once it was born.

It was an increasing concern to others of Lallie's people that Jack was the main reason for the police hounding her. Tjirrgulu and her people could feel the Moore River net tightening around Lallie and them. The elders needed to think of an interim solution that could give Lallie better protection and safety from the police until Jack secured legal permission to marry her.

By early 1926 many of the Wongai in the Laverton-Linden-Morgans area were familiar with the existence of the mission 11 kilometres out of Morgans. When the missionary first came to Laverton in 1921 and from there moved to Mount Margaret, the local Aboriginal people were very suspicious of him. They would approach him with curiosity, listen to his strange words for a while, wait around to see if he would give them any food, then would leave. Over time circumstances encouraged the Wongai to return to the missionary and for some to camp with him. The effect of World War One on the goldfields was to attract many miners to enlist in the Army. Small mining settlements closed down. The closing down of many mines meant there were very few opportunities to earn a wage and very few places around which hungry Aboriginal people could beg. During drought there was very little game to hunt in the bush. So the Wongai went to the missionary at Mount Margaret who promised them physical and spiritual nourishment. The missionary, Rodolphe Schenk, gave them food, shelter, medicine and kindness when few other colonists did. He did not chase after them to drive them away. He wanted them to stay as long as they could. The police did not seem to raid his camp trying to catch children as much as they did out in the bush. The Wongai came to learn that it was most likely safer to leave their children with him, as he was asking them to do, than to keep them out in the bush with them all the time.

There was another attraction to the mission for the Wongai. Since 1905 their children were not permitted to enrol in schools, and what education was available at Moore River Native Settlement, which was very far from the eastern goldfields, meant living a life in an institution. By the mid-1920s Mount Margaret mission had a school for Aboriginal students. The age of the children in its classroom tended to be from about five to twelve, the upper age of compulsory attendance. By the time the school was established at this mission it was too late for Lallie to attend classes as in 1926 she was already almost sixteen years old.

Since 1921 several of the Wongai children had come to live at the mission. By mid-1926 Tjirrgulu knew that staying deep in the bush was not the solution to keep her unmarried, pregnant, part-European daughter and future grandchild safe and well fed. She also knew that when Lallie emerged out of the bush to walk into a ration depot the police were likely to apprehend her and her infant.

Tjirrgulu took more and more heed of the comments her people made about how much safer it would be for her daughter to go and stay at the mission. Many of the Wongai had come to perceive the mission as a haven of safety. They took their children to stay at the mission because some of them saw Schenk as their real protector[51]. A modern Aboriginal descendant summarised the relevance of the mission to his parents' people by commenting that the mission ground was the only place to avoid the murderous onslaught of white settlers[52].

It is calculated that by September 1926 Tjirrgulu received advice from the elders that it would be acceptable for her to take her pregnant daughter to the mission. To go there Tjirrgulu would have to walk 129 kilometres with her heavily pregnant daughter from Linden to the mission out of Morgans. Snowy Bradley would go with them.

A trek this long in this country was dangerous. It was a journey that Tjirrgulu had not chosen. Ironically it had been precipitated indirectly by Jack's desire to marry her daughter. Tjirrgulu would have been constantly afraid of a surprise approach by the police. She was worried that either local police informants or traps, or the police themselves would see her travelling with Aboriginal children of a fairer skin colour, or perhaps even recognise Lallie. Much of her energy on that journey, as during the entire childhood of the two offspring, would have been spent concealing her children's fairer skin. Tjirrgulu was the sole protector of her pregnant daughter and part-Aboriginal son until they reached the Mount Margaret Mission.

CHAPTER FOUR

Lallie arrives at Mount Margaret Mission

When Tjirrgulu and her two adolescent children emerged out of the bush they may have felt some trepidation about what sort of person would welcome them. Mysie Schenk, the wife of the manager of Mount Margaret mission, would have been drawn to the girl particularly. Lallie's appearance would have contrasted with that of the neat, groomed girls on the mission. Mysie noted how the girl's face had been rubbed over with charcoal and that her legs and arms were coated in fine bush dust[1]. Mysie would have been most concerned by the advanced stage of the girl's pregnancy — a condition to be reported. So as to have sufficient details for a report, the missionary couple would have to ask questions to find out who they were, if there was a father for the child, from where they had come and why. The arrival of Lallie made such an impression on Rod and Mysie Schenk that they gave it a particular mention in one of their letters sent out to Church members in other states[2].

Lallie would have been cleaned and given a fresh dress. While the acceptance onto the mission of Lallie was arranged, Mr Schenk suggested to Tjirrgulu that should Snowy stay a while also he could be trained in basic labour skills. When Tjirrgulu left the mission she may have had peace in her heart regarding the safety and future of daughter. However, the total way in which the missionary helped to care for and 'protect the children' of the Wongai was more complicated and subtle than Tjirrgulu or her people were aware.

Rodolphe Schenk, the founder of the mission, and his wife Mysie were guided in their work by regulations of the same Aborigines Act that drove Tjirrgulu to bring her daughter Lallie to their place. The Chief Protector of Aborigines was the terrestial authority who granted the missionary permission to conduct work for his celestial authority. In turn for this permission one of Schenk's duties was to report promptly to A.O. Neville, through the local protector Constable Perks in Morgans, the names of Aborigines who arrived, departed or became residents at, his mission. Tjirrgulu could not have known this. While the mother thought she was outwitting the police by taking her daughter to a place representing safety and freedom, she had compromised the safety and freedom of her daughter by bringing her closer to a man who collaborated with the police and the Aborigines Department, both of whom were on the look-out for Lallie.

Rodolphe Samuel Schenk, one of ten children of a railway worker, was born on 29 October 1888 in Macoona, Victoria. A few years into their marriage Rod's parents converted to evangelical Protestant Christianity. When a teenager Rod chose the same path and decided to live his life doing the work of Christ. Rod left Victoria for a few years during the 1910s to study at the Missionary and Bible College in Sydney. After completing his studies Rodolphe Schenk returned to Melbourne to practice his religion in his parents' congregation. During the late 1910s and the 1920s when an international and national missionary movement peaked, Rod attended meetings addressed by guest missionaries who had worked with indigenous people in other parts of the British Empire or the world. This period stimulated Rod's ambition to work as a missionary in the field for his spiritual Lord.

At a prayer meeting in 1917 Rod, aged twenty-nine years, met his future wife, Isobel May Johnston, aged nineteen. Isobel, nicknamed 'Mysie', was one of five daughters of a Scotsman named William Johnston who was a Presbyterian Church elder. Mysie, like Rod, had decided in her teenage years to dedicate her life to serving Christ and she was prepared to go anywhere. By 1919 Rod had to leave Melbourne to work as a probationary missionary with the Aboriginal people in the Walgett area of New South Wales[3].

Rod did not believe this farming district was the place for him to work permanently and waited for God to reveal to him what his calling might be. He kept himself informed of the experiences and 'successes' with indigenous people of other missionaries. One journal delivered regularly to Rod Schenk was *Missionary Tidings*, a missionary newspaper published monthly in Melbourne. In one issue he was drawn to an article that reported the plight of some Aboriginal people living in the eastern goldfields on the edge of the Great Victoria Desert of Western Australia. These people were so desperate that they were plundering, fighting, begging and stealing. The author of the article pleaded that one of his readers might find enough piety and love to go out there to help them[4]. Rod Schenk wrote to the author, who lived in Perth, to inform him that he believed he was the person whom God had called to go to the goldfields[5]. To take up work in Western Australia Rod would have to resign from his current service and enlist with the Australian Aborigines Mission (A.A.M.)[6].

Rod Schenk would have been elated to know his calling. He would model the work of the international speakers who were pioneers in their areas. In Melbourne Rod Schenk made his arrangements to go west. In 1921 when he boarded a west-bound train with his motor bike Mysie was at the railway station to see him off. A promise was made to maintain their friendship.

In his early days in Perth Rod had two significant meetings. One was with the author of the article which had drawn him to this state[7]. Though there are no surviving notes of this encounter, in the days in Perth Rod would have gained some insight into the relationship between missionaries and the government in Western Australia. To work with, or even visit, any Aboriginal people, a missionary had to have the authority of the Chief Protector of Aborigines, A.O. Neville, who was the executive head of the Aborigines Department of Western Australia. An Act of Parliament, titled the 1905 Aborigines Act, in effect gave the Chief Protector control over almost every aspect of the lives of the Aborigines. Rod would need Mr Neville's authority in writing to get to the eastern goldfields Aborigines who he had come a long way to work with. He would need the Chief Protector's permission to stay out there and start a mission, and his cooperation to recieve any subsidising funds or supplies. That same Act, which incorporated missionaries as local protectors, bound the missionary to collaborate with the Police Department.

The second important meeting for the Victorian missionary was with , the Chief Protector of Aborigines himself. The meeting of Neville and Schenk brought together two men who were committed to working for the 'benefit' of the Aboriginal population. Their backgrounds, motivations and personal applications caused them to have different interpretations of their work. Both Neville and Schenk were very committed and dedicated to their respective careers and were most earnest about how they went about it. Both had their personal beliefs and philosophies about what was best for, and the best way to protect, the Aboriginal people. Neither saw this from the point of view of the Aboriginal people. Many years later Rod Schenk's daughter related the impression Mr Neville made on her father on that occasion, which was that of 'a man of unlimited power'[8].

It would be to the advantage of the Chief Protector that the eastern newcomer fully comprehend how dependent he was on the Chief Protector and the Aborigines Department. Rod would have to know that the 1905 Aborigines Act made all Aboriginal children who were 'full - blood' and 'half-caste' the wards of the Chief Protector until the age of sixteen. Ultimately the Chief Protector had control over the majority of Aboriginal people. The regulations required missionaries, who could be local protectors, to regularly inform Neville of any young Aboriginal person brought into their care. The work with Aboriginal children was most vital to Neville's policy of assimilation and the missionaries were was expected to cooperate with it. Subject only to the Minister for the 1905 Aborigines Act, who in 1921 was William Kitson, the Chief Protector made Schenk aware that he controlled the indigenous population of Western Australia.

As his department's facilities for educating Aboriginal children were very inadequate, Neville could find a place for mission settlement in his assimilation program. They could provide basic education for children and job training for adolescents. In Perth Rod would have begun to appreciate that in order to commence a spiritual program with a group of tribal Aborigines, he would be required also by the regulations of the 1905 Aborigines Act to pursue just as devotedly a practical teaching program and would be responsible for that to the Chief Protector. The missions were expected to submit regular and annual reports. Neville did not regard highly the status of missionaries and believed in the need to monitor them closely. Another regulation of the 1905 Aborigines Act maintained the missionaries' subservience to the Aborigines Department. Section 5, under 'Reserves or Stations', stated that 'the Superintendent or Manager of a station or reserve for Aborigines shall be responsible to the Chief Protector of Aborigines for its administration and welfare and control of the Aborigines thereon'[9]. Neville saw himself as a rational administrator, while he believed that missionaries dealt with emotions. The difference of view, i.e., what was the practical, logical way versus what was the spiritual, humanitarian way of caring for the Aborigines, would have been a basis for conflict between the Chief Protector and the missionaries in Western Australia.

An issue fundamental to both the 1905 Act and thus to Neville's policy of assimilation of the Aboriginal population was the distinction between 'half-caste' and 'full-blood' Aborigines. It was essential for Neville's assimilation program that Schenk understood the need for the Aborigines Department's practice of separating 'part-Aboriginal' children from their Aboriginal families. One procedure to implement this was for the police, as local protectors, to raid Aboriginal camps and remove the mixed-race children for conveyance to distant institutions. Some hundreds of youngsters had been gathered up already and sent to government settlements for Aborigines. The belief was that there they would be saved from a heathen and uncivilised destiny that otherwise awaited them. To avoid any setbacks in the process of assimilation Schenk would have to understand that he could take any child from its Aboriginal mother at any stage of its life, and that he had to keep that child at his mission. It would be expected that Schenk would disallow such a child to return home[10].

The role of the missionary was fundamental to another provision of the 1905 Aborigines Act. The Act made education of Aboriginal children the responsibility of the Aborigines Department. Before 1905, when these children were mostly 'full-blood', that responsibility was discharged by the government to the missions who in turn were financially subsidised by government funds. Many of the increasing number of 'half-caste' children in the southern part of the state were enrolled in State schools. Before 1905 there were an increasing number of protests from European parents about the presence of part-Aboriginal children in their schools. The government responded to their repeated requests to have these children removed from State schools by introducing an amendment to the 1905 Aborigines Act which banned all Aboriginal children from schools. The consequence of this was that the Aborigines Department had to provide the facilities for the education of Aboriginal children.

It did not concern Neville so much that full-blood children were deprived of an education. It was the part-Aboriginal children whom he wanted educated and trained, so that they could be absorbed into the wider society by the program of assimilation. Because his department was small in manpower and resources he saw the role of the missions as being fundamental to education of his wards, and thus in the process of assimilation. Section 6 of the Act stated that the Aborigines Department was expected to maintain all its programs of education; training for employment; distribution of rations, clothes and blankets; management

Rodolphe and Mysie Schenk, the missionary couple who established and managed Mount Margaret mission from 1922 to the late 1930s. Photo 70391p. Battye Library, Perth.

and regulation of all 'native' reserves and 'settlements'; medical assistance and supplies - all with the limited funds of about ten thousand pounds per annum. This amount was not sufficient for the Department to take on the building of its own schools. The religious institutions continued to be the only avenue of education of the 'native' children, and from the time of his appointment in 1915 Neville welcomed the participation on that level of the Australian Aborigines Mission[11].

One item of information the missionary must have found encouraging was to be told that he would be given some small financial and practical assistance in the form of rations by the Aborigines Department. He knew that whatever supportive funds he received from the Australian Aborigines Mission would be small and erratic. However, Neville informed Schenk that the provision of assistance from Perth and its timing was conditional. The impression Neville had of the remaining tribal groups in the eastern goldfields was that they were idle, not yet civilised or settled. He wanted someone to reform them into 'productive people', and that someone had to be beyond those few who were his small staff. He advised Schenk that he was expected to pursue a practical and teaching program with as much zeal as his religious program. Neville expected to see positive results in the conversion of the goldfields Wongai from an 'indolent, unpractical lot' to an educated and skilled society of productive citizens within a certain period of time[12].

Another matter Rodolphe Schenk was expected to be aware of was the practice of Aboriginal people collecting around a church or mission site in or near a town. This was not condoned in Western Australia. The locating of a mission in a town would attract Aboriginal people into the settlement and this would antagonise the citizens and pastoralists who were concerned that the Aboriginal people would make a nuisance of themselves. Then the police would have to shift both the Aborigines and the mission[13].

Further research into the relationship of Neville and Schenk revealed that the one particular place the former had in mind for an additional branch of the Australian Aborigines Mission was the area in which the Victorian misionary wished to work. The tribal people of the eastern goldfields, some of whom were called the 'Wongai', included desert fringe dwellers who the Aborigines Department assessed as needing to replace their nomadic existence with a sedentary lifestyle in which individuals would do regular work and were capable of earning a wage. Neville's plan was that a mission sited around Laverton and Mount Margaret goldfields district would be the chief vehicle for the policies of institutionalisation of children and assimilation. His vision for that mission branch was that it would be more successful than any other Western Australian mission of the same period in providing educational and technical skills, and instilling in the graduates a Christian and European view of the world[14].

The need for a mission or government native settlement on the eastern goldfields had been apparent to the Aborigines Department for some time. There had been a gradual westerly and south-westerly drift of Aboriginal people from the semi-arid regions further inland. By 1917 the goldfields had a fair-sized Aboriginal population. Aborigines were moving in from the Gibson and Great Victoria Deserts. Neville wanted Aboriginal people living on the fringe of the nearby mining towns of Laverton, Morgans and Leonora to have a more permanent residence.

By 1920 the Moore River Native Settlement was showing signs of making satisfactory progress in institutionalising indigenous people. He was convinced that the 'reserve and settlement system' was the only true solution to the 'native question', and he sought opportunities to establish additional stations of this kind in the future. An assessment from his field trips had revealed that one or two such settlements were 'very badly required' in the goldfields[15]. The establishment of a mission in the Margaret goldfields district would become the goldfields' much-needed station to absorb part-Aboriginal children. The location around Laverton was strategic in extending the Aborigines Department's policies to those members of the indigenous population not yet sufficiently 'civilised'. Schenk's arrival in Western Australia, with his desire to work with the wilder Aborigines in the eastern goldfields, was timely. Though the evangelical worker believed he was to do missionary work in the goldfields because that was God's calling for him, his presence there would be serving the needs of the Chief Protector of Aborigines[16].

Rod Schenk's daughter many years later proposed that Neville wanted Schenk to go to Laverton and not one of his 'show missions' such as the Violet River mission, because he was from the eastern states and not indoctrinated in the ways of the west, and a mission in the goldfields would 'break Schenk'[17]. When Rod believed he had to undertake to work among the Western Australian Aborigines he may have expected a degree of autonomy and limited interference in how he applied himself to his task. During his time in Perth it was made clear to him that he would have to acknowledge the ultimate authority of the Chief Protector and in any Aboriginal affairs be a collaborator of the police. It would not be acceptable for him to take an individual stance 'morally' on issues such as the forced removal of Aboriginal children from their families and tribal areas. Schenk had two masters to consider, the celestial God he worked for and the terrestial administrator on whom he depended for permission, support and funding to achieve the work for the other.

In April 1921 Rod Schenk left Perth by train for Kalgoorlie in the goldfields. After an overnight stay he continued his journey to Laverton on the rail branch line known as the 'mulga express'. Heading north-east across mulga plains, the train pulled into rail sidings at Comet Vale, Niagara and Kookynie, stopped for lunch at Menzies and paused intermittently to service some old mining centres in the Margaret goldfields district such as Malcolm, Leonora, Murrin Murrin and Morgans, which service the old Mount Margaret mining site[19].

This was a drought year[20] so Schenk did not see much surface water or wildlife from his rail carriage window. The mining towns still had some human life in them, but they had seen much better days. He saw a few pastoral dwellings, railway workers' cottages and abandoned mining shows. Pepper trees indicated where streets of towns had once been. His initial observations indicated to him that life out here would be demanding, that there was bush rather than cultivated fields, that distances between substantial settlements were greater, and the quality of roads which were more like tracks would be trying on his motor bike.

The end of the rail line was at Laverton, the largest town in the Margaret goldfields district. Its size, position as a railhead town and its regional central location warranted the posting of two staff to the town's police station. Services listed the Laverton inclusive of the Mount Margaret Roads Board and the Laverton hospital; businesses included the Clarke and Lamont forwarding agents. Rodolphe Schenk arrived with his motor bike on 22 April 1921. One of his first obligations was to present himself to the local protector. Sergeant Thompson, the police officer in charge of the town's police station, had come to Laverton in 1918 as a constable.

In the conversation which ensued between the missionary and the Sergeant aspects about the numbers, character, movements, traditional camping sites and habits of the local Aborigines surfaced. Thompson wanted to impress on the inexperienced, eastern state 'do-gooder' that he should not expect to make much progress with the Aboriginal people of this district. It was the Sergeant's opinion that, in comparison to other tribes in Western Australia, even the Aboriginal people of the Far North who were considered to be wild and unruly, the eastern goldfields Aborigines were the wildest and laziest tribe. He warned Schenk that nobody was safe from them. They stole from residents in the town and they would rob a lonely prospector or squatter out in the bush. The local Aboriginal population, known as the 'Wongai', were 'a bad lot', and he advised the Victorian not to go too far into the bush and to keep around the town[21]. To make the missionary cautious about going into the bush to find the 'natives' the Sergeant informed him that many Aboriginal people, about 450 to 500 Aborigines, still inhabited the district[22]. Many years later Rod Schenk's daughter commented that Sergeant Thompson was considered to be a policeman who did his job and accordingly would have given Rod Schenk what he considered to be 'good advice'[23].

Fired on by his Christian zeal and the belief that working with the Wongai was his calling, Schenk was not alarmed but inspired by the Sergeant's figures. Nor was he intimidated by the policeman's comments about the local indigenous people. However, to not venture into the bush and to stay near the town would be in opposition to the advice of the Chief Protector, so Schenk had to clarify why he should not venture out into the bush where he would find the Wongai.

Constable Hunter, the second policeman based at Laverton, contributed his view of the behaviour of the Wongai. He claimed that if Schenk went far away from the town the Wongai would spear him 'as quick as look at him'. The Constable patted his hand gun while he commented that he himself would not go amongst them without being armed and mounted. The control of the Aborigines was to be achieved out in the goldfields by the rule of the gun[24]. This comment came from a policeman who, according to Schenk's daughter Margaret Morgan, was considered by Aboriginal and non-Aboriginal people to be a very cruel man, compared to Sergeant Thompson and Constable Perks. 'He was unfeeling'[25]. In an interview with one of the Wongai descendants, Reggie Johnston, one of the topics he covered was police harassment of Aboriginal people in the 1920s and 1930s, and the only policeman he chose to be specific about and name was 'Dave Hunter'. Reggie summed him up as 'one policeman pretty bad'[26].

The issue of sufficient food for the Aborigines entered the conversation between the missionary and the two policemen. The police viewed it quite simply. Ration depots, which were operated fortnightly by the police, supplied a basic amount of certain foods to the Aborigines. If the rations did not last them the whole fortnight the Wongai could go out into the bush and hunt native wildlife. That practice also complimented the efforts of the police to keep the Aborigines out of their towns as much as possible. They told the missionary that if the Wongai were in towns they were idle and made nuisances of themselves. They were better off out in the bush where they could occupy themselves in hunting. It was even more satisfying for the police and residents to know that the Aboriginal people were moving deeper into the bush in drought times, as wildlife was more likely to be found there due to less disturbance by settlers or pastoralists.

Another matter Schenk needed to address was the best way to make contact with the Wongai. The Sergeant explained that the Wongai were a nomadic people and did not have permanent camp sites for Schenk to visit. The police did not want them to establish any, and they did not want anyone to encourage them to do so. The police preferred them to remain nomadic.

The policemen pointed out to Schenk that keeping the Aborigines out of towns was driven by government regulations. A Section of the 1905 Aborigines Act declared that when a policeman, acting as a protector, saw it appropriate, he could move any 'natives' who were 'camped within or near the limits of any town or municipal district, from their camp at such a distance as he may so direct'. Any 'natives' refusing to obey such an order would be guilty of an offence. The police would then attempt to catch the offenders, put them in the lock-up, transfer them into a rail cattle wagon and then would send them to a native settlement out of the district. From 1918 any eastern goldfields Aboriginal people transferred out of their district were conveyed in police custody to the Moore River Native Settlement.

With the words of warning of the Laverton policemen, the condition set on Schenk by the Chief Protector, and the calling on him by his Lord Jesus Christ in the back of his mind, Rod Schenk commenced his pursuit of the Wongai. He would have tackled the commencement of his work with a mixture of trepidation and excitement. At first it was difficult to talk with the 'indigents' because they were often on the run from the police. After spending some months in the goldfields the Victorian Christian concluded that what the Chief Protector and the local police considered to be 'nuisance' behaviour was actually the behaviour of people who were frequently hungry and thus desperate. The colonists had eliminated much of the wildlife and native vegetation that nourished and bred the wildlife. The traditional food source of the indigenous population was more scarce in times of drought such as now. So they could not stay in the bush for too long without becoming hungry. Though the Aborigines knew they were not welcome in the town, hunger forced them back.

Two months after Rod Schenk's arrival in the Laverton area he communicated his concern over the insufficient amounts of both rations and bush tucker to an authority superior to that of the local protectors. In a letter he sent to Deputy Chief Protector of Aborigines Copping on 21 June 1921 he pointed out that if 'three white men with good dogs and rifles took a three day hunting expedition but did not get one kangaroo [which was Aboriginal tucker as well as a sporting prey for the settlers], how could the natives exist?'[27].

Rod Schenk developed another concern about the state of the Aboriginal people that the police also took for granted and as status quo. Rod had witnessed the constabulary's methods of keeping the Aborigines out of their towns. They would mount their horses and wielding whips or batons they would chase and hound the people. They showed no concern if the weapons they swung menacingly about heads and bodies of the fleeing people made painful or injurious contact. Sometimes the police would persist in their pursuit well beyond the boundaries of their town into the scrub in their municipality. They made the Wongai feel unsafe even in the bowels of the bush that fed and secluded them.

The police were not odd in their attitudes towards the Aborigines. Their actions had the support of the whole district which at this time was generally intolerant of Aborigines. The regular concerns Sergeant Thompson had about the 'the hungry natives' returning to his town were reflected in the letter he sent on 24 March 1921, to Police Inspector Duncan in the Kalgoorlie district headquarters. In that letter he also referred to the concern held by the two policemen at Laverton about the number of Aborigines around their district:

> It's hard to get the natives back into the spinifex country. There are about 450 of them, the majority being born and reared here. Some of them are semi-civilised, and others wild. They can't be got together. As soon as the police move on them they scatter into small camps.
>
> There has been no rain for the last 12 months, so there is an absence of native waters in the bush country. The natives are dependent on towns for water.
>
> The decline of small mining settlements means less food available for begging...the natives used to get food for cutting firewood and cleaning up about the premises. The pastoralists' stock is driving native game further afield, so hunting is inaccessible to them.

> It is no good to drive natives from one camp to another as they become a menace to persons in outlying districts.[28]

The police were very confident that they were doing their job as law enforcers. Like Constable Perks in Morgans, Sergeant Thompson was very proud of his record of clearing Laverton of the local indigenous people and he conveyed this to the missionary on several occasions.

Perhaps it was inevitable that the missionary would come into some conflict from the beginning of his work with the constabulary, town residents and pastoralists. The first stage in Rod Schenk's plan to evangelise the Wongai was to give them some sort of preliminary, basic camp site from which he could coax them to him by offering some sort of food supplement. When he had their trust and confidence he could start the next stage, the work of nurturing their souls. He would prefer to set up his work about Laverton where food and other supplies for his mission site were accessible and where he could select premises from amongst the abandoned buildings. However, this did not seem possible. Rod Schenk had witnessed how the police purged the town of Aborigines and how the local residents resented their presence. He remembered Mr Neville's advice about not calling the Aborigines to assemble near the towns.

Until Schenk could think of an alternative site, his missionary work enticed the Wongai to congregate around Laverton, and hence in the path of the charging mounted constables. Quite early in his relationship with this municipality many of the local residents became intolerant of him. They set about to make Rod Schenk feel that with his ideas to settle the indigenous people nearby he was unwelcome. When he made enquiries at the Town Clerk's office about what land was available for him to lease from the Laverton Roads Board he met non-cooperation. In raising the subject of Laverton's Common around the outskirts of the town as a possible site for a mission he was informed by the staff that there was no land available for leasing. He was advised further that none of the useful land beyond the Common was available for leasing either. It had been taken up by pastoralists who had been able to select enormous holdings at very cheap prices[29]. The President of the Laverton Roads Board, Mr Harris, was a successful local pastoralist and prominent community member who led local opposition to Aboriginal presence and Aboriginal sympathisers. He was not in favour of the missionary's presence in his district.

The local townspeople also tried to convince Rod Schenk that he was wasting his time if he thought he could do anything good for this 'lot of ratty natives'. Their impression of these indigenous people was that they were 'like brumbies' and could not 'be tamed'[30].

In becoming familiar with the local Wongai Rod gradually learned some details about their origins. They came principally from the Gibson and Great Victoria Deserts[31]. A significant number of these were 'Mandjundja' from the Warburton region[32]. Schenk was later told by Tjirrgulu that her people came south to Laverton many years ago from the Warburton Ranges and settled on the edge of the Great Victoria Desert[33]. Wongai came to the mission at the Mount Margaret site from Morgans, Linden, Burtville, Menzies and Karonie east of the goldfields. Laverton people joined up and eventually visitors from the spinifex country were brought in from a radius of over 100 miles (160 kilometres) by Wongai who had befriended the missionary[34]. The Wongai who came to Schenk's mission were of the eastern goldfields Laverton-Linden tribe who were considered by colonists to be 'the lowest type of native'[35]. When Schenk saw them about his mission aspects of their appearance indicated they still practised ancient customs. They had maimed limbs such as broken toe joints and dislocated hips as part of initiation ceremonies[36]; they feared the emufoot man and practised infanticide. They still practised spear fights, at least one every week up until 1924.

From the early days of his arrival Schenk also aggravated the pastoralists who had a working relationship with the local police. Schenk's work was drawing the Aborigines out of the deeper bush where the pastoralists preferred them, and his words were encouraging them to congregate around Laverton. The resentful pastoralists commenced to spread rumours that questioned Schenk's conduct with the Aborigines.

Pastoralists had relied on the indigenous people to be a source of cheap and pliable labour. They did what they were told and seemed to demand little in the way of shelter and food. The 1905 Aborigines Act barred Aboriginal labour from contact with trade unions and so Aboriginal station hands never agitated for improved conditions. In the summer 'lay off' season the Aboriginal people received food supplements from the ration depots which were supplied by the Aborigines Department. This took that load off the pastoralists and made Aboriginal labour still cheaper. Schenk started to teach the males how to earn an income and what to expect as a wage. By involving them in collecting dingo scalps and pulling and cleaning sandalwood, Schenk was providing cash wages when few Aboriginal stockmen or women in household duties were receiving cash for their labour[37]. So Schenk was attracting Aboriginal labour off pastoral stations[38]. Pastoralists spread rumours among the 'natives' about Schenk so as to create prejudice about him[39].

Schenk further aggravated residents, miners and pastoralists over the matter of illegitimate babies. When the ardent missionary found out the names of biological fathers of 'half-caste' babies he would attempt to confront the father with his responsibility by suggesting that he take care of his baby and its mother[40].

Rod could not let his work be obstructed by the attitudes and the opposition of the Laverton townspeople. The condition placed by Neville on Rod Schenk, that he had to show a degree of progress and success within a certain time in order to have continued support and authorisation of the Chief Protector, was constantly on his mind. Neville expected to hear that the missionary out at Laverton had established a base for his evangelical work. Schenk was having to search well beyond Laverton, and the site would have to have certain prerequisites. It would need a source of permanent water; to be close to a settlement with a ration depot so that he would have a guaranteed source of food for his new congregation; and there had to be a police station within a reasonable distance because of the regular need to be in touch with the police as protectors.

He also had to establish a rapport with the Wongai. It had been difficult and frustrating to make headway in such a relationship. The Wongai were difficult to find and to approach. After a couple of days of being chased by the police out of settlements they moved deeper into the bush where they would disperse into small groups and move their camps regularly so that the police could not find them.

A letter written by the Chief Protector in September, five months after Schenk's arrival in Laverton, was brought to Schenk by Sergeant Thompson. The Perth administrator was reminding him that he was anticipating news from him soon. The communique was frank and curt. If Schenk did not achieve 'something practical' very soon, his authority to work with the 'natives' would be withdrawn[41].

Rod Schenk found his site. He discovered that there was a town Common 32 kilometres from Laverton which was lying idle. It was attached to the now defunct Mount Margaret diggings, one of the earliest gold mining towns in the Margaret Goldfields District, and was situated on a saltbush plain near the Mount Margaret hills about seven miles from the larger, old mining and rail town called Morgans. The Common had a source of permanent water at the site called King's Well and there was a police station and a ration depot in Morgans. Rod

Schenk applied for permission to lease the land. Though bureaucratic procedure held the decision up, permission was granted eventually during January 1922.

Mount Margaret's location would please both Schenk and Neville. It could provide a point of focus for the Aboriginal people moving out of the interior of the Western Desert region and from the Warburton Ranges. It was a good buffer between the pastoral stations and townships on one hand, and on the other the remaining local Aborigines from which men could be absorbed to be trained as pastoral hands[42].

Once Schenk's rapport with the Wongai was established he had to identify the means by which he could make the Aborigines 'productive'. The devout evangelist applied himself to gaining experience in one of the popular industries of the goldfields, sandalwood pulling. The sandalwood plant was plentiful in the district, freely acquired and with a guaranteed market for its products. There were many men about the district who were skilled in this trade and all Schenk had to do was find a man who was willing to teach a preacher how to pull, clean and stack sandalwood. Once Schenk had mastered these skills he then could train some of the Aboriginal folk to labour at the same business.

Within two months of receiving Neville's letter Schenk was ready to make his response. The missionary could report to the Chief Protector where the site for his mission was to be, and that he had commenced the erection of its first main building and of fencing for goat yards. He could outline the commencement of the training program to make the Wongai productive. Wongai men and women were learning the trade of sandalwood pulling; males were learning fencing, shepherding and building, and the women household duties. In December 1922 Schenk reported to Deputy Chief Copping that since June he had 'from five to fifty natives at Mount Margaret working sandalwood and money went back to them'[43].

In the first year of the mission Schenk attempted to deal with the hunger of the Wongai. He wrote in September 1922 that, 'It is a joy to do something in the way of providing food for the bodies of these poor souls, but it takes up so much time supervising that less time is left for the greater joy of helping them spiritually'[44].

As well as being provided with basic assistance from the Aborigines Department Schenk's mission was to receive donated funds from the A.A.M. Schenk saw his mission as a refuge for Aboriginal people from the problems they faced in living on the fringe of the nearby mining towns of Laverton, Morgans and Leonora. Schenk shared Neville's view of assimilation. He accepted that the best future for the Aboriginal people lay in the combination of their education and vocational training, and their evangelisation, so that they would take their place beside Europeans in the wider Australian society.

Schenk regarded all traditional Aboriginal customs and beliefs as the 'works of darkness', to be discouraged. Preaching and conversion were to be in English and he forbad members of his staff to attempt to learn any of the local indigenous language[45]. Schenk maintained that, apart from their language being a heathen tongue, their knowledge of English would enable the native to gain better work and to fit better into the wider Australian community[46]. Schenk contributed to eliminating the Aboriginal culture and language, though later he softened his policy on Aboriginal language, and some of his staff and his own daughters learned much of the Wongai vocabulary.

Community resentment against Schenk's presence and work persisted even after he left Laverton and opened his mission station at Mount Margaret in 1922. Police Constable Warren, who replaced Sergeant Thompson and Police Constable Hunter in Laverton during 1923, wrote to Inspector Duncan at police headquarters in Kalgoorlie in that same year to alert his superior to the nuisance Schenk was making for the community in regard to the Aborigines. He reported that Schenk was causing the natives to be restless and troublesome. It seemed he could not control the movement of natives in and out of the mission. Warren's perception of the situation was affected by his ignorance of it.

During the first years of the Mount Margaret mission the Wongai went through a period of transition from their nomadic lifestyle to one increasingly sedentary. When the Aboriginal people first came to the mission, they left their children in the bush. As they came to trust and accept Schenk they started to leave their children with him. The missionary was offering them food, safety and accomodation and eventually a basic education. The Wongai parents had learned from their own experiences with the local police and from the stories of those who escaped Moore River Native Settlement that the mission was a kinder place for their children to be, if they had to part with them at all. They would be very likely to lose their children if they kept them in the bush.

Though the children were left with Schenk to escape the Moore River net, the fear of police boots and horses' hooves was entrenched in them and kept them company there too. When an unexpected approaching sound was heard some of the younger children who were already skittish or nervous would flee to a hiding spot in the hills just beyond the boundary of the mission[47].

Though the Aboriginal people experienced how the missionaries aided in the destruction of Aboriginal culture and language, their views were compromised by the situation that the mission also offered some security for the children. At a mission their children received regular meals and somewhere safe from the police to sleep. Their experience was that no other colonists' groups were prepared to help them to the same extent[48].

The mission was not entirely free of police attempts to remove children to the Moore River Native Settlement. Neville intended that Mount Margaret would suit his plans which ever way was most appropriate. Intermittently Schenk did request of the Chief Protector that he guarantee no more children to be taken from his mission to Moore River.

The police view that Schenk was 'having difficulty' with the local Aborigines reached the Aborigines Department, who in turn viewed his success with some reserve. At times it was reluctant to be prompt with some of its cooperation. In January 1923 Rod Schenk wrote to Deputy Chief Protector Copping to request 'any medicines be sent by the Aborigines Protection Department', because quite a few of the Aboriginal people attending the mission were ill. Schenk requested 'especially pure carbolic acid and mercurial ointment, and other general items such as boracic acid, carbolic oil, eucalyptus, vaseline, epsom salts, iodine, ointment for sores, etc.'[49].

Before deciding how to respond to the request Copping sent a letter to the Commissioner of Police to get an opinion. In his reply to Copping written on 5 April 1923, the Police Commissioner said, 'At Mount Margaret mission Schenk has no proper control of [the natives] as there is no stronghold to retain them. It's wasting good medicine to give it to them [there] as they never stop more than a few days at the mission then they take to the bush again'[50].

At this time Inspector Duncan received additional correspondence from an anxious Constable Perks at Morgans. The latter wanted to draw the Inspector's attention to how the number of Aborigines coming into Mount Margaret mission was causing an overflow into his town. The same matter was causing Police Constable Warren at Laverton some anxiety. The latter reported to the Inspector in Kalgoorlie that the mission 'is 7 miles [11 kilometres] from Morgans and 17 miles [27 kilometres] from Laverton' and that it was 'still too close to both towns for a native settlement'. The police and settlers would have preferred that the mission was many more kilometres away from these two towns, a few hundred kilometres away out in the spinifex country or the desert[51].

The pastoralists never ceased in opposing Schenk's presence in the Morgans district. They persisted in spreading their rumours, in attempting to get Schenk's mission lease cancelled and in arguing for the mission to be moved far east of Laverton. They were not successful in either, but the public disturbance they raised in opposition to Schenk gained the attention of the authorities wanting to investigate the mission. In January 1925 District Inspector of Police Duncan and Deputy Chief Protector of Aborigines Copping travelled to Mount Margaret to investigate the complaints by pastoralists against the mission. They did not find any grounds for the complaints or to close the mission, and instead provided a favourable report to the Chief Protector on the progress being made there with the local Aboriginal people[52].

Within twelve months of founding his mission at Mount Margaret Rod Schenk's affairs were progressing sufficiently for him to be able to focus on his personal life. Rod proposed marriage to Mysie and asked her to share his life of missionary service in the place that he had chosen. Her personal dedication to God, fused with Rod's compelling love for her and his vision for the Aborigines, combined to help Mysie make up her mind. She agreed to be his 'helpmeet'[53] and was prepared to go anywhere God called them. Leaving a missionary couple, Jim and Gladys Jago, in charge of the completion of the construction of his marital house and of the mission, Rod travelled from the Western Australian goldfields to Melbourne, a journey taking about a week.

While Mysie prepared in Melbourne for her marriage to the Mount Margaret missionary and to start her life doing work for the Lord she gave her role on the mission and her working relationship with Rod some serious thought. From Rod's correspondence Mysie comprehended that he was planning to have Aboriginal children staying at his mission and that the Aborigines were expected to be given education and skills training. Mysie wanted to have a purpose of her own that could be offered to the work of the mission. She contemplated becoming involved in training the Aboriginal girls and women. If there was a program established to train the girls in skills that gave them a means of earning an income then they should not have to resort to cohabitation in miners' camps. She considered it would be suitable to teach raffia to the Aboriginal girls.

Rodolphe Samuel Schenk and Isobel May Johnston were married

among family and friends on 14 October 1922 in the Protestant Hall of the Melbourne Gospel Crusade. Within three weeks of their wedding, during November, they were in their new home at the comparatively remote Mount Margaret mission.

Mysie worked by her husband's side for nearly two years before they commenced a family. Mysie's first two pregnancies resulted in miscarriages. During a miscarriage Rod was away in Laverton and Mysie was alone on the mission. The nearest hospital was that at Morgans, but it was not as well equipped as the one in Leonora, which was ninety-eight kilometres away. When Mysie became pregnant a third time Rod sent her to Melbourne. In August 1924, Mysie gave birth to their first child, a girl they named Margaret, after her father's mission. Rod travelled to Melbourne in November to collect Mysie and Margaret and to bring them home[54].

When Mysie became pregnant again Rod took her and little Margaret to Melbourne in May 1926 for the birth. Their second child, a girl who they named Esther, was born on 18 June 1926. Their third child was due in August 1927. As the conditions on the mission and in the Leonora hospital were improved by then Mysie felt confident in having her baby in the goldfields. The baby decided to come a few days early and Frances Elisabeth was born at the mission itself on 18 August 1927. In 1932 when Mysie became pregnant with their fourth child she had the three girls Margaret, Esther and Elisabeth, aged eight, six and five respectively, to care for. Rod and Mysie decided it would be best for her to take the children to Melbourne where Roderick William was born on 10 December.

During the years of caring for children at the mission Mysie attempted to prevent acts of infanticide. She observed that sometimes pregnant Aboriginal women would go away from the mission into the bush and return to it without their baby[55]. As a Christian, Mysie attempted to help these women by getting to their infant in time. Their daughter, Margaret, commented that her mother saved babies when she could and mourned for those who were lost. Mysie had come to understand that the Aboriginal people practised infanticide as a 'tribal thing for population control'. Once an Aboriginal youth came running into the mission yelling, 'little red baby born in camp'. Mysie sensed that that baby would not be brought to them so she went out to the camp to look into the situation. She was able to save that baby, named Gladys Simpson, from strangulation. Gladys still bears the marks on her throat today from that attempt[56].

By September 1926, when Lallie in her pregnant condition arrived at the mission with her mother and brother, Wongai families had become more accepting about leaving their children with Rod and Mysie Schenk. The Wongai had noticed over time that the police seldom raided the mission settlement, compared to the frequency with which they raided the Aboriginal camps in the bush. If the parents took their children voluntarily to the mission they were deprived from having them at home again, but it was the only option left to them; at least they would have them close by[57]. Once the local Aboriginal people learned that missionary Schenk was opening a school to give some education to their children the parents would walk great distances to have their children placed on that mission. The parents came from the south, north and west to bring their children to Mount Margaret. They would arrive at the mission during the night, having come from distant places like the Mulga Queen, a significant meeting place for the Wongai. Some came from the Warburton Ranges and some from the spinifex desert[58].

Mothers were prepared to take risks to get their sons or daughters, particularly if they were part-Aboriginal children, to the school at Mount Margaret mission. One mother who had a job as a washerwoman in a hotel in Laverton was able to provide for her fair skinned boy, so did not have to fear being assessed as neglecting her child. However, there was nowhere in Laverton for her son to go to school. When she heard that a school was being started at the mission near Morgans, she left her job in Laverton and walked with her son to the mission, though in fear of the police[59]. The additional benefit of their children being left on the mission was that the police would not consider them neglected, as they did the children growing up in the bush camps, and would have less cause to remove them[60].

Knowing that the appearance or status of neglect would motivate the police to attempt to seize Aboriginal children, the welfare of the children was a high priority to the Schenks. They kept strict control on the absence of the children on their settlement, rarely permitting them to leave and in effect detaining them there. The Schenks' rule at their mission was that their child residents could go back to their families only once a year, usually around Christmas. They had a few reasons for detaining the children on the mission. One was that the children did not return to their bush lifestyle nor permanently to their people. The Schenks were concerned that if these part-Aboriginal children were allowed to go back to their people at any time, particularly those who were given full-blood fathers, they might be taken further into the bush country and there was a chance that they might then remain with their people. They would grow up to live a nomadic existence and be lost to both the Schenks' evangelical congregation and the Chief Protector's assimilation program. If such children did not have a father the Chief Protector would consider them to be uncared for and neglected. They could then be at risk of a police raid on their camps and of having the Moore River net gather them. Appreciating that Aborginal parental loved was sacred, the Schenks encouraged the parents of children boarding at the mission to remain near the mission and have degrees of interaction with their children. This overall attitude towards parents' proximity provided an atmosphere of security at the mission[61].

Another reason was that the Schenks knew that it was very likely that girls aged sixteen or over who went out working, for example as duty girls on pastoral stations, would get pregnant and be left unmarried. The Schenks did not want them to face that risk[62]. The outcome of this could be that the pregnant girl abandoned by the biological father would be taken by the police to Moore River, or another case of infanticide would occur, or the girl would be directed into cohabitation to contribute to her own support.

There was the concern for the part-Aboriginal girls who were required under regulations to not marry a promised husband who was full-blood. If these girls were allowed to return too often to their people there was the possibility that while the girls lived their people's traditional ways they might be given to their promised tribal husband. Those girls would not return to the mission and this would displease the Chief Protector. With or without a tribal husband the girls might still be expected to practise cohabitation which was unacceptable to the missionaries.

If Schenk let too many girls escape his religious flock and not be turned into productive people capable of being assimilated into the wider Anglo-Saxon society, Neville might view the missionary as failing in his duties outlined by the Aborigines Department. Neville might withdraw Schenks' authority to continue his practical, educational and spiritual work with the Aborigines.

Another aim of the Schenks was to make certain that a girl at puberty did not become a wife, or second wife, to an older man to whom she had been promised. They knew that the girl could experience the tribal custom of painful discipline such as a beating or spearing by their husband, and some girls were afraid of this[63].

The Schenks kept their girls at the mission up until the age of sixteen, and kept older girls for as long as possible, permitting them to leave the mission only under certain conditions. The missionary couple preferred that the girls stayed on the mission until they had sufficient training in skills so that when they left they could earn their own income and not have to resort to cohabitation to survive. They also preferred that the girls did not leave until one of their tribal men, who they preferred to be mission educated, married them at the mission in a Christian ceremony and then took them to a marital home.

Another circumstance in which the police viewed a girl as neglected was when a girl's tribal husband had three or four wives already. Then it seemed quite likely that the young wife with her child or children could not get sufficient food and care for herself or her dependents. The police were aware of the Aborigines' lack of provisions and that it was quite easy for physical neglect of the children to occur.

The distinction over the skin colour of Aboriginal children was less a concern to Rod Schenk than it was to Auber Neville. The missionary was prepared to care for any Aboriginal child who was brought to him, whether full-blood or part-Aboriginal. He was not manipulated entirely by the Sections of the 1905 Aborigines Act and the advice of the Chief Protector. There were occasions when Rod Schenk took 'full-blood' children into his mission and did not include their name and presence in any report he sent on to the Chief Protector. Mysie and Rod were aware that some of the full-blood children died because they had no immunity to gastric trouble and influenza. So they attended to their medical, nutritional and other needs just as they would any child. They appreciated that to give some education to some full-blood children would aggravate the Chief Protector. This man believed that educating full-blood children - who were of limited intelligence and of a race which was 'dying out' - was squandering the limited resources of the Aborigines Department. Rod and Mysie would have been cautious when the Chief Protector or his Deputy visited their mission to observe and assess how the programs of education, of assimilation and of making the Wongai productive were progressing there. A Wongai descendant, a girl on the Schenks' mission who received a sound education there, remembered the Schenks hiding some 'full-blood' children because they did not want Neville to prevent them from caring for those children as well as the others[64].

By the time Lallie came to Mount Margaret mission in September 1926, which was five years after it had opened, Rod Schenk had made significant progress in establishing a mission, a teaching program and evangelising many of the eastern goldfields Aboriginal people, despite his tense relationship with the Chief Protector of Aborigines. Schenk still faced the unrelenting opposition of the pastoralists, a most influential group in the community whose voice was heard in the halls of Parliament House and the Legislative Assembly, as well as at the administration level of the Police and Aborigines Departments. To achieve his personal and religious ideals Rod Schenk had to walk a fine line between doing what was outlined for him by the 1905 Aborigines Act and doing for the Aboriginal people what he believed to be Christian and humane.

When Mysie and Rod Schenk took Lallie in they wanted to protect her from the police, and keep her at Mount Margaret if they could, rather than for her to face cohabitation, mistreatment by an older tribal husband or being sent by the police to Moore River Native Settlement. Nevertheless, Rod still filled in the form that he had to whenever new wards were taken in at his mission. It was particularly important that he communicate to the Chief Protector if a new girl was single, pregnant and 'half-caste'.

When Tjirrgulu and Lallie arrived at the mission the girls' quarters had been built, with separate accomodation for the young girls and the teenage girls. There was a room in which children had their schooling. An estimation of Lallie's age, older than sixteen, determined that she was too old to be enrolled in the school lessons. In her advanced pregnant state the Schenks thought it inappropriate to locate Lallie in the girls' dormitories. Rod and Mysie decided that Lallie would be placed in their private quarters where she could look after their two small children, two-year-old Margaret and two-month-old Esther, thus enabling Mysie to be of more assistance to Rod around the mission. While they awaited the birth of her baby Lallie would be taught basic skills in domestic duties.

In such close proximity to Lallie, Rod and Mysie Schenk became very fond of her. Her character and demeanour were very appealing. They were impressed by her sensibility, reliability and cheerfulness, by her modest and friendly nature. They noted exceptional aspects about her character. Although they had not known her before when she came to the mission she could already sing some hymns, such as 'I am So Glad That Jesus Loves Me'. Lallie told the Schenks that she was taught by other Wongai who had stayed at the mission for a while and returned to the bush[65]. The Schenks were very confident about their decision to have her in their home and trusted her totally with their children.

Over the next four weeks while awaiting the arrival of Lallie's baby

Mrs Schenk taught Lallie how to take care of her grooming. She gave her instruction in how to set the table for a formal meal, how to sweep a floor and how to fold serviettes. Lallie learned a few more hymns such as 'Nothing but the Blood' and 'At the Cross'. Lallie sang these songs about the house and made the atmosphere of the Schenks' home more pleasant and cheerful. To take Lallie further into her transition from a bush life into a 'civilised, Christian life', and from her indigenous culture into the colonists' society, the missionaries called her only by her Christian name Lallie, and Lallie heard only English spoken around her. The Wongai on the mission at this time were discouraged from speaking their own language[66].

Eventually Jack Akbar found out the decision of the elders in removing Lallie to the mission at Mount Margaret. This was the second time that Jack had sought the permission of the elders to marry Lallie and he had unexpectedly lost her. The news may have evoked mixed feelings in Jack, perhaps similar to those in the hearts of some of the Linden people. Jack could comprehend how placing Lallie at the mission could protect her from police capture, and would provide her with proper care during the delivery of her child. However, he may have been under some apprehension that Lallie was now out of seclusion. Jack may have felt anxious and alarmed because the future he hoped to have with the woman he wanted as his wife was continually being obstructed by decisions which concerned them but which were being made by others. He had helped to seclude Lallie in the bush from the knowledge of the police. Now her people had moved her to a place which did not give her any cover.

It is most likely that Tjirrgulu, the Linden mob and Jack Akbar did not know of the reporting requirements placed on Schenk. Because Lallie was now on the mission the Aborigines and Police Departments and the Chief Protector's office all had a collaborator who would provide them with regular reports on her health, condition and location. The police now had easy access to her and could come instantly on receiving the order to take her into custody.

When Chief Protector Neville made the major decision that was to alter Lallie's future, her people and Akbar had no warning of it. Upon receiving the report of Lallie's arrival at the mission and her pregnant condition, Neville seems to have had no need of further convincing that it was time to place her into police custody and have her transported from the district. To initiate this formal process Neville sent through the Police Department a request to the local protector Constable Perks to visit the Schenks and to have an interview with Lallie[67].

The main intention of the interview was for Perks to verify whether or not she had a provider, and to ascertain the state of her health so as to confirm that she was fit to travel as soon as the order to remove her came through. Constable Perks had not seen Lallie since July, two months before, when Jack Akbar and the elders had brought her into Morgans to show her to him. Since then all the stealth that Perks had mustered with his network of informants had not led to any success in locating the girl. It may have been humiliating to learn that the wanted girl's own mother had walked her into the mission which was part of the Constable's area of responsibility. Rather than continue to allow the impression to stick that he was not doing his job effectively Perks wasted no time in going out to the mission to observe Lallie's state and to interview her.

Before talking with Lallie Constable Perks asked the Schenks for their impressions of the girl. The few comments they could offer Perks were that they estimated her age to be about nineteen and the time of the birth could be within three or four weeks. They stated they were very fond of her and that they were willing to take care of her until the Chief Protector decided to authorise her removal. In the report that Perks prepared consequently on 16 September he reflected the couple's fondness for Lallie and their desire to keep her at the mission[68].

Perks then had an interview with Lallie. The only time Lallie's own words are contained in her DCS File in the time she lived in Western Australia is during this interview in September 1926. Even in this case her exact words are derived from Perks's interpretation of them. On only one other instance in her whole file, which features police enquiries and interviews with herself, her mother, her brother, the elders and Aboriginal police informants, are the exact words spoken by an Aboriginal person recorded officially. There could be several explanations for this absence of the voice and thoughts of the Aboriginal person: it could be a reflection of the evolutionary philosophy regarding the intelligence level of indigenous people; their side of the story was not considered valid, even for the law courts. Reporters like police and public servants may have preferred to represent their interpretaion of what they heard, rather than attempt to record the words of Aboriginal people whose grasp of English was often rudimentary.

Perks recorded that in the conversation between himself and Lallie she stated that 'she is willing to now live with the Missionary couple'. Though the reason why Lallie expressed this is not verifiable, it may have indicated that she wished to settle permanently somewhere, as opposed to continuing her nomadic life as a 'bush native', which could bring her risk. At the same time she would not want to give up her people. Privately she may have hoped that her life would become settled and safer when she became Akbar's wife. At this moment she knew the Schenks wanted her to stay with them. For the moment all she could tell Perks was that she was willing to stay at the mission with her baby and not return to her past life.

Through her interview Lallie alerted the police to another circumstance of her life that caused some alarm. She declared that she was 'afraid of the Linden Natives coming over and spearing her'[69]. Though some of her people wanted her safe from the police and agreed that being at the mission would keep her free from raids, there were others who still believed that her rightful place was with Burtville Jack. She was still the promised wife of a tribal man, and by not being with him she has left his company without his consent. They would regard even her presence at Mount Margaret mission as inappropriate and would be the group of the Linden mob expecting an emufoot man (also called a featherfoot man) to be sent there to spear her. It was quite likely that this group also perceived Akbar as interfering in a partnership arranged according to tribal law. This would have placed the Afghan in a position comparable to that of an adulterer, and thus deserving of a spearing. If the emufoot man was prevented in any way from getting to Lallie and punishing her, a proxy such as Lallie's mother could be chosen to experience the punishment.

Lallie may not have expected Perks's interpretation of her fear of harm to work against, rather than for, the hopes that the Schenks, her mother and her people, and Akbar had for her. Perks was concerned that the arrival of an emufoot man at the mission, intent on carrying out a spearing on one person, could be a threat also to the welfare of others in the vicinity. Perks had now discovered another alarming point regarding the Akbar-Matbar case. Perhaps now the administration would be provoked into promptly ordering the girl's detention in his cell in Morgans and then her removal from the district.

The contents of Perks's report on his interview with Lallie at the mission made a profound impression on Inspector Spedding Smith. He sympathised with Perks's anxiety about what might be the possible consequences on the mission's population of the continued presence of the Linden girl. Within twenty-four hours he had sent a succinct telegram to the Chief Protector of Aborigines in Perth and advised prompt action; 'I think it would be advisable to have this woman removed from the District altogether'[70].

Both Perks's interview report and the Inspector's wire reached Neville's desk about the same time. The Chief Protector's attention was taken by the wider perspective of Lallie's case. Lallie's behaviour over the previous several months could be a negative influence on Aborigines and be seen by other members of the community as a flagrant disregard of the regulations of the Aborigines Act. Neville had been advised earlier that the continued freedom of the girl was having an unsettling effect on the local indigenous people. The file does not provide any details on what kind of unsettledness there was, or who were the leaders amongst the Wongai, at least around the time of September 1926. The conclusion of the Chief Protector and the police was that her placement at the mission could be a threat to others.

Perks's report of a possible spearing on a mission was still not enough, however, to have Lallie removed from the district. Constable Perks was left to continue to observe Akbar's movements and Lallie's situation so as to accumulate more concrete evidence of breaches by those two of sections of the 1905 Aborigines Act. Due to the earlier episode of suspecting them of spreading a venereal disease and of Akbar's more recent volunteered confession that he was the father of the baby Lallie was carrying, Perks hoped to witness the Afghan actually breach a regulation of the Act. Perks saw Akbar with Lallie during September and October while she was at the mission[71]. The police suspected that Jack's visits to the mission, though they were primarily for his business, had an ulterior motive. They suspected Jack Akbar of being devious enough to attempt to remove Lallie and her baby after its birth from the mission, and to take them to a secluded place deep in the bush.

While Akbar was able to visit Lallie on the mission he could still hope to persuade the Chief Protector to grant him an exemption. He was contemplating his next angle of appeal to the Chief Protector before the birth of her child. He was not aware that in Perth at this same time the Chief Protector was ready to make the decision for which Perks had been hoping for so long. On 25 September 1926, Neville sent a despatch by courier to the Under Secretary of the Colonial Secretary's Department, James Hickery. It contained a request for the Honourable Minister Kitson to sign a warrant for the arrest of 'a young half-caste girl named Lallie Matbar, who has been leading a nomadic existence in the Linden district'.

To prevent his request being put aside the Chief Protector included in the despatch a comprehensive letter which explained to the Minister why there was an urgency about the girl's arrest. The police had been trying over a long period of time to get hold of Lallie and remove her. She had been living a life of prostitution, and she was a further nuisance to the police because an Afghan was persisting in proposing to marry her even though he had been directed that a marriage between an Aborigine and an Asiatic was prohibited. She had been given in temporary charge to the missionary people at Mount Margaret but this was not an appropriate solution because there was the threat of danger to all there due to some of 'the Linden natives' planning to spear her. Neville emphasized the need to effect her removal from the district altogether[72].

While the Chief Protector in Perth awaited the authorisation for the arrest of Lallie, Jack Akbar met with with his solicitor Mr Cook. On 30 September Cook sent another letter on his client's behalf to Chief Protector Neville. In the letter Jack reassured Neville that he had been keeping company with Lallie for eighteen months, and when he found out that she was in a certain condition he was willing to marry her so as to make an honest woman of her. The solicitor backed up Jack's admission by declaring to the Chief Protector that he knew Akbar was trying his hardest to do his duty towards her. The letter was completed with a request from Akbar to the Chief Protector to arrange matters so that he could 'marry her within six weeks, the latest possible date'. Jack Akbar hoped very much that this time his solicitor would rally the very best of his persuasive and argumentative talents to finally achieve the Chief Protector's agreement to an exemption. Perhaps reflecting his desperation and determination, Akbar offered a bonus to his solicitor:'P.S. If this [exemption] can be arranged by you [very soon] I will willingly add an extra ten pounds to your account for your good work'[73].

It may have been this gesture of a bonus perhaps viewed as a bribe, or the adamant persistence demonstrated by his Afghan client in not respecting government regulations or in not taking the advice of the Chief Protector or the police, that eventually caused the solicitor to become somewhat nervous about the implications for himself. Cook wished to retain his reputation in the community and with the Aborigines and Police Departments. He knew that Akbar's request was illegal and had been denied by executive authority more than once. Cook was a servant of the government as well as of its citizens. He did not wish to risk incurring the government's wrath and criticism by being perceived as aggravating, argumentative, and as refuting and challenging its laws. Though Akbar came initially with good character references, his repeated petitioning for an exemption to which he was forbidden, could draw the authorities to both Cook and Akbar.

Cook decided that the letter he wrote on 1 October would be his final service in support of the petitioning by his Asian client of the Chief Protector of Aborigines. The solicitor proposed to the Chief Protector that he reconsider the genuine appeals Jack Akbar was making in seeking permission to marry the pregnant Wongai girl. If Akbar was responsible for Matbar's condition then it might be desirable that the two should be united in marriage. At the same time Cook understood the regulations of the 1905 Aborigines Act well enough to realise that the Chief Protector of Aborigines had no choice in deciding what would be in the best interests of the Aborigines. He concluded his letter to the Chief Protector by asking him once more to reconsider the application Akbar made to marry Matbar[74].

The arrival of the solicitor's letter in Neville's office had no effect. It came too late. The procedure set in motion by the Chief Protector to prepare the warrant for the arrest of Lallie, unbeknownst to the solicitor and Akbar, was complete. By 4 October 1926, the Chief Protector was able to supply the Commissioner of Police Connell with the signed warrant that authorised the Police Department to send Constable Perks to take a pregnant Aboriginal girl off a mission. Lallie Matbar was to be sent to the place the Wongai dreaded and feared, the place the Linden mob had tried for so long to keep her from, the Moore River Native Settlement[75].

A.O. Neville may have hoped that the exercising of the warrant would demonstrate convincingly to his critics and the indigenous population what influence and power he could wield in dealing with offenders of the 1905 Act. He would be seen to be an uncompromising and effective administrator whose portfolio and position in the government was vital. At the same time it would not serve Neville's purposes to appear to his public to be overly authoritarian, unapproachable and unreasonable. If he could clarify that there was no other option but custody and removal of Lallie Matbar his public image would reflect an efficient and responsible yet compassionate administrator. The alternative solution needed to be acceptable under the regulations of the Act and not require an exemption.

To get clarification of Lallie's marital status Neville contacted District Inspector of Police Spedding Smith in Kalgoorlie to find out if there was any objection still in existence, from either the police or her people, to this girl going back to her promised tribal husband, Burtville Jack. The

Protector's logic was that if Burtville Jack would be willing to have her back then Lallie would have a provider. With this arrangement neither Lallie nor her baby would be considered as being neglected. Also, there would no longer be the need for the emufoot man to be sent to punish her with a spearing. This arrangement with Burtville Jack and Lallie could be the solution[76]. Inspector Spedding Smith was not able to obtain the solution the Chief Protector was prepared to consider.

As soon as the warrant for Lallie's removal was sent on to District Inspector Spedding Smith in Kalgoorlie, A.O. Neville could turn to other business. One job he had yet to do was to respond to the letter from the Kalgoorlie solicitor. He informed the solicitor that he recently issued the warrant for Lallie's removal from the mission and her people, and advised him that the girl would be railed far away to 'Moore River Native Settlement where she will remain pending the birth of her child or during the Minister's pleasure'. He further advised the solicitor to warn Jack Akbar that he may yet be prosecuted for cohabiting with Lallie[77].

Before Perks received the warrant Lallie went into labour. Mrs Schenk attended the birth as a midwife. On Thursday 7 October 1926 at 7.30 a.m. Lallie 'gave birth prematurely at the Mission House to a boy. He weighed 3 1/2 lbs and was stillborn'. The Schenks arranged for Lallie's baby to be buried at Mount Margaret near the Mission House[78]. There is no mention in Lallie's file how she felt about the loss of her infant, just as the whole issue of the death of Aboriginal babies was never considered by the police to be worthy of investigating. Nor is it known how soon after the death of the infant that Akbar got word, or how it affected him.

On the day of the birth of Lallie's little boy Mr Schenk sent an assisting missionary, Mr Reichenbach, into Morgans to report the birth to Constable Perks. Reichenbach was also to request the policeman to visit the mission immediately.

In requesting Perks's presence at their mission they wished to pursue more than a duty. Their fondness for Lallie had deepened. As well as providing a formal report on her baby boy's death, they wanted to persuade Perks and the Aborigines Department to leave Lallie with them. They understood the options for Lallie. Though they had witnessed the devout suitor Jack Akbar spending some time with Lallie around the mission they knew that it was illegal for an Asian and an Aborigine to marry, and that there was no hope that Jack would be permitted to be a provider and husband for her. It was also their understanding that there was no promised tribal husband among her own people who could provide and care for her. If the police took her it would be to Moore River Native Settlement. The missionary couple believed that the best thing for Lallie's future was for them to be Lallie's providers and care givers, to have Lallie stay with them.

When Perks arrived at Mount Margaret mission the Schenks reported on Lallie's state of health. Though Lallie was on the way to recovery, if her condition worsened over the next three days she would have to be removed to the Morgans hospital. The Schenks then put their case to him to keep Lallie with them. When Perks returned to his station he sent off a report on the birth of Lallie's son. The contents did not include the Schenks' request to Mr Neville to leave Lallie at the mission[79].

On the sixth day after the birth of Lallie's son Perks returned to Mount Margaret mission to serve the warrant for her arrest and to commence her removal from the district. After transferring Lallie to the Morgans cell Perks telegrammed Inspector Spedding Smith to report that Lallie Matbar was in police custody and that he considered that she was fit to travel[80].

Constable Perks must have felt a sense of vindication and victory when he sent that telegram. In his holding cell he had the girl who had taken so long for the police to secure. Because of his experience with removing children forcibly he presumed that Lallie would show herself to be, as many of the frightened and desperate children had been, conniving and to know a lot of tricks about escape. Perks did not want to see all the work and effort gone into tracking and collecting Lallie undone, or his reputation damaged, by her slipping from custody. He wanted the head office to transfer her promptly. At the bottom of his report on Lallie's arrest Perks warned his superior that, 'This native will probably make her escape if given a chance'[81].

The police removed Lallie irrespective of her state of health. There is no record of Lallie's state of mind or physical needs during this ordeal, nor of her expression of the loss of her son and being separated from his burial place. Police Constable Capstick arrived in Morgans to collect Lallie and escort her to Kalgoorlie where policewoman Constable Fogarty took over custody. At 5 p.m. on 18 October, the two women left the Kalgoorlie railway station for Midland Junction, a major rail intersection to the east of Perth, where Lallie was kept in a police cell overnight[82].

The next day Constable Fogarty handed Lallie and the warrant to another officer who would escort Lallie from Midland Junction to Mogumber, the final route stop of her imposed and sad journey. A telegram, sent ahead to the current Superintendent of Moore River Native Settlement Mr Gaffy[83], advised him that a police escort was bringing Lallie Matbar to his institution and that he was to meet her personally. He was to arrange that she be 'isolated and cleansed' before she was allowed to mix with others[84].

The file does not contain a description of the 14 kilometres that Lallie had to travel from the Mogumber siding to the native settlement constructed on the banks of the Moore River. There are no details of the greeting by Superintendent Gaffy of the Linden girl and the process of cleansing her. What was documented was that during the cleansing a nurse noticed that Lallie's leg was afflicted with a wound that had become poisonous. When the police had finally placed Lallie in custody for removal from the district, they were concerned with noting the state of her health, so there was not any mention of the wound in the telegram received by Superintendent Gaffy. There is no record in Lallie's file of any questioning of Lallie about the occurrence of the wound, so it is not known whether she had been uncooperative and not said how it came to be, or if she was asked. The matron did not provide an explanation for what had caused its mysterious appearance. As the Chief Protector seemed to have a particular interest in this ward's case, the Superintendent thought it most prudent to notify him of the wound. As it was in the interest of the Chief Protector to keep all his wards in good health Neville authorised the staff at Moore River to send for the local doctor from Moora to come to the native settlement and treat Lallie's leg. The wound healed within a few days[85].

A copy of the doctor's report was not included in Lallie's DCS file so it is not possible to identify the cause of the wound. It is tempting to wonder if the emufoot man had in some mysterious way caught up with Lallie and given her the spearing some of her people considered she deserved.

In October 1926 Mr Neville changed Lallie's life. She was now to be an 'inmate', as residents of Moore River Native Settlement were labelled by the Aborigines Department, of an Aboriginal institution. A supplementary part of her DCS File was commenced on this part of her life and it states that her age at the time of her intake was eighteen[86].

Meanwhile, in the goldfields Lallie's family, people and Akbar had learned of her swift removal from the mission and the district. They had tried very hard over a few years to prevent the police from finding and taking her. They were not prepared to give up yet. There was one solution left to them. A conspiracy was born as a last effort to have Lallie released from Moore River and returned to her people. It was never confirmed who exactly was responsible for planning, designing and coordinating the conspiracy, and the known details are in fragments. The surviving records of dialogue and correspondence produced around the conspiracy implicate the Schenks, Lallie's mother, brother and the Linden people. The impact of what the sympathisers attempted, and the involvement of the Police and Aborigines Departments, evoked a set of correspondence of its own, though whatever investigation occurred did not find any infallible answers.

A few days after Lallie's removal from Mount Margaret mission Perks received an irregular request from the missionary. Mr Schenk enquired if the Constable could write to Mr Neville requesting a pass for Snowy Bradley to visit and stay a while at Moore River Native Settlement. Rod Schenk added that as Snowy was Lallie's brother she would not be so lonely if he went over there to be with her a while, and Snowy would be a very proper resident at Moore River[87].

Perks suspected that the request for permission for Snowy to visit his sister at Mogumber may have arisen out of duplicity. Rather than follow up the request, the policeman decided to collate some details he had collected already with some additional enquiries.

When Perks had gone to Mount Margaret to interview Lallie he had raised with her the subject of the likelihood of her marrying again with one of the tribal men. On these lines it appears that Lallie agreed to cooperate with Perks. It was either when she was at the police station that she dictated a letter typed by Perks, or on the mission that she provided the words that he typed on his return to his office. The brief letter was addressed to the Chief Protector and stated that 'Aboriginal native Locky had given me permission to marry my cousin, Snowy Bradley, a half caste aged 22 years. "Chilgoo" alias "Polly" has given me her word that I can marry my cousin'. Lallie signed the letter with an 'X' as her signature[88]. The wording of this letter implies that the words were chosen from a combination of what facts Perks had and what information Lallie was attempting to convey to him. These would not have been Lallie's exact words.

To clarify the appropriateness of Lallie being permitted to marry her 'cousin' Snowy Bradley, Perks raised the matter with his superior in Kalgoorlie Inspector Spedding Smith who in turn instructed Perks to interview Burtville Jack. The latter told Perks that he had returned Lallie to her people, and that he was not opposed to her marrying some other 'blackfellow' living at the Mount Margaret mission station. He was even satisfied that she could marry Snowy her cousin if she wished[89].

The main aim of the conspiracy was to convince the police that there was waiting for Lallie a tribal husband who would marry her if she was released from Moore River Native Settlement and be allowed to return home. As a married woman the Aborigines Department would consider that she was provided and cared for, so she could remain with her people. Lallie remained interned instead.

Shortly after Lallie's arrival at Moore River Native Settlement Mr Neville was scheduled to visit there for an inspection and other business. His itinerary was revised to include an interview with Lallie Matbar, the Linden girl. He may have thought that once he had personally seen and questioned her it might be easier for him to assess what should be done in the future about her welfare. His own impression of her character and manner could indicate to him what would be the appropriate length of internment in the institution to wean her from her less than moral standards, and her Aboriginal bush ways.

Within two weeks after Lallie's arrival, in early November 1926, Neville arrived at Moore River Native Settlement. Superintendent Gaffy arranged a venue for Neville's interview with the goldfields girl about whom he had received so much correspondence from Perks, Spedding Smith, Cook and Schenk.

While having the opportunity to question the girl himself Neville wanted to clarify conclusively the possibility of her marrying a tribal man. Such a possibility could influence the length of Lallie's internment. The Chief Protector learned that Burtville Jack wanted nothing more to do with Tjirrgulu's daughter. The only yardstick left to the Chief Protector by which to determine the period of internment was the quality of her character.

The qualities that the Schenks saw and valued in Lallie were not so readily apparent to the Chief Protector. After the first interview with her he took into consideration the evidence about her contained in her file in Perth. When he returned to his office in Murray Street, Perth, he made a report of his assessment of Lallie Matbar. He recorded that she was 'pleasant looking and well spoken, but absolutely immoral and the victim of lustful men'[90].

Lallie's DCS file reveals that in the next few weeks Neville received police reports from the goldfields that continued to attempt to slur Lallie's character. This did not make it any easier for Neville to decide on how long Lallie should be kept as a resident at Moore River. His curiosity about this girl's case was maintained and fed.

To assist him to come to some firm decision about the girl's future the Chief Protector arranged to have a second interview with her. In his subsequent report he commented that Lallie was 'getting along quite well at present'[91]. His perception of Lallie's progress was that institutional life seemed to be developing a strong moral fibre in this girl and to be educating out of her the more undesirable qualities. Another Aboriginal youth was soon to be suited to settling into Anglo-Saxon society. This was all the more reason to keep Lallie here for as long as it suited the Minister.

About this time more public criticism appeared about the way A.O. Neville handled Aboriginal affairs. This criticism came not from his more regular critics, the press or the politicians, but from some Aboriginal people themselves. William Harris was a 'half-caste' farmer from the Morawa district. He was the son of an Aboriginal mother and a European shepherd who had paid to have his boy educated at the Swan Native and Half Caste Home. William and other educated 'half-castes' felt a great loss of rights when the 1905 Aborigines Act included 'half-castes' in the term 'native', and were concerned about the treatment of Aboriginal people in Moore River Native Settlement. He and eleven other men decided to form a Native Union, the first Aboriginal voluntary organisation in the South-West, in order to fight for their rights as British subjects and actively protest against government policies. William Harris wanted 'one law for us all' and the right to vote to be given to the Aboriginal people [92]. The Union functioned only for a short time. William Harris's concern about the government's treatment of Aboriginal people manifested itself in November 1926 when he wrote to the editor of the *Sunday Times*. In his article he stated that the southern Aborigines were tired of being robbed, shot down or run into miserable compounds.

A.O. Neville must have thought that the less the wider community were aware of Aboriginal cases that were deserving of some irregular humanitarian consideration the less material they would have with which to criticise him. He would certainly not want the matter of an Afghan genuinely seeking permission to marry an Aborigine to become public. He was confident that he had grounds to warrant Lallie's arrest and internment. However, the man who wished to provide for her was financially established and had the respect and sympathy of many, in spite of the attempt by the police to slur his character and reputation. There might be some people in the community, such as religious groups, philanthropists and liberationists, who might think this was certainly one case in which it would be reasonable for Neville to make an exception. However, the Chief Protector wanted all Sections of the 1905 Aborigines Act followed to the precise word. He also wanted as much control as possible over 'half-caste' people so as to maintain the pace of assimilation. He would not concern himself with critics.

In spite of Neville's efforts to keep Lallie and Jack apart, and their case out of the limelight, Akbar did not cease in his cause, and there came a time when a newspaper published the Akbar-Matbar story.

CHAPTER FIVE

Internment

From November 1926 to October 1927, Lallie Matbar resided in an alien place, the Moore River Native Settlement[1]. The settlement included accommodation for the Superintendent and staff, dormitories for the young inmates, a chapel, a hospital and a compound. Three hundred metres from the compound was a camp occupied by 'indigent natives' and their families[2]. The staff at the settlement were trained in professions such as nursing and missionary work.

The people around Lallie were from a range of tribal groups and were thus most likely intimidating to her. By 1926 the calibre of the 'inmates' was not that of what was originally intended when the settlement opened in 1918. According to the historian Anna Haebich, the inmates had become 'a mixture of terrible characters'. Inmates came from all parts of the state, either sent there under special ministerial warrant, that A.O. Neville had passed successfully through the legislative assembly, or as minors under the legal guardianship of the Chief Protector of Aborigines[3]. Moore River Native Settlement had become a dumping ground for all kinds of odd or difficult cases - discharged prisoners, pregnant single girls, old derelicts, troublesome youths, orphans, waifs and strays[4]. The residents of Carrolup settlement who were accommodated there in 1922 added to the overcrowding.

The location of the eight-year-old 'native settlement' was remote in a number of ways. It was a great distance from the various tribal homelands of the Aborigines interned there. Because they would be unfamiliar with the local landscape and they had no family nearby it was anticipated that there would be almost no 'absconding', as well as few visits by relatives and friends. It was sufficiently isolated from Perth so as to avoid the eyes and ears of any philanthropic or critical members of the public who might find some cause to raise questions or debate about the purpose, conditions, standards and practices of the institution.

One can try and imagine what impressions this settlement had on Lallie who came to it from an open bush life growing up in an Aboriginal culture and society. Life at the Moore River settlement was regimented, disciplined and unfriendly[5]. The staff never used Aboriginal vocabulary and prohibited the young residents from speaking the indigenous language with which they had grown up. The children were addressed by the names given to them by police, missionaries or the Moore River staff.

When Lallie arrived, the institution had been deteriorating for some time. There was less time allowed for the children and the younger adolescents to play. It was advocated that time for play left children in a state of idleness and unproductivity. It was better for them that they be allotted chores around the settlement. By 1924 the Superintendent had arranged that when the children were not participating in vocational training they were being occupied with work. During the six years between 1921 and 1926 when Fred Aldrich administered the division of the Aborigines Department south of the 25th parallel, standards at the Moore River Native Settlement deteriorated[6]. With a background in marine and freshwater biology and other aspects of the fishing industry, Fred Aldrich had become Chief Inspector of Fisheries in 1911. When the Aborigines Department was divided in 1920, Fred Aldrich, being in charge of the southern division, became Deputy Chief Protector of Aborigines. He had minimal knowledge of Aboriginal affairs. As the Aborigines were for Aldrich of secondary importance to his other areas of responsibility, he left much of his work regarding Aboriginal people to the Secretary of the Aborigines Department, Ernest E. Copping. This person made tours of inspection to the Aboriginal settlements and towns in the southern division and dealt with Aboriginal people seeking assistance from the Aborigines Department. Between 1920 and 1926 there was not much consultation between Neville and Aldrich. When they did communicate their views generally clashed and Aldrich showed no inclination to yield to Neville's comparatively greater experience. Of the State's annual grant for Aboriginal affairs Aldrich's southern division received one sixth, while five sixths went to Neville's northern division[7]. Aldrich's administration had clearly suffered in the merging of the departments, and with a reduced budget his instructions to the native settlements were to cut back strictly in all areas. Consequently, conditions generally at Moore River Native Settlement suffered[8].

The skills taught to the inmates reflected the contemporary assumption that indigenous people were of limited intelligence. The girls were taught sewing, culinary skills, table setting, cleaning tables, basic cooking and the correct disposal of waste. Some of these skills Lallie may have been introduced to when she lived in the Schenks' quarters at Mount Margaret mission. They were shown how to make a bed properly, to sweep a room and to do laundry. All children had nose cleaning drill. When an assembly of the inmates was ordered, they would form ranks in order of darkest skin to fairest skin, or of 'full - bloods', 'half-castes' and 'quarter-castes' (or 'quadroons')[9].

The diet of the inmates was reduced to a minimum. Food was very basic. Funds for these items were very limited. The vegetable crop program that the institution had originally planned, which was intended to make the institution self-sufficient to some degree in its food intake, and thus contribute to 'paying its own way', had failed. The soil proved to be too poor and the rainfall was too unreliable. What the children were given actually to eat and drink were not the items that were shown on the menus perused by the Chief Protector, or his representative such as the Deputy Chief Protector, when he came to the settlement to conduct inspections. Breakfast was often dry porridge. Lunch was soup made out of bone, sheep heads and other offal, with vegetables included occasionally. Dinner was often a slice of bread with jam and a cup of tea[10]. With financial cutbacks during the Aldrich administration cutlery was dispensed with.

The inmates' experience of a poor diet was preserved in a song that many of the inmates learned and that was sung in later generations. They had taken the melody of a very popular Christian hymn and changed the words;

There is a happy land far, far away,
Where we get bread and scraps three times a day.
Bread and butter we never see
No sugar in our tea
While we are gradually starving away.[11]

Lallie learned these words during her period of 'internment'. Many years after her time at Moore River she was heard by her own children around their home to sing the same tune and words[12].

Unhappiness and the desperate anxiety to locate and rejoin family members led to a sharp increase in absconders. By the time Lallie arrived at Moore River, abscondment by adolescent girls particularly was frequent and repetitive, despite the fact that escapees were almost always tracked down by the settlement's skilled Aboriginal trackers and brought back[13]. Recaptured absconders were punished in a variety of ways. Sometimes the girls' hair was shaved off, or they were 'dressed' in old sacks[14], or they were belted in front of everyone with a cat o'nine tails[15]. They could be given a beating before being sentenced from seven to fourteen days in solitary confinement in the 'Boob'. This was a small, square wooden room founded on posts driven into the ground, a floor of white sand[16], roofed in corrugated iron, fenced with barbed wire, scarcely allowing a gleam of light, with little ventilation, and located out in the open in the middle of the compound. Its exposure made it susceptible to the extremities of seasonal temperatures, and provided a constant visual reminder to the children of what terrible punishment would befall them if they offended Section 9 of the 1905 Aborigines Act. That section forbad any inmate under sixteen years of age from leaving a station or reserve without permission of the Superintendent or Manager[17]. The food which the native trackers brought to offenders confined in the Boob was usually dried bread and water. The Boob was present in Lallie's time at Moore River, and there is no documentation surviving that states she was ever confined in it.

Nor is there evidence that Lallie received any painful treatment. Recaptured escapees were disciplined, often drastically, by the Aboriginal trackers who acted as 'policemen' for the Settlement. Over time the Boob proved to have limited effectiveness in deterring some of the older children from repeating absconding. So habitual absconders were occasionally sentenced to imprisonment in Fremantle Gaol[18]. When Commissioner Moseley reviewed in 1935 the effects and conditions of the Boob as part of his enquiry into Aboriginal conditions, he stated that 'it is a barbarous treatment, and the place should be pulled down'[19].

No documentation preserving Lallie's personal experiences or thoughts at Moore River Native Settlement have surfaced. Details in Lallie's DCS file record that after being at the settlement for about four and a half months, the Linden girl developed a close affinity with one particular female inmate who had three children. When Lallie heard the mother speaking she recognised her dialect. The mother spoke the language of the Darlot people, a tribe that neighboured the Linden mob. The new inmate, whose indigenous name was 'Nimmer', was addressed in the institution as 'Laura'. She was quite fair skinned, petite in build and also quite pretty in appearance[20].

A group of children play beside the chapel at Moore River Native Settlement. The building erected for the punishment of children, 'the Boob', is the white building, front right of chapel. Photo 368/5 Battye Library, Perth.

Laura was born in the Edjudina district of the Laverton area in 1898. Her parents were a 'full-blood' mother named 'Biddy Binyoon', and a Caucasian father known as 'Teddy Bird'. When Biddy's daughter Laura became pregnant Teddy was not willing to take care of her. It was left for Laura to put the care of herself and her baby, and most likely her mother into that of her mother's people.

A man named Jack Quince, a part-Aboriginal man, was not Laura's promised tribal husband, but he was prepared to be a provider to Laura and her infant. He earned a regular income from sandalwood pulling and prospecting and was prepared to spend it on his family, on Laura's mother Biddy and any children he and Laura may have had.

Laura and Jack had three children altogether to raise. Their eldest was Jack. Three years later a girl called Toodie was born. Their third child Dede, who was born in March 1926, was a significantly fair part-Aboriginal child. It was the youngest baby in particular who would draw the attention of the police. Laura, Jack, their children and Biddy lived out in the bush, close to their people, and so continued to adhere to many traditional practices. It was arranged that their older girl Toodie would be given as a wife to a man named 'Jinner Jindoo', alias 'Jacky'[21].

While Laura and her children lived with a provider they satisfied the requirements of the 1905 Aborigines Act and were left alone by the local protectors. This all changed when Jack Quince became ill very suddenly. During one of his trips to Kanowna in his cart and horse to get food and other stores for his family, he had a sudden attack. When help came Jack was transferred to a motor truck and driven to the Government Hospital in Kalgoorlie. The stores were taken to Laura who was told the news and the doctor's report. The doctor who attended Jack said he had experienced a stroke. The patient would live, but the consequence of the stroke was a severe degree of paralysis. Jack Quince had become an incapacitated invalid and would need to be cared for permanently in a convalescents' hospital.

The police in Kalgoorlie considered then that Laura and the three quadroons' were without a provider and proceeded to investigate her situation. In May 1926, Sergeant McGuiniss of the Kalgoorlie police station instructed Police Constable Goldie to go out to the Mulgabbie area to ascertain the circumstances surrounding Laura Quince and her children.

Constable Goldie found Laura Quince, 'an unmarried half-caste', camped in a 'mia mia' with her three children and her mother. There was no reliable source of income and one of the three children was particularly fair. Before leaving Laura's abode Constable Goldie warned her that because her youngest baby was so fair she could expect her to be taken from her.

On his return to Kalgoorlie Goldie made out his report. He recommended that the two older children he removed from their bush home and placed in an institution. The fairer baby Dede was still young enough to need her mother's care and should not be removed from her mother quite yet. Goldie's report on Laura and her children was sent to the office in Perth, but no action regarding that family was taken[22].

As the months passed Laura's situation deteriorated into desperation. Nine months after Goldie's visit, in February 1927, Mr E.C. Mitchell, who in 1924 had become an Inspector in the Aborigines Department, went out to Mulgabbie to examine the standard of living of Laura's family. The office of Inspectors for the Aborigines Department was comparatively new, and due to its small budget there were very few. In his first Annual Report of 1916 as Chief Protector of Aborigines one of the changes to the provisions of the 1905 Aborigines Act that Neville pushed for was the establishment of the office of travelling Inspectors. The provision was granted in 1924 and E.C. Mitchell was the first Inspector. He travelled in the north during Neville's time as administrator of territory north of the 25th parallel. Before this appointment E.C. Mitchell had been manager at Carrolup Native Settlement, and in 1921 was appointed Superintendent at Moore River Native Settlement. Few of the staff of the Aborigines Department had any special experience or training in working with Aborigines. Mitchell was the exception. He had a wide knowledge of Aboriginal traditions and could speak to some of the Aborigines in their own language[23]. He was the sole travelling Inspector of the north until his retrenchment in 1933.

When Inspector Mitchell met Laura and her children his attention was attracted particularly to the youngest child with the notably fair skin. In his evaluation of their circumstances - the absence of a provider, the children being 'quadroon' and therefore dominantly of Anglo-Saxon genetic traits, and the youngest being so particularly fair - the future of this family was very clear.

Before departing from Laura's camp Inspector Mitchell made a suggestion to Laura that would be beneficial for those to be served with it and acceptable for the official who was to serve it. He advised her that as the standards of her bush camp were not adequate it would be a matter of time before the police at the Kalgoorlie District Office would be ordered to ride out to her camp to seize her children and remove them to another place for their own good. He suggested to her if she wanted to be near her children an alternative was to take them to Mt Margaret mission near Morgans. There she would have to give her children up to the missionary, but she could still see them, be near them and on the odd occasion have them home with her[24].

On learning more from Mr Mitchell's report about the case of Laura Quince and her three children near Mulgabbie the Chief Protector of Aborigines was struck by both the family's very basic living conditions and the reference to the baby Dede's fairness. For him there was no doubt about what was the best solution for these children. The potential of the 'Anglo-Saxon' elements of the three quadroons needed nurturing, civilising, educating and Christianising. However, the Chief Protector did not value Mitchell's recommendation that the family go to the Schenks. Laura's children were three quarters 'white' and there were many Aborigines at Mount Margaret mission. In responding to the Laura Quince case Neville recommended to Police Inspector Spedding

Smith in Kalgoorlie that as Laura's children were so 'white' they should be taken into custody and transferred to Moore River rather than being placed in a mission where they would be brought up with 'natives'. It was a policy of his Department that children who were 'three quarters white should be brought up as white'. He advised the Inspector to arrange a warrant for their arrest and transfer to Moore River[25]. To activate the arrest of Laura and her three children Neville sent a despatch to the office of the Under Secretary of the Colonial Secretary's Department[26].

By 10 March Inspector Spedding Smith had the authority to order the removal of 'Nimmer alias Laura Quince and the three children, Jacky, Toodie and Dede, from Mulgabbie'[27]. On 25 March 1927 the Superintendent at Moore River Native Settlement was advised by Mr Neville of the pending arrival of Laura and her children[28].

Laura arrived at Moore River a month after Lallie. Like Lallie, Laura and her family had been taken from their home with little warning and forcibly removed to a distant, alien and unfriendly place. Neither of these women were subversive or insurgent by nature. As they passed their time of internment together the notion of getting back home to the goldfields crept into their thoughts and desires, and perhaps into the content of their conversations. Nested in the back of Laura's mind, most probably, was the advice from Inspector Mitchell regarding the reason to get her children to Mount Margaret mission. Lallie would have told her how the Schenks respected and encouraged Aboriginal parental love. During their internment they would have heard a number of stories of other girls who before them had felt so desperate and homesick, so intimidated and afraid of conditions in the settlement that they had attempted to abscond.

Conditions at Moore River Native Settlement were intolerant, particularly for girls. The Wongai women in the goldfields who gave oral histories in the 1980s were relatives of some of the girls who escaped successfully and made it back to their people in the 1920s. They suggested that the girls who were the lucky ones at Moore River were the ones who ran away. The female escapees related their experiences and observations of the institution to the older Wongai women back home. Some of these tales were recorded many years later when Lallie's own two adult daughters visited the goldfields to meet some of the Wongai women who themselves were teenagers or young mothers in the 1920s to learn what they could about their mother's life. The phrases these women had inherited from the escapees to sum up their experiences in that dreaded southern place may seem vague, as the teenage escapees would not have been literate enough to know the terminology of authorities at the settlement. The phrases they repeated included 'a rotten place, a terrible place'. The young escapees claimed that 'the man who was looking after the place' [most likely the Superintendent] used to [sexually] interfere with all the girls there. They alleged that some of the girls became pregnant by 'the man who was in charge there', and that man never acknowledged any of the babies who were his. When he realised that an Aboriginal girl was pregnant as a result of his impregnation of her he would marry her off to one of the Aboriginal youths so that people would not be able to accuse him of being the father[29].

The girls who returned home to the goldfields from Moore River told of another circumstance in which girls were interfered with by the man in charge. There was a means by which the Superintendent could learn of the girls who had boyfriends at the settlement. For instance, when a couple came to considering marriage they had to get permission, and in writing, from Chief Protector Neville. So they would have to go to the man in charge of the settlement to state their wishes to him to get that permission. That man would interfere with the girls before they 'ever went to their bloke'. One can understand why the girls often wanted to run away from Moore River Native Settlement[30]. The fact of many of the absconders being recaptured and punished did not outweigh the desire of Lallie and Laura to one day themselves make a run from this place.

Laura would have been concerned with the welfare and future of her two daughters particularly. The friendship of the two women gave them the courage and determination to try.

It was about five months after Lallie's arrival and about two after Laura's arrival, in late May 1927, that the two goldfields women attempted their first abscondment with three children from the settlement. They planned to depart under the cover of darkness with two other Wongai girls, ten-year-old Ada Taylor and Enid[31]. Ada, who had a Caucasian father, was born in Ida H., a settlement beyond Laverton. Her Aboriginal mother's people had found it difficult to hide her because of her straight blond hair. They had many near misses with the police. The police in Laverton caught Ada at the same time as Enid, another 'half-caste' girl, was caught. Enid was motherless because her young mother had died by wounds inflicted on her by her tribal husband Bungara who did not accept her cohabiting with a white man[32]. After two days in the lock-up in Laverton the two girls were transported to Moore River Native Settlement.

Before the four Wongai women could be truly free of this settlement they had one particular fear to surmount, the crossing of the Moore River. Deep, permanently flowing rivers were not a common part of the natural features of the red mulga country of the tribal lands of the Wongai. Inmates of other tribal origins at Moore River who fished quite fearlessly alongside the river would tell the superstitious Wongai that there were bad fish in that river that would try and eat them if they swam in it. They convinced the Wongai that there were evil spirits in those waters[33].

The possibility of evil spirits in the river, the darkness, the fear of discovery by the Aboriginal trackers who worked for the institution and consequent punishment, took their first two victims. Losing all confidence, Ada and Enid could stand the tension no longer and retreated to their dormitory beds. Lallie and Laura continued to try to work out a way to cross the river[34].

Once they had crossed the river the two women hustled the children straight into the cover of the grass and shrubs so that the moonlight would not reflect off their fair skin and expose their presence to any mounted trackers on guard duty. With Laura holding the baby in her arms and Lallie taking the two other children firmly by their hands, the two women moved swiftly and as silently as possible away from the institution. They attempted to put as much distance as possible between themselves and Moore River before morning. They dared not stop. Once the alerted trackers were on their mounts they would travel the same country at three or four times the pace at which this party of fugitives was moving. The two young women used their knowledge of the stars to guide them in the direction they believed was towards their tribal lands[35].

They would keep away from the roads. The Native Settlement would alert the Aborigines Department which would in turn alert the police stations out in the districts of their escape route. They wanted to ellude the Aboriginal trackers, the constabulary and any police informers who would be watching out for them. If they could get to the Coolgardie district they planned to hop on a train and eventually travel the Kalgoorlie-Laverton branch line.

Lallie, Laura and the three children did not make it over the Wongan Hills. Their progress had been slowed considerably by the advent of daylight which required them to cling to shrubbery, to dodge and weave and lie low so as not to be spotted. They were unsure of where there were houses or roads to avoid. It would have been increasingly difficult to keep the children quiet, as they would have been extremely hungry and tired. The thought of getting some food for them would have distracted the women from their target of gaining distance.

By late morning of 2 June 1927, the Aboriginal trackers from Moore River caught up with the party of absconders and escorted them back to the Native Settlement[36].

The Superintendent of Moore River Native Settlement Arthur J. Neal sent a wire to the Chief Protector to notify him of the recapture of Lallie, Laura and the three children. Mr Neal had been a farmer and his wife was a trained nurse who had worked at the Carrolup Native Settlement. At the Mogumber settlement his wife became the matron of the hospital.

Neville was very annoyed with the insolent action of these two women whose warrant for their internment he himself had organised. He may have felt also that he had been tricked by the Linden girl. Lallie had given Neville and the staff the impression that she was settling well into institutional life and would be a model subject of assimilation. Between November 1926, when he first interviewed her, and May 1927, he had not been given reason to reconsider her case.

The event of Lallie's daring attempt at abscondment implanted doubts in Neville's mind about Lallie's character. He may have begun to suspect that he had been duped. Perhaps she had hidden cleverly the more 'undesirable' elements of her character from him during the interviews. She may have been more cunning, rebellious, uncooperative and stubborn than he suspected. Perhaps this institution was too lenient with her. The friendship she had developed with the Mulgabbie woman needed investigation. It needed to be ascertained which of the two women had been the conspirator and ringleader, who was responsible for inciting the other, and who was the lackey. Once it was established who was the real culprit of the crime, Mr Neville could decide then what would be the appropriate length of internment for each of them.

In response to Superintendent Neal's wire, and as an outcome of the doubts he had now acquired about Lallie's character, the Chief Protector decided to go to the Moore River Native Settlement and to talk with Lallie himself. On 10 June Lallie was interviewed for the third time by the Chief Protector[37].

The file on Lallie Matbar states that her attempt at abscondment in late May from Moore River Native Settlement was her second one. It does not contain any details regarding her first attempt. Whatever her motivation she had become daring. According to his comments recorded after his interview with Lallie, the Chief Protector had hoped to find that

Lallie was a naive and misguided character who had been manipulated by a more clever, older female. It was apparent to Neville that Laura who had three children would need assistance if she was to consider an act of abscondment, and perhaps she had sensed both the naivety in Lallie and that there was enough guile in the Linden girl for Laura to be able to persuade her to join her in making a break for it. Neville could not comprehend that the behaviour exhibited by Lallie occurred not as a reflection of her character, but more likely because of her personal experiences of suppression, harassment, loss of freedom and deprivation. The accumulation in her life of extraordinary experiences was evoking extraordinary reactions in her.

Whatever he learned about the character of these two women, their repeated offending suggested to Neville that he had to give some serious thought as to what would be the most appropriate degree of discipline and punishment for them. The two women had twice flouted Section 9 of the Aborigines Act which stated that it was against the law for an Aborigine to leave a native station or reserve without the permission of the Minister for the Aborigines Act, or his second in charge, the Chief Protector. He would discuss with Superintendent Neal how drastic they should make the degree of punishment for offenders who repeatedly attempted escape, such as these two women.

The Superintendent agreed with the Chief Protector that confining repeat absconders, such as these two women, to the Boob did not seem to be an effective deterrent, and that another method of discipline was needed. The Superintendent suggested that another punishment might be to cut off the hair of these older girls. The Chief Protector was not convinced that this measure was suitable. He responded to the suggestion that the idea of cutting off the girls' hair as a punishment was repugnant to him, and he would not agree to it.

The Chief Protector preferred the strategy of removing the girls much further afield. He had in mind a place at Port Hedland (most likely Violet Valley which was in the Kimberleys) which was a remote coastal settlement reached by travelling several days by steamer from Perth. Not only was the landscape arid and hostile to humans but it was thousands of kilometres overland. Should he and the Superintendent agree to employing this method of punishment Neville would be able to get the women on the ship called the 'Koolinda' which was leaving for that place within the next two weeks. The 'Koolinda' travelled regularly from Fremantle northward along the coast to the Kimberleys and was used occasionally by Neville to visit Aboriginal settlements in the far north[38].

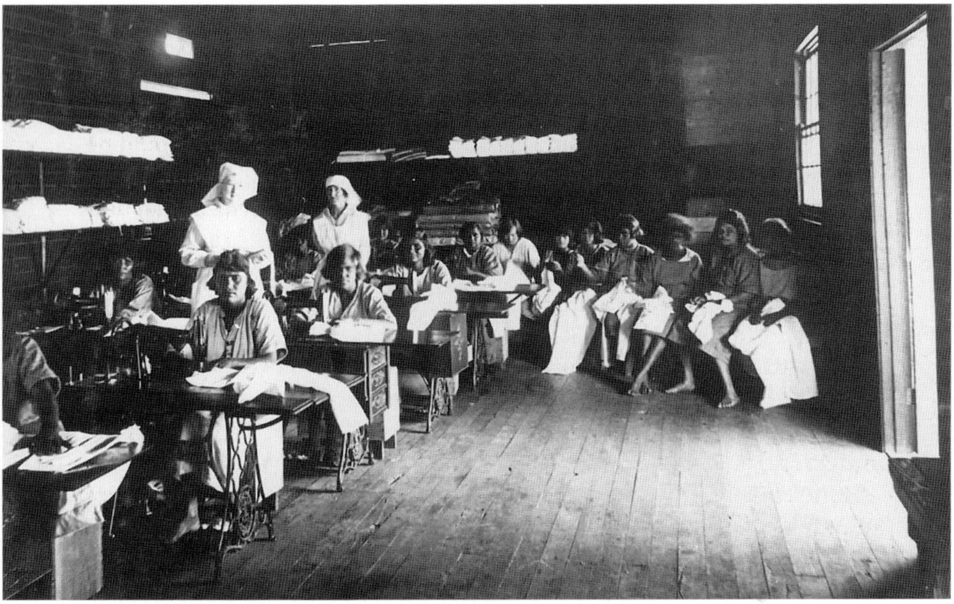

Lallie would have been old enough to have attended practical skills training in the sewing room at Moore River Native Settlement. Photo 368/5 Battye Library, Perth.

There were other extremely removed institutions Neville pointed out to the Superintendent where they could send the older girl. Even further than Port Hedland was the far north Forrest River Mission Station. It was the distance from Perth to Port Hedland once again, and would take more than a week of travelling along the coast by steamer to get to it. The nearest port was Wyndham and the mission was many miles from there in quite an isolated position. The police considered the Aborigines up that way to be still very wild and maintained a control on them by carrying out punitive expeditions occasionally. The staff at that mission may not be so tolerant with their charges. The strategy behind this proposal was that the girls would be so far from their own people, feel so alienated and intimidated that they would be very disinclined to dwell on any thought of escape and would be willing to revert to being submissive and cooperative.

The Chief Protector and the Superintendent did not decide on an alien destination for the girls. On this occasion the Chief Protector was agreeable that the Superintendent should warn the older girls who repeatedly ran away that they would not be given another chance. The next time they ran away they would undoubtedly be sent to Fremantle Goal, a prison located at the port of Perth in which most inmates were hardened male criminals. It was surrounded by a high, very thick stone wall topped with broken glass, to discourage inmates from contemplating mounting. The reason for A.O. Neville not making the decision at this time to send his two wards to a maximum security penitentiary may have been to avoid attracting criticism. Some members of the public might consider this reaction to the girls' offence as being disproportionate. The Chief Protector may have hoped that by threatening Lallie and Laura with imprisonment in Fremantle Gaol he would intimidate them sufficiently so that they would not attempt again to abscond[39]. After Neville returned to his office in Perth, Superintendent Neal imparted the warning.

The warning did not have the impact on the girls from the eastern goldfields as the Chief Protector had hoped. Laura's determination to keep her children and to attempt to get them to Mount Margaret mission predisposed her to eventually defy once again this system of authority that used its power to break up families and intern children. Lallie and Laura lived daily with the threat that it was only a matter of time before the order would come for their removal to a penal institution, an action that would separate Laura's children from her.

About five months after their second abscondment, the two goldfields women with the three children executed their third. On the night of 29 October 1927, Lallie and her desperate party crossed the Moore River again and headed eastward through the scrub. Within twenty-four hours Superintendent Neal had sent a wire to alert the Chief Protector of the latest action by the two eastern goldfields women. Neal suspected that the fleeing party would take the same route as they had before, so he sent another wire to the Goomalling Police[40].

Once notified of the abscondment the Chief Protector wanted each police station between Mogumber and Coolgardie to be alerted to their escape. He sent two wires to the police east of Moore River. One wire was sent to Inspector Spedding Smith in Kalgoorlie who could coordinate the search from there, and another was sent to the Police Inspector at Northam[41].

Though a number of police were alerted, and they in turn could notify local farmers and pastoralists to keep an eye open for a fleeing party of two women and three children, the absconders covered significant distance. In seeking out sustenance the absconders acquired what they could. What was available to them depended on what time of the year it was and in what landscape they were. The escapees could consume lizards, goannas, eggs, emu, mallee hen, silky pear, bush honey and honey ants, and feral life such as wild cats and rabbits. If they had a spear to break up the hard soil they could dig up the bulbs of roots of the young currajong tree. These bulbs would give water and food. Sympathetic farmers could give them eggs or dry bread. Lallie and Laura found some allies in farmers' homes[42]. One farmer's wife who felt some sympathy for them gave them some pullet eggs and a drink of water. Another place gave them some bread. This time, the fleeing group survived several days out in the scrub, crossed the Wongan Hills and passed the settlement of Wannamal[43].

In Perth, Neville was very anxious to receive any news of a sighting of the absconders. He had been aggravated extremely by their sustained insubordination and defiance. In spite of his threat to punish the women more severely, they had not feared him and had dared to escape again.

In spite of the presence of several police out in the field making enquiries about the absconders and various district inspectors passing on to the Commissioner what information their constabulary collected, the police network was ineffective. The reports from the police either referred to possible sightings of the girls or were not useful at all. Two weeks after they escaped, on 24 November 1927, Inspector Mitchell informed Neville that he received word that two 'half-caste' girls were travelling on foot between Dowerin and Mininvale, two settlements east of the Wongan Hills, and they had asked for a drink of water at a farm house. They were some kilometres north off the Dowerin-Merredin rail line and were walking parallel with that line in an easterly direction. They appeared to be making for Merredin[44].

The police were still watching out for Lallie and Laura four weeks later. On 27 December, Police Constable Geoff Woods in Dowerin reported to Inspector Johnston that after making enquiries regarding the two absconders he could not get any trace of them and that it seemed there were no Aboriginal people or 'half castes' in his sub-district[45]. On 10 January 1928, Police Constable C.L. Polak at Wyalkatchem reported to Inspector Johnston that his enquiries on the same persons were fruitless, as no one had sighted the absconders in his sub-district[46].

There seemed to be a time lapse between when Lallie and her party were actually in an area and when a report of someone sighting them in that area arrived at Neville's desk. This made it difficult to alert police promptly to the likely presence of the girls in their area. So the approach of the fleeing women to their tribal lands was not impeded. By mid - January 1928, about three months after their escape, Neville had a sense of their proximity to their homes. On 12 January he sent two wires. He informed Inspector Spedding Smith at Kalgoorlie that Lallie Matbar and her party may have left Kalgoorlie for the Morgans district about a fortnight earlier[47]. The second wire was sent to Rod Schenk to alert him to the possibility that Lallie Matbar and party would be making towards his mission[48].

Mr Schenk was able to promptly confirm the Chief Protector's suspicion. Having received word himself just recently through the local Wongai about Lallie's return to her people, on the same day as receiving the telegram from Mr Neville he was able to reciprocate with positive news. In a letter dated 12 January Rod Schenk informed the Chief Protector that Lallie had arrived in Morgans by the last train and after a few days in the vicinity went to Linden. Rod and Mysie had not themselves seen Lallie, but they had heard that there was another woman and three children with her. The missionary completed his telegram with the request for either the Chief Protector himself or Inspector Mitchell to come out to the Morgans-Linden area to make further enquiries as to what the situation might be[49].

This time Lallie and Laura were successful with their attempt to abscond and with their bid to regain their freedom. The police had not been able to catch them. Now they were in the Linden area, back in Lallie's home and with her family and people. It is very likely that Lallie had lived at Moore River in fear, both for her personal safety and her future, and in sadness thinking that she might never see her mother, brother and people again, and that they themselves might give up eventually on seeing her again, or might even forget her. Her attempt at being daring had brought her home again.

The two fugitive Wongai women had endured much in the three months they had been on the run from the constabulary. Though Lallie and Laura with her three children were back in their country their lives as liberated people were compromised and there was more to endure. The happiness would become dissipated. They could not go with Laura's children immediately onto the mission, as Lallie's people would not allow it. The memory of how Lallie was originally taken into custody by a policeman riding into the mission was fresh in their minds. They had learned that the missionary would be required by the police to report to them as soon as he had sighted the girls and children. They could not go into any ration depot to get food because the police on duty

Inmates and environment at Moore River Native Settlement c. 1927, the year in which Lallie was residing there. Photo 368/5 Battye Library, Perth.

would need to know their names before they could pass the food rations to them. To stay out in the bush continually on the run and in hiding was becoming more and more difficult. Laura was tortured with worry for the welfare of her children. She had come to the Morgans area with Lallie hoping to get her children into the care and comparative safety of the Mount Margaret mission and instead they would have to stay in seclusion in the bush for some indefinite time. While they were out in the bush and not at the mission the possibility of a police raid on their camp caused continual anxiety for Laura who would have constantly worried about the seizing of her childen. The police would be relentless. These women were repeat offenders and they had now managed a successful escape. The extent of their accumulated offences would be considered to be very serious.

The stories about conditions, discipline and treatment that successful absconders such as Lallie and Laura brought back to their people made Moore River Native Settlement more than a fearful, dreaded place to the Aboriginal people of the goldfields. The potential to lose a child permanently was a constant anxiety. Many of the inmates did not escape while they were children and over time did forget their indigenous language, the identity of their Aboriginal mother and the location of her people and their tribal land. By keeping the inmates at the institution until they were sixteen and sending them out from there to service in home duties or pastoral work, the staff made these people dependent emotionally, culturally, socially and morally on the institution which became their 'home'. Years later when some of the ex-inmates had 'family reunions' it was to the native settlement at Moore River, rather than the district of their mother's people that they returned. Their 'parents' were neither of their biological parents but ex-nurses and government staff who had looked after them as wards of the State in an institution.

The benefits anticipated in the 1920s and 1930s of institutionalising part-Aboriginal children at Mogumber's settlement were put precisely years later in the 1970s when they were viewed in retrospect by a Christian citizen Reverend Clarke: 'As primitive natives they lived not a happy life but a life of fear. At Mogumber the natives were taken out of their misery by being taught the Gospel and being kept busy at work and sport...under the influence of Jesus Christ they could cut out some of the evils of their life'[50]. It is quite likely that the views given in retrospect by Aboriginal people, who in the past experienced displacement, family and social disintegration, spiritual deprivation and harsh discipline and deprivation in institutions, would be worded differently.

From the time of their return to their people, until something happened to undo their situation, Lallie, Laura and the three children would have to live like outlaws, remaining out of sight and on the run.

CHAPTER SIX

Lallie as a fugitive

Lallie and Laura with her three children commenced a life as fugitives from November 1927. As single women in the bush they could be faced with the predictable ordeals. They could practise cohabitation for the survival of their children and themselves. That would most likely culminate in one, if not both of the women, becoming pregnant again. A pregnancy could require either woman to experience another act of infanticide. If a baby survived, certain pursuit by the police would follow, thus precipitating the cycle of pain, separation and tragedy that characterised these women's lives.

One measure that could prevent the police from removing the two women or any of their children from their tribal lands would be for the elders to arrange for either of the women to be given to a tribal husband. Such an arrangement would satisfy, at least temporarily, the regulations of the Aborigines Act and the expectations of the Chief Protector, as well as that of the Aborigines' tribal customs. Without a male provider Lallie and Laura would have to live as fugitives, and often witness the three children experience hunger.

The Linden mob and Lallie's mother wanted Lallie and her company safe and free with them, but the law enforcers were not going to give up their search for the fugitive party. It became a priority for the elders to assess what would be the best action to take to keep Lallie secluded from the police. The passing of time was now very precious to Lallie's people. Every day they had to be aware of the proximity of the police. They hoped that the longer they could outmanoeuvre the officers the more likely Lallie would be left with them.

The elders had not forgotten that the Afghan storekeeper from Morgans still wished to marry Lallie. In considering all options to keep the police from seizing Lallie the elders needed to evaluate quickly the appropriateness of Lallie's marriage to Jack Akbar. On reviewing all that had happened to Lallie during the last six months, the elders began to view the Afghan's proposal from a different perspective. The association of Akbar and Lallie, that once seemed to be of benefit to the girl, had recently seemed to evoke trouble and danger. Though the elders may have believed that the Afghan was genuine in his aim to do the right and honourable thing by the Linden girl, they and their people had experienced how his persistence with seeking official permission for his marriage to her had ironically tightened the Moore River net around them. Since Lallie's third escape from Moore River Native Settlement the constabulary had regularly ridden out to the Linden mob to ask questions about the whereabouts of Lallie, Laura and the three children. In their exchange of words with the Wongai they implied that they knew Jack Akbar would have knowledge of her whereabouts and suspected he would be collaborating with the Wongai in secluding her[1]. When Jack visited Lallie the police, who were watching his every movement, would track him to her. This information intimidated and alarmed the Wongai. The regular presence of the constabulary, on horseback or in the recently introduced motor vehicles, would require Lallie's people to be constantly on the alert and at the ready to conceal their other part-Aboriginal children. A surprise police raid that might take Lallie or any other children away could come any day. Lallie was a fugitive and her only protectors now were the elders.

One elderly surviving Wongai man explained that for the Linden mob there was more to the subject of the marriage of one of their girls to an Afghan than the issue of the police possibly tracking Jack to catch Lallie. Some of them considered that even though Jack was their friend and would not intentionally put them at any risk, he was not a tribal man. According to the Aboriginal people's ancient rules about who was an appropriate partner for whom in marriage, Akbar's marriage to Lallie would constitute a mixed marriage. This would not be acceptable[2]. Another female Wongai descendant of the Leonora area, whose mother was alive in Lallie's time, could not recall much about Lallie's early years around the eastern goldfields; however, one memory that did remain with her was that 'Lallie's people were against her going with Jack'[3].

An effort was made to understand why some of Lallie's people were not tolerant of Jack Akbar. According to tribal customs Aboriginal

The troopers who participated in the discipline of the inmates at Moore River Native Settlement were themselves Aboriginal. Photo368/5 Battye Library, Perth.

society incorporated an amount of reciprocity. At times the rules of cohabitation were relaxed so that intercourse was permitted between a couple not normally accessible to each other. The elders, as guardians of their society and figures of authority, would supervise sexual privileges. The rights of older men and reciprocal sexual privileges were governed by a fairly strict although broad moral code. In demanding their privilege the old men could demand the right to spear an offender, one who did not have rights to this reciprocity. Perhaps some of the older Linden people suspected Akbar of cohabitation with Lallie, perhaps with one of their other younger women, and wanted a spearing carried out on Akbar[4]. If they suspected that Akbar had sexual intimacy with their girl Lallie during a time when the elders were deliberating the passing of her to one of their tribal men, then they could compare this behaviour to adultery, and this offence was traditionally punished with a spearing of either or both partners.

Perhaps due to discord amongst the Linden people about the suitability of Lallie's marriage to the Afghan, the elders' latest assessment did not lead to a new decision about Lallie's relationship with that man. They remained cautious about the whole notion. Keeping her out of Moore River Native Settlement or a worse institution was the higher priority and one that the Linden people were united on. This would be threatened if Jack Akbar renewed his persistence in seeking their permission for his marriage. Rather than give their consent to her marriage to their friend the Morgans Afghan storekeeper, they would now keep her well concealed from him. Jack's presence around their people and the regular monitoring of his movement by the police would jeopardise their efforts to keep the fugitive women safe. Jack and Lallie's marriage would be forbidden because it would bring too much trouble and unhappiness.

This decision by the elders was law. Lallie, and her mother Tjirrgulu, both understood that the elders had decreed that she should not associate with Jack Akbar. Should she not adhere to their instruction a punishment would be served on Lallie and possibly her mother. The method of punishment would be a spearing carried out by an emufoot man.' Once Jack had been told by the elders that he was forbidden to see or associate with Lallie then he was also liable for a spearing if he disobeyed their direction.

The elders now resumed discussion on the subject of a suitable tribal husband for Lallie. They understood that if the police could see that bush teenage girls had a tribe-given husband who was able to provide for them then the girls would not be considered by the police or

Aborigines Department as being in a situation of neglect. If tribal men could be found for Lallie and Laura this would remove the urgency to have them taken into police custody and transferred out of the district to a remote institution. However, the selection of a man amongst their people to whom Lallie could be suited could not be decided upon quickly. The elders would require more time to resolve this problem, precisely when timing was critical.

The need for Laura to get her three children to the mission illuminated to the elders another possible means of keeping Lallie safe from rearrest and institutionalisation. Sine her arrival amongst the Linden people Laura had talked with them about Inspector Mitchell's suggestion, that to take her three children to Mount Margaret mission would be a possible means of diverting authorities from separating her from her children, or even the three siblings from each other. It had been a main motive for her attempts at escape with her children from Moore River Native Settlement. If she could still get her children to Schenks' mission, while she was living as a fugitive, there was less likelihood of the police taking her children to a place that would be far from her.

The elders considered taking Lallie with Laura and the three children to Mr and Mrs Schenk at Mount Margaret mission. They had not forgotten that the police had earlier gone onto the mission to remove Lallie. The elders hoped that if there was the promise of a tribal husband for Lallie, Schenk might be able to persuade the Chief Protector to allow him to keep Lallie. The elders needed further advice to calculate thoroughly the advantage of this strategy. They would go and sit with Mr Schenk at the mission and seek his advice. In their circumstances they considered that he was one colonist who was willing to sit down and talk in council, and who would respect their authority amongst their people. In later January 1928 the elders went to the Schenks to discuss with them Lallie's return to their mission, as well as admitting Laura's three children[5].

Rod and Mysie Schenk had retained their fondness for Lallie. The proposal that the elders put to them, regarding keeping her with them at the mission, would have been welcomed and earnestly encouraged by the Evangelical couple at any other time, but this one. There were circumstances about Lallie's case that would make it difficult for the Schenks to obtain permission to keep her with them. Rod would have had difficulty normally getting permission to keep Lallie on his mission after such an escape by her. Apart from the fact that she had committed an offence by leaving a native settlement without the written authority of the Chief Protector of Aborigines, Lallie was over sixteen years old and Neville was not in favour of any young Aboriginal women being kept at the mission after that age. He believed they would become too complacent and dependent. It would be better that from the age of sixteen they be made to go from the mission to do domestic work and thus develop into productive members of society. By now Lallie was about eighteen. The only way the Schenks could get authority to keep her at Mount Margaret mission with them was for her to become a monitor in their school, and Lallie did not have enough education to take on that role[6].

If the Linden mob's elders had come at any other time to appeal to the Schenks for their help regarding Lallie, the couple may have attempted to help her. The timing of the elders' request was most inconvenient. An authorisation provided very recently by the Chief Protector for a project that Rod Schenk had waited a long time for predisposed the missionary to inaction in this matter. During the time of Lallie's escape from Moore River, the Chief Protector in Perth had finally agreed to authorise a request that the missionary had been putting earnestly and formally for five years since 1922. Rod Schenk had a long-term goal to obtain permission from the Chief Protector of Aborigines, in writing, to have a ration depot sited at his mission. Schenk saw this as crucial in increasing his influence over the Wongai.

Not long after Rodolphe Schenk founded his site for his mission he had difficulty in eliminating the Wongai's custom of being at the mission for a while then decamping. In the first few years at Mount Margaret mission he had to understand the various motives for them leaving his settlement and avoiding his influence. It frustrated him to see the local Aborigines emerge out of the bush, spend a little time on his site, then retreat. Rod realised early that one of the dominant reasons for their regular departure was the requirement to be present fortnightly at one of the ration depots at Burtville, Morgans and Laverton or at the occasional 'Linden relief camp'. The missionary realised that more Wongai would come to him, more would be likely to stay with him for longer periods of time, if he had a ration outlet on his mission.

By April 1923, two years after his arrival in Laverton, Rod had achieved some success in encouraging a number of Wongai to stay at Mount Margaret for extended periods. He was able to report to Chief Protector Neville that about one hundred Wongai were staying at his mission for some time. About fifty of these had become so settled at the mission that the other Wongai called them 'Margaret blackfellas'. The Aboriginal male known as the 'king' of the whole district let it be known to Schenk that he intended to 'sit down at Margaret 'til he dies'[7].

Schenk viewed the dependency of the Wongai on the ration depots as an interference of his influence over them. In late December 1922 the missionary attempted to convey to the Deputy Protector of the Aborigines Department Ernest E. Copping how the ration depots encouraged the nomadic patterns of the Wongai, and thus obstructed his plan to make progress with converting the Wongai not only to Christianity but also to a 'productive people', an objective placed on him by the Chief Protector himself[8].

Rod Schenk perceived that it was crucial to his progress that he be in a position in which the Wongai would depend on him for all their basic human needs. He wanted to be able to demonstrate to the indigenous people that he had enough food and blankets for them all. Mysie and Rod expected they would have an increasing number of Wongai to support as their programs to make the Aborigines more productive were established. While Mysie commenced her raffia work classes for the girls and young women at the mission[9], Rod trained the young Aboriginal males in sandalwood cleaning, shepherding goats, building fences and dwellings, and mustering. Establishing these programs in skills training so as to provide the Aboriginal people with a means to earn a wage implied that the Schenks would need to be prepared to be able to feed and clothe as many Wongai as they took under their care, or growing influence[10]. He and Mysie also planned to open a school for the children of the Wongai. With a ration depot located at his mission Rodolphe Schenk would be able to impress effectively on the local Aborigines that through his love and the love of his God he could care for them in every physical, as well as spiritual, way.

Another motivation Rod Schenk had for requesting authority to distribute rations was to take care of the elderly Wongai. Once Aboriginal people reached an age at which they were not so capable of walking long distances between the nominated ration depots, their traditional camp and religious sites, and recently the mission, they were left behind. Schenk's letter of 19 April 1923, in which he again raised with the Chief Protector the subject of giving authority for ration distribution from the Mount Margaret mission, focused on care for the elderly[11].

A request from Schenk to Neville for any addition to the mission was not always responded to promptly. There were a number of reasons for this. Over the years that Neville and Schenk collaborated their own professional relationship was not always on the positive side. Neville's political and administrative goals and Schenk's evangelism at times brought them into conflict. Neville did not like the missions to have too much autonomy, yet at the same time his department, with its limited expenditure, after 1905 came to depend on them more for support in achieving the gradual assimilation of the part-Aboriginal population and in setting up education and training programs.

Another reason for Neville resisting Schenk's appeal for a ration depot for a long time could have been his awareness of opposition in the wider community to the Aborigines Department granting a ration depot at the mission. Many residents and pastoralists in the Laverton and Morgans municipalities were against a ration depot being located at the mission because they perceived it as attracting nomadic Aborigines to settlements. They ran a minor campaign to oppose any decision by the Chief Protector of Aborigines to locate a ration depot at the Schenks' mission. They spread rumours about Schenk and made complaints about his mission. Mr Harris, a local pastoralist who was chairman of the Roads Board of Laverton, spearheaded the opposition which sought the cancellation of the mission's lease. The number of complaints provoked a visit to the mission in January 1925 by District Police Inspector Duncan of Kalgoorlie and the then Secretary of the Aborigines Department Mr Copping. In conducting their investigation Duncan and Copping first went out to Laverton to meet with the pastoralists before visiting the mission. After inspecting the mission thoroughly Copping was very impressed by what he saw in the work being done for the Aborigines. In his report to the Chief Protector, Copping advised that the mission remain open[12].

Schenk also aggravated the pastoralists in his attempt to find out the name of the biological fathers of any part-Aboriginal babies that were brought to him to be put in his care, thus implicating pastoralists. And, he taught Aboriginal lads what the value of a wage was and how much they should expect to get paid when working for a pastoralist. This was contrary to the means by which the pastoralists preferred to 'pay' their Aboriginal labour.

The biggest annoyance caused by Schenk to the pastoralists would have been his talk about giving land back to the Aborigines. Schenk understood that the 'natives' had been alienated from their land by the spread of cattle and sheep runs. Near the mission was the Mount Margaret Native Reserve, which was only about 200 acres (81ha). Schenk summed it up as 'a small home for many hundreds of natives whose only home between the Great Australian Bight and the Tropic is there'. The Reserve was surrounded by huge sheep stations. Schenk questioned how hundreds of natives could live on such a restricted area which could not even support three hundred goats. They could not provide enough milk for the seventy to eighty children cared for at the mission. Schenk proposed that either Parliament would have to raise vast sums of money for rations to 'avoid starving the natives to death in their own country - or else restore land where they would be safe from molestation by whites and safe from official deportation'[13].

The local constabulary also had reasons to resent the placing of a ration depot at the mission. They were affronted by the idea that a missionary and not them should be the distributor of rations. The Constable in charge of Laverton and of Morgans believed that to give a ration depot over to the mission would reduce the power the police exercised over the Aborigines. Through the control of their food supplements, which the police could withdraw at will, they could intimidate the Aborigines. Constable Warren of Laverton, who advised the Aborigines Department not to locate rationing for the natives at Mount Margaret mission, explained to the Chief Protector:

> The police will lose all power over the natives and they will be stealing again as usual, and causing no end of trouble. When a native does anything wrong a policeman can threaten to stop his rations. I have done so and it has had a great effect on them...It is only by the Police issuing the rations that keeps the natives in check around Laverton. Schenk is causing the natives to be restless and troublesome. He can't control the movement of natives in and out of the mission. They get rations at Morgans then come up to Laverton and worry the people there and go to the [Laverton] police station and ask for more and go back again[14].

The Wongai's experience and perception of ration distribution was summarised by an elderly Wongai descendant: 'When the police issued rations they would look to see who looked frightened'. When such a person approached the Constable distributing the flour he would have that person seized and put in jail[15]. The police were convinced that their influence over the Aborigines through their control of issuing the rations had a great effect regarding keeping the Aborigines in check.

The Aborigines Department may have had some sympathy for the police who had the duty of maintaining order among the Wongai. After his trip about the State as Inspector for the Aborigines Department in February 1927, Mitchell declared that Mount Margaret had the most difficult tribe in Western Australia[16]. Their lack of conventionality was confirmed by Wilf Douglas, a retired missionary in Kalgoorlie, who added that in the 1920s the Aborigines who resided around Mount Margaret mission still had featherfoot men, circumcision, and 'witch doctors'[17].

The general community's opposition to his campaign for a ration outlet on his mission did not deter Schenk. By 1927 there were demographic changes in the eastern goldfields that served to support his cause. The pull on human resources of World War One had caused quite a few mining settlements and other towns to close down. More buildings became empty as some of the remaining population relocated to where there were jobs or economic activity. As settlements closed down the continuation of some of the police stations in the goldfields became impractical and economically non-viable. Under these circumstances the future of some of the ration depots had to be questioned.

During September 1927 Neville himself went to the goldfields to view the current sites of the depots. His itinerary included a visit to Leonora, Linden, Laverton, Morgans and Mount Margaret. He observed demographic changes and the redistribution and numbers of the remaining Wongai in the eastern goldfields. He noted that as there were fewer settlements around which the local Aborigines could congregate to get odd jobs or beg for food, that more and more Wongai were 'sitting down' on or making quite permanent camps outside Schenk's mission.

The impression Neville had gained of Schenk after this visit was very favourable. He had observed that Schenk of the Gospel Mission for the Australian Aborigines was doing very good work at his mission. He had succeeded at erecting quite a number of buildings on the 6000 acres that he had leased. Eighteen of the 30 children present were receiving education. Neville was convinced that the establishment of the Mount Margaret mission supplied a long-felt want and was as good as any departmental settlement Neville might have himself arranged in the district[18].

From his recent tour the Chief Protector deduced the need to review the distribution and number of ration depots in the goldfields and the status of the Mount Margaret mission. Neville decided that the ration depots at Laverton, Linden and Morgans would be closed down before November 1927, and all those Aborigines receiving rations would have to go to Mount Margaret, making it a ration centre for 250 Aboriginal people[19]. It appeared to him that this one main ration depot would be geographically most suitably placed for all Wongai. As the mission was 7 miles (11 kilometres) from Morgans and even further from the remaining larger communities, another advantage of choosing Mount Margaret was that it would keep the Aborigines away from any of those settlements.

On 29 September 1927 Inspector Mitchell reported that 'all Morgans and Linden indigent natives requiring assistance shall be rationed hereafter at the [Mount Margaret] mission. Perks will still exercise supervision on ration days. The butcher at Morgans will deliver meat at the mission'[20]. The weekly government ration was to be '454 grams sugar, 28 grams tea, 8.8 kilograms flour and a plug of tobacco'[21]. The rationing at Mount Margaret caused the Linden people to join with the Laverton people, and Mount Margaret which had once been a buffer zone became common grounds. Though Schenk had been granted the ration depot by October 1927 it would not be operating fully stocked until early 1928.

Because of his satisfaction with Schenk at this time Neville considered making Schenk a Protector for this district[22]. If this occurred it would mean that a policeman may not always have to be present to supervise the distribution, thus effectively removing a potential source of intimidation of the Aborigines at the mission.

In October 1927 the Morgans ration depot was closed down. By late 1927 the Mount Morgans mine had ceased operations and the population of Morgans town was reduced to 35 men, women and children, with a total of about 60 men, women and children in the whole district. From 27 October 1927 the Morgans police station was closed and the Morgans sub-district came under the jurisdiction of the police constable at Laverton. Police Constable S.E. Perks was transferred to Gwalia station near Leonora. Laverton-Morgans police business was communicated by Police Constable Warren to District Inspector of Police Spedding Smith in Kalgoorlie[23].

The addition of a ration depot to the mission would give Rod Schenk a tighter grip on his indigenous congregation and a greater influence over their lives. From Neville's perspective it would give the mission a more crucial role in the assimilation of the Aborigines.

It was one month after Inspector Mitchell's announcement that the mission would get a ration depot that Lallie escaped with Laura and her three children from Moore River. The Linden girl returned home as a fugitive. This event did not affect Schenk directly until about two and a half weeks later when the elders of the Linden people came to speak with him. The elders had come to seek protection for their girl, and accomodation for a fugitive mother's children, at a mission which was about to be granted the authority to open a ration depot. The elders wanted the Schenks to believe that Lallie wanted to resume a most moral and law-abiding life. They were emphatic that Lallie was not going to be associating with the Afghan again, and that she did not want to mix with 'white men' again. 'The Linden people as a whole would be against her if she did'[24].

The request the elders were making at this particular time could have put the missionary couple in a dilemma: a choice between the welfare of two adults and three children of their indigenous congregation, or the benefits to all the Wongai of a ration depot at the mission. If he was to work for the good of all Wongai then there was only one decision he could make. As Schenk gave no assurance that he could take Lallie into his mission and keep her safe and free, they remained unsure and suspicious of the exact consequences of putting Lallie into Schenk's charge. They left him without telling him exactly where they had the girl and her fellow fugitives concealed.

The presence of the fugitives Lallie and Laura in the area had another ramification for Mr Schenk. The ration depot could be used against the Wongai people in a way the missionary had not ever anticipated. All Wongai in the district would have to come in from the bush at regular intervals to collect their rations. Their names had to be checked against a list and their attendance registered. Until Schenk was made a local protector his ration outlet would be visited by the local policeman, who would from now be Constable Warren. With fugitives in the bush the police would be watching the new ration depot for the appearance of Lallie and Laura. The police knew that it would be only a matter of time before the fugitives would be so hungry that they would be desperate enough to risk capture by coming out of the bush to collect their share of food. Rod Schenk would have realised that the ration depot he had wanted for so long to improve his capacity for caring would be used for the opposite cause; to ambush and remove two hungry women and three defenceless children.

The visit by the Linden elders to the mission inadvertently assisted the police in finding out more about Lallie's whereabouts. They had verified for the missionary that the two female fugitives from Moore River were definitely in the Linden-Morgans area. On 17 January 1928 he reported the visit of the elders and the contents of their conversation to the Chief Protector through the local police Constable[25].

After their visit to Mount Margaret mission the elders accepted that Lallie and her party would not be safe there. The Wongai had no choice but to keep Lallie and Laura as fugitives in the bush living in desperate circumstances.

Rod and Mysie Schenk knew the elders would not bring Lallie in. They became concerned about the impact of the resumption of her people's ways on the quality of her life. They realised that Lallie, Laura and the children would be very short of food: the bush did not always have sufficient game. Lallie was forbidden now to associate with a man who had hoped to marry and care for her, and it would take time before the elders could secure a tribal husband for her. As circumstances deteriorated around her and her company they could see that Lallie's life would revert again to one of immoral behaviour with all its dire consequences.

Back in their camp the elders became concerned that their visit to the mission to discuss Lallie's safety may not have been a wise move. The close liaison between the missionary and the police had led to the removal of Lallie from the mission once before. The elders had thought then that she was safe there. Schenk by now may have informed the police of their recent visit to the mission. The response by the police might be to organise a raiding party within the next few days and ride out from Laverton into the bush in search of her. The elders now had to devise a strategy that would confuse the police about the precise location of the fugitive party. They decided to use a ruse and instructed their people to spread the rumour through the bush that Lallie and her companions had left the district. The elders anticipated that when the bush Wongai talked with the Mount Margaret Wongai, word of Lallie's departure from the district would eventually get back to the missionary and thus to the police.

The rumour that Lallie, Laura and the three children had left the district got back to Mr Schenk as the elders hoped. However, the missionary was not entirely convinced of its credibility. Schenk did report to A.O. Neville that he heard from the Wongai that Lallie had left the district. However, he added the comment that he and his wife had reason to think that there was some collusion about the matter[26].

When Jack Akbar learned that Lallie was back with her people his hopes would have rallied once again for them to have a future together. However, the Wongai did not want the Afghan to resume his relations with their girl.

Throughout January of 1928, while establishing a building for the ration depot and awaiting the stock to fill the shelves, it was the missionary more so than the constabulary who provided the Chief Protector with the more reliable and current news regarding the location and condition of the fugitive party. Since the five had escaped from Moore River in May 1927, A.O. Neville had been plagued by a frustration about Lallie Matbar's case that was aggravated over the subsequent eight months by the comparative ineffectiveness of the police. Reports sent by those constabulary on the lookout for the absconders passed on details that were either out of date, uncoordinated or contradictory. Because of this inefficiency and unwieldiness of bureaucratic red tape, Neville could not advise on the time to act, or where exactly the police could find Lallie.

While Lallie remained at liberty but secluded in the bush the Schenks worried about the path towards cohabitation that her life was destined to take. They felt that the circumstances around the situation of the Linden girl were too complex and were taking too long in being resolved. They were aware that the desire of Akbar to find her and marry her could provoke trouble with the Wongai. Though they did not want to see her arrested the Schenks did not want to learn that she had resumed sexual company with the 'white men' or that she and her young fugitive companions were starving. The Schenks concluded that this particular girl's case required the expertise of a government executive administrator who knew more about rules and regulations and the means by which to resolve more difficult cases. By mid-January 1928 Mr Schenk wrote to Mr Neville requesting him to send a senior officer to the Morgans-Linden area to deal with the case[27].

The Chief Protector in Perth had assessed that the Schenks' position was more advantageous than that of the police in attempting to locate the five fugitives. The missionary had a very close relationship with the local Aborigines, particularly those that came intermittently out of the bush to visit the mission and collect rations. He was directly in contact with the Wongai who knew exactly where Lallie and her party was. Neville noted Schenk's alarm and responded.

On the 2 February 1928 Inspector Mitchell was assigned to the Lallie Matbar case. His instruction was that after returning to Kalgoorlie from Karonie he was to take the train to Morgans and from there travel out to Mount Margaret mission to visit and interview Rod Schenk. The main object of his visit was to make arrangements for the return to the Moore River Native Settlement of Lallie Matbar, Laura Quince and the three children, who were being harboured by the Laverton Aborigines.

Neville provided the Inspector with a line of reasoning that could persuade the Aborigines to cooperate with him. Mitchell was to meet with the elders and make them understand that as Lallie had absconded thrice from Moore River, she must be returned. The Inspector was to persuade them that the government must be obeyed, and that its will was paramount in all matters, even though every consideration would be given for 'tribal laws and susceptibilities'. If they cooperated in bringing in Lallie with Laura Quince and family so that they could be returned to the Moore River Native Settlement, Inspector Mitchell could give them the Chief Protector's word that in due course Lallie would be permitted to return to the mission, providing that the elders agreed to her remaining there for the future[28].

Neville conveyed ahead to Schenk that he would send Inspector Mitchell equipped with particular instructions to deal with the fugitives' case. Once the missionary heard that the Inspector had arrived in Morgans he sent word on to the elders that another man was coming from the Aborigines Department who wished to discuss with them the best measures to take for the future of Lallie and her companions.

Word was sent back to Schenk from the elders that they accepted the offer to meet with the government department man. Inspector Mitchell put the views and offers of the Chief Protector to these most respected heads of the Linden people. To gain the facts from the elders of her exact whereabouts Mitchell used very subtly posed questions that might elicit from the Wongai where the elders had the absconders concealed.

The Inspector did not gain the facts he sought. The elders overall contributed very few facts and their dialogue in the discussions was frugal and non-committal. The Inspector related later to his superior that he thought the meeting was more 'politic than candid'. All that Mitchell was able to learn about Lallie's whereabouts was that she was away in the bush somewhere between Burtville, Linden and Laverton, and he suspected that already.

By the end of the conference Mitchell had not gained any information by which he could give the police directions to collect the fugitive party. The terrain of the eastern goldfields was too inhospitable in which to send police off on a hunt without specific directions. There was an enormous dried lake bed between Laverton and Morgans which the police would have to circumnavigate. There were many miles of trackless scrub and hilly areas in which Lallie and Laura could be kept hidden. The Wongai knowledge of the location of natural waterholes and some soaks in the area, and how to find food in the more remote spinifex country, meant that Lallie and Laura could outmanoeuvre the mounted constabulary and could survive out there for a long time.

Mitchell did not want the elders to leave before he could salvage some achievement out of his visit to Mount Margaret. Mindful of Neville's proposed strategy, the Inspector ultimately made an offer to the elders which he hoped they would consider reasonable and would thus convince them to either reveal the location of Lallie and Laura or even to surrender them. His offer comprised a barter of two humans for two other humans. Dion and Ada Taylor were two Wongai youths who were inmates of Moore River Native Settlement and who were due for a 'holiday' from that institution. During their release they would come back to the Laverton district to visit their family. Mitchell suggested to the elders that once the police were told where exactly to find Lallie, Laura and the children, and the police had this fugitive group in their custody and on its way to Moore River, the elders and the parents of Dion and Ada could then be assured that their children would be freed for a while and would come home to visit them. The Inspector then added the condition that once Dion and Ada returned to Moore River from their holiday, then the Aborigines Department would release Lallie and Laura so that they could return to their own people. However, if the elders and their people did not cooperate with Mitchell and inform him now of the present location of the absconders, then Dion and Ada would not get a holiday from Moore River Native Settlement. As the elders prepared to leave, the Inspector informed them that he would give them a certain amount of time in which to get back to their people, particularly to the mother of Dion and Ada and of Lallie, so that they could all discuss his offer[29].

A few hours later the elders returned to Mitchell bringing with them a few other persons. These included the mother and father of Dion and Ada.

The parents had come back to the mission with the elders because they themselves wanted to speak with the government man. They had been encouraged to believe that their children would be home soon and now that seemed to be merely a probability and dependent on another parent turning in her child to the police. When the parents urged the Inspector to maintain the promise his department had made and to arrange to have their children sent home to them, Mitchell's reply was that it was in the hands of their elders to decide the future of their children. He informed them that he would give them still more time by delaying his departure. He expected that the Wongai would come to their senses about what he proposed, and thus on this day some cooperaton from the Wongai in locating and catching Lallie and her companions might yet occur.

The elders and the parents left the mission settlement and discussed the matter at a distance. What Mitchell considered to be cunning did not achieve the outcome he desired. The Wongai did not consider his offer of bartering with human beings to be fair. No representatives of the elders were seen again by the Inspector of the Aborigines Department. When Mitchell left the mission and Morgans he had not made any progress in the recapture of Lallie and Laura.

Mitchell believed that the attitude of the elders indicated that the police would continue to have a difficult time in catching Lallie. The recapture of the fugitive party seemed to the Inspector to be less and less likely. In his report to the Chief Protector, Mitchell encouraged the administrator to hesitate before incurring any further expenditure over the capture and return of the women to Moore River Native Settlement[30].

Neville was committed to the pursuit of Lallie until recapture and internment. In his instructions to Mitchell to meet with the elders at Mount Margaret the Chief Protector had stated to him that the government's orders were to be followed to the end. At the mission Mitchell had passed on the Protector's word to the elders and to Schenk. The statement had committed both the Aborigines and the Police Departments into combining their manpower and resources to pursue the absconders until recapture. Even if it took a time, and was hampered by a lack of cooperation from the community, the Aborigines Department had made a promise that had to be kept to maintain its integrity.

It seemed by now that Neville was motivated to keep Lallie's file open by more than the required boundaries of his job and position. It would not be beneficial to his public image for him to be seen to have been outwitted by, and loosing a case, to a mob of 'native desert fringe dwellers'. For the sake of the reputation of his relatively small government department, Neville wanted it to be acclaimed publicly for being the victors, a success reflecting their dogmatic persistence and true control over the indigenous population. So as to ensure that his and the police departments were the eventual victors, Neville would now have to give more serious thought to what resources he could muster, to what methods he could resort to so as to widen the net that would catch the two women and children.

Meanwhile, the Schenks continued to collect fragments of information from the Wongai in their effort to keep abreast with Lallie and Laura's movements. Since the ration depot at Mount Margaret had begun to function Lallie and her company had not come in from the bush to collect their rations. There were no other sites left at which Lallie could collect food. Considering the amount of time in which Lallie had now been in the bush in hiding Rod and Mysie suspected that she had begun 'to trade again with white men'. They eventually heard rumours through the Wongai to that effect[31].

This news was a concern to both the Schenks and to Neville. Both parties believed that something would have to be done to get that girl away from her people and back into an institution. The Wongai had attempted to keep Jack Akbar out of Lallie's life as they did not want anyone to draw the attention of the police to Lallie. For a while even Jack could not assist her with food and thus reduce her need to practise cohabitation.

While the police hunted for Lallie and Laura these two women with the three children lived the life of outlaws. Lallie and Jack endured life without each other for some time. In Perth A.O. Neville would have been very frustrated still by the inability of the Police Department to coordinate its actions on the whereabouts of the absconders. Even though missionary Schenk and Inspector Mitchell had both recently confirmed that Lallie was in the Linden-Morgans area, the Chief Protector was still receiving occasional reports from the constabulary which indicated that they were not yet aware that Lallie and her fugitive companions were back with their own people north-east of Kalgoorlie. The police were still watching out for the fugitives in areas west of Kalgoorlie.

Just after Mitchell's visit to Mount Margaret, Police Constable White of Mukinbudin reported to his district's superior Inspector Johnston that he had recently been making enquiries amongst a few part-Aboriginal people in his district about the wanted Wongai absconders. He ascertained that no such persons had been seen around Mukinbudin[32]. On 17 February, Police Constable J.B. Allanson of Trayning reported to Inspector Johnston that he had only just learned that the two female Wongai absconders had passed through North Trayning about two months previously. They told a farmer at whose house they called in to get some food that they were on their way to Merredin[33].

About two and a half weeks later Police Constable Reilly of Merredin reported to Sergeant Nisbet that he had had just learned from J. Hughes the butcher, who had a good deal to do with Aborigines in the district, that several Aborigines came through Merredin a few months previously but they did not stay any time. They were supposed to have gone to Kellerberrin[34].

Neville had a concern that the daring of Lallie Matbar might incite other Aborigines in the Laverton-Linden area. The story of Lallie was potentially volatile and thus it was becoming imperative to act with an impact so as to curb any indigenous protests, demonstrations or insurgency. Knowing that the constabulary in the country and goldfields areas were not effectively coordinated or up-to-date in their reports, Neville considered that the energies of the police out in the fields would have more of an impact if their Commissioner committed his men more earnestly to the task of tracking down and recapturing Lallie and Laura. From Neville's point of view, the matter of the significant increase in expenditure of both the Aborigines and the Police Departments would have to be seen as secondary to both the seriousness of the case, due to the repetition of offences committed by the Linden girl against the State, and to the potential of the case to incite Aboriginal unrest and revolt.

The Chief Protector of Aborigines set about attempting to persuade Police Commissioner Connell that the case of Lallie Matbar, absconder and outlaw, needed prompt attention. In the very explicit letter he wrote to Commissioner Connell on 20 February 1928, Neville attempted to demoralise the character of Lallie by referring to incidents of the past and declaring that she was a 'well-known half-caste prostitute', she had had an immoral relationship with an Afghan and that the three children she gave birth to were all dead. Neville perverted the truth about Laura's situation by stating that she was well known in Kalgoorlie as being 'the paramour of a white man', this man being the part-Aboriginal man who had lived with her and cared for her and their three children. Neville hoped to insense the Police Commissioner into believing there was a need for his men to take immediate action against these two women.

The Chief Protector pointed out to Connell which regulations of the 1905 Aborigines Act Jack and Lallie were suspected of breaching. He argued that from the point of view of the Aborigines Department the unresolved cases of the two women were a serious matter, and it was time for both he as Chief Protector and for the Police Commissioner to take a firm hand in dealing with them.

What had been done so far had not been sufficient or successful. Warrants already existed in the cases of the two women. The Chief Protector claimed he had dealt fairly with the tribe and that they had not responded. He warned the Police Commissioner that if they did not take firmer action now it would be impossible to intern and then keep any Aborigines from the goldfields at the Moore River Native Settlement. Neville suggested to the Police Commissioner that one way in which he could be 'good enough to support' him would be by ordering the formation of a police expedition which would go in pursuit of the two women. This organisation of man power would definitely secure the runaways and in turn demonstrate to the tribe that the government's wishes could not be flouted in any way[35].

The Chief Protector's letter did make an impression on Commissioner Connell. His preliminary response was to send a brief, interim note to the Chief Protector informing him that he would discuss the contents of the letter, particularly the formation of an expedition, with some of his own senior men and then make a decision.

Just at the time when Neville felt he had accumulated enough evidence against the Linden girl to be able to justify to Connell the manoeuvring of a volume of constabulary in a full-scale search, some of the correspondence he received from the police and the missionary in the goldfields halted him in his stride. Their content could possibly serve to reduce the sense of urgency propelling his petition to the Police Commissioner. The news from Rod Schenk was of the nature that would have been appealing to the missionaries, but at this precise time did not serve the purpose of the Chief Protector, though once it would have. Schenk reported to Neville that he had learned from the Wongai that three or four tribal men were prepared to have Lallie for their wife. Earlier in the case Neville would have accepted such an arrangement as meeting the regulations of both the Aborigines Act and Lallie's people, and therefore reason to cease the pursuit by the police of the girl. Now it came almost like an impediment to his plans. Schenk had added that 'the natives say that she is not with the white men yet'. This news would indicate to Police Commissioner Connell that Lallie was, at this time, not breaching any regulations of the 1905 Act.

The missionary also had encouraging news in regard to the circumstances around Laura Quince and her three children. He learned from the Wongai that she had become partnered with a tribal husband who was keeping her and her three children out in the bush with him where he was able to care for and feed them. He would be a good provider for them as Laura was his only wife[36].

The news that might have been once in Lallie's favour at this time was irritating, inconvenient and almost insolent. That Linden girl was a repeated absconder, and a successful one at that. If at this time Neville recognised the partnering of Lallie with a tribal husband then let her stay on at the mission, such an agreement on his part would in a sense be a victory to her and her people. It would also negate any justification for returning Lallie to more strict confinement and punishing her for past offences.

At this same time the Chief Protector of Aborigines also received reports from police in the Laverton area that they suspected that a certain number of Wongai in the district were becoming subversive and rebellious[37]. There is no other documentation of this potential for widespread insurgence. There were still many of this tribe in the area and they were considered to be quite wiley. Neville perceived that the pardoning of Lallie Matbar now, after all that she had done since May 1927 that was offensive in the eyes of the law, would add fuel to the fire.

Neville's belief that it was imperative that Tjirrgulu's daughter be removed from her surroundings was confirmed by news of the restless 'natives'. The initiation of a police expedition sent to capture her and remove her to Moore River Native Settlement, or to a more punitive institution such as Fremantle Gaol, seemed to be essential. Once she was interned the Aborigines Department would keep her there for a length of time to be determined. That time would be long enough for that girl to have succumbed to the influence and authority of the Chief Protector's position, and for the process of assimilation to have been more internalised within her. On her eventual release she would be little trouble. Also, with the passage of time the goldfields Aborigines might forget the successes of the Linden girl, and would see through her altered behaviour and attitude the effectiveness of the Chief Protector's authority and guardianship. When she was handed back to her tribal husband, it would be under Neville's terms. The ultimate benefits of having Lallie brought back to confinement would be the reinforcement of the fear of his authority, and the heeding of his regulations and his local protectors with more compliance and submissiveness[38].

While Commissioner Connell considered the Chief Protector's request to form an expedition, both he and Neville were provided with further details on Lallie from Constable Warren of Laverton. He had been maintaining his investigations among the Laverton and Morgans Aborigines on the location of the two absconders. Constable Warren told his senior officer that after interviewing a couple of Linden Wongai he learned that the two female fugitives were 'in the bush between Linden and Yarri'[39]. It might be difficult for the police to catch them by surprise because they were said to be on the look-out for the police and were keeping well in the bush.

Though the details from Constable Warren were very encouraging, another part of his report raised another issue, the subject of excessive wastage of government, and thus taxpayers', money, and eventually motivated a Perth newspaper, the *Mirror,* to publish an article on the Akbar-Matbar case[40]. By late February 1928 the searching for Lallie and her party had gone on for four months. Much money had gone into manpower, paperwork, horse feed, petrol, tyres and other maintenance. The 1920s witnessed the arrival of motor vehicles in the outback and with those came a revised budget for the police who used cars from their outposts. The costs of fueling and maintaining early model vehicles was significantly higher than horse power. Constable Warren was responsible for the budget of his station at Laverton and was aware of the cost in fuel and car damage that accrued with numbers of sorties in the vehicle. He attempted to impress upon his superiors that he was very willing to go out into the bush and pursue his enquiries, but he was mindful of the costs the case on Lallie Matbar was incurring. He gave the Commissioner and the Chief Protector a choice, to be based on finances, for his next action. He was willing to drive out to the Yarri area, a distance from Laverton of '170 miles' (274 kilometres), to try and arrest the offenders, but would expect the Aborigines Department to pay car hire for 170 miles (274 kilometres) at one shilling per mile. The alternative action was to wait until the Linden mob came to Laverton for their annual corroboree, and if Lallie and Laura were amongst them Constable Warren would attempt to catch them then[41].

Constable Warren was supported in his concern for budgeting by his superior, District Inspector Spedding Smith, who looked also at the pursuit of the Moore River fugitives in view of financial considerations. He was very familiar with the fact that police based out in the goldfields had extensive areas to patrol and vast distances to travel. The conversion to motor cars was increasing the transport expenditure of the Police Department, significantly so when the vehicles were used for patrol or reconnaissance work out in the goldfields. Inspector Spedding Smith included some advisory comments of his own to Constable Warren's latest report. He suggested to Commissioner Connell that the sending out of an expeditionary party, as proposed by the Chief Protector of Aborigines, would involve a very considerable expenditure and would not be likely to achieve the arrest of these two women. It had been shown already that considerable effort and cunning had to be used in getting these women, so if the expedition were to be authorised the Police Commissioner should consider who would be liable to pay the bill. Just as Constable Warren proposed, Inspector Spedding Smith suggested that if vehicles were needed to travel great distances to make enquiries about Lallie Matbar or to seize her, it should be the Chief Protector who approved of and paid for the expenditure for car hire[42].

Commissioner Connell put a query to the Chief Protector regarding covering the expenses of pursuing the Matbar case. The sole content of the Police Commissioner's correspondence to the Chief Protector early in March was the query that, with the knowledge of the journey costing at least one shilling per mile and that 340 miles would be travelled by the expedition, would the latter be prepared to cover the expense?[43]

Neville was committed officially to achieve a victory with the case of Lallie and Laura. He had given his word to the Aborigines through Inspector Mitchell. There was only one response he could make to Connell. Neville replied that his Department would be responsible for the cost of the Police Department's expedition.

At this time an unexpected piece of news concerning the case of Lallie arrived in a police report and caused further vexation to the Chief Protector. Continuing police enquiries revealed that the Afghan Jack Akbar had resumed keeping company with Lallie Matbar. This had redeveloped in spite of the orders of the Chief Protector, of those of the Wongai and the wishes of the Schenks who all knew what trouble it could bring the girl. It was Rod Schenk who had told the police of the renewed association.

When Jack Akbar occasionally carted meat and other stores from Morgans to the mission he did not generally say much about events in his personal life. There is no note in any of Schenk's reports regarding any conversations he had with Akbar.

Rod and Mysie Schenk had been the first informants to confirm for Neville the latest presence of Lallie after her escape from the Aboriginal institution. Schenk was more useful to Neville than the police were, to some extent, because he had a duty to the Chief Protector and to his Lord in heaven to protect the girl, and that duty made Schenk an accessory to the Chief Protector's ambition to recapture her. The Schenks believed that Akbar's renewed association with Lallie would bring her danger in the form of a spearing. In order to protect her they asked local Wongai who came in from the bush to tell them what they could on Jack's specific movements with Lallie. They would then convey those details to the police in the hope that they might curtail Akbar's companionship with the Wongai and thus defer any trouble from brewing with the elders towards him.

The Schenks learned from the Wongai that the Afghan suitor was helping Lallie's people to keep her secluded. He would visit her about once a week and would bring her provisions. Schenk was able to eke out of the Wongai the details of the precise route that Akbar travelled to visit Lallie where he had her secreted.

By 7 March 1928 Rod Schenk was able to outline for the Chief Protector the route Akbar took to Lallie. It started with the Afghan's regular, customary drive to Linden and from there he would drive to Hicks Well. It was in the vicinity of Hicks Well that Lallie was hiding. When it was a trip in which he had visited Lallie, on his return to Morgans he would go through Linden, instead of coming by the straight road from Hicks Well which passed the mission.

Rod Schenk made it possible for the Chief Protector and the police to know where to go to find Lallie, and to catch Akbar in the act of aiding and abetting a repeat offender and wanted fugitive, perhaps even in cohabiting with an Aboriginal girl. Schenk was able to give further assistance to the police by suggesting to them the best time to go out to catch the Afghan at his unlawful activity. If Constable Warren went out at the end of the week he could quite easily pick up Akbar's motor truck tracks near Hicks Well.

The missionary also offered to keep Constable Warren well informed on the activities of Jack and Lallie through his contact with the Wongai. He advised the Chief Protector that some of the Wongai were very displeased that Jack had renewed his relationship with Lallie, and it was those who were likely to supply the missionary with information about Akbar[44].

The Perth administrator could not perceive the actions of Akbar with any sympathy or compassion at all. Rather, he saw it as a public demonstration by the Asiatic of his disregard of the laws that were instituted to protect the Aborigines. He could not be obedient, was defiant and was an offender himself.

The next piece of news the Chief Protector received about Akbar may have quite astonished him. A police report informed him that the Afghan suitor was coming himself from the goldfields to have a meeting with him. He was coming to discuss personally the subject he had been forbidden several times to talk about or contemplate. No record of the dialogue between Jack Akbar and A.O. Neville has survived. The only referral to that personal encounter is in a letter written by Neville to the Commissioner of Police. He stated simply that Jack Akbar visited him on the morning of 12 March 1928[45].

The Chief Protector would have hoped that the media would not learn of the Akbar-Matbar case which he suspected they would use to direct criticism against his administration. Akbar's visit had been very close in time to a deputation that put complaints to the Premier of Western Australia regarding Neville's administration and that media had given publicity to that event. The deputation led by William Harris a 'half -caste' was significant in that it was the first organised, official protest by Aboriginal people on record in Western Australia and its focus was the unjust treatment by Neville's administration of Aboriginal people.

On 9 March 1928 a 'unique deputation consisting of half-castes and full blooded aborigines', headed by Mr William Harris, a 'well educated half caste', came to the office in the Treasury Building in Perth of the Western Australia Premier the Honourable P. Collier. Harris's delegation sought the alteration of the existing laws governing Aboriginal people. The deputation, nearly all men of education, requested that all their people be placed under the same laws as the colonists. They had significant criticism of Moore River Native Settlement, incorporating rare documentation of the Aboriginal people's view of their experiences of that institution. The deputation asked that the 'Mogumber prison' be done away with; that the Protector be stopped from moving natives from different parts of the state to Mogumber station where they were forced to live in dirty conditions. The rule of the 'native' police was too stern. 'Native' police at Mogumber, who were described by the deputation as 'cut throats and gaol birds from the North', should be abolished.

The journalist of the West Australian newspaper who reported on Harris's deputation, included a section in his article for the *West Australian* continued the next section of his article sub-headed 'Killing Them Out'. The deputation suggested that the Protector should be a man who had a practical knowledge of the 'natives', their habits, customs and manner of living. They claimed that Chief Protector Neville was the worst enemy the 'natives' had. Harris added that his people believed that under the present [1905 Aborigines] Act Mr Neville owned them body and soul. If he was allowed to continue in control he would soon be responsible for the extermination of the race. The department which was established to protect the 'blacks' was killing them out.

The Premier provided the deputation with lengthy, possibly convoluted replies to the various points raised. The Premier was prepared to state that Mr Neville merely administered the laws and was not responsible for them. Nevertheless, he promised the deputation their points would receive an official response from his government, and if he could help then he would.

The journalist's description of William Harris was that 'he spoke in perfect English and showed no signs of erudition'[46].

The details of the Premier's meeting with the Aboriginal deputation were passed on to the Aborigines Department for comment. The Chief

Protector's response shows how he used eloquence and bureaucratic explanations which were non-committal and blameless, to deflect criticism of himself and his administration. Amongst the content of the eight pages he wrote as the government's response he attempted to derogotise Harris's character. Neville proposed that as William Harris was 'brought up as a white' he did not speak for the Aborigines who looked upon him as a 'white man'.

Regarding the term used by W. Harris of 'dumping' Aborigines in any place, the Chief Protector replied that Section 12 of the Act gave the Minister power to remove Aborigines from one place to another and place them in reserves which were used to safeguard women and children'. The warrants issued under Section 12 intended to remove to Moore River Native Settlement young girls leading a loose life, women with 'half-caste children from undesirable and vicious surroundings, or issued in the interests of the community generally'. Neville may have included this point to pre-empt any criticism his administration may get from the media should they show an interest in the Akbar-Matbar case. As Lallie's presence in the Laverton-Linden district had the potential to create a disturbance he had cause to move her.

Regarding the 'cut throats from the North', Neville stated that the 'people from the North are clean, moral, law abiding'. He continued that Mogumber was a community of three hundred inmates and that the 'Native Police' were actually 'orderlies, not police, who are appointed from the inmates, and their operations are severely restricted. Any abuse of their power is followed by instant removal from their position'.

Towards the end of the eight-page response Neville added details that inferred he was accepted by the 'natives' of his State, perhaps more so than Harris. He reiterated that Harris did not speak for the 'natives', while 'natives from Wyndham to Esperance welcome me, and constantly appeal to me and tell me things they will tell no one else'.

In conclusion, Neville used the event of the deputation to reinforce to the government the need for the Aborigines Department to strengthen its control over the Aboriginal population. Neville proposed to Premier Collier that in view of 'stirrers' like Harris, it would be better if the government increased the powers of the Aborigines Department so as to provide further protection and to see that justice was done. On the basis of Neville's response Premier Collier shelved the matter and the Honorary Minister of Aborigines William H. Kitson told journalists that the Aborigines Department had nothing to be ashamed of[47].

Neville may have been concerned that giving publicity to criticism of his administation by educated Aboriginal people could provide a cause around which could merge the potential for restlessness reported by the police in the eastern goldfields. The Harris deputation could become a springboard for organised protest by some of the Aboriginal population of Western Australia.

However, this did not occur, and there could be some explanation for this. Aboriginal people generally at this time were inarticulate. The dispersed nature of the Aboriginal population prevented them from developing a united front. They had limited organising experience. To speak out publicly for Aboriginal people would be seen not as a civil right but as inciteful and would mean for them incarceration in Moore River Native Settlement or imprisonment in Fremantle Gaol. They could not vote for change[48].

With the response to the Harris deputation out of the way Neville could focus on the ramifications of Akbar's visit to Perth. He may have seen Akbar as another source for inciting Aboriginal people. The Aborigines Department was aware that Jack Akbar was deliberately and willingly practising most undesirable collusion with Aborigines who were sympathetic to harbouring a fugitive. In spite of all the instructions and warnings that Akbar had been given by both the Aborigines and Police Departments to cease his quest to marry the Linden girl, he had adhered obstinately to his goal and remained undeterred. The Chief Protector's word and authority was to be accepted without question or debate and this Afghan would have to be taught to have regard for and fear of the King's laws. While in the Commonwealth, he was a subject of the British Empire and not aloof from the government and laws of Western Australia. He was not a citzen and could be deported at any time.

After Jack's visit to Perth the Chief Protector was more determined to build up the case against Akbar that would move the Police Department to exercise more authority over the Moslem upstart. Five days after his meeting with Jack Akbar Neville composed another lengthy letter to Commissioner Connell. He included points that would provoke the opinion that there were some questionable and undesirable aspects of Jack Akbar's character and behaviour. He was harbouring an escapee from Moore River to whom he was secretly providing provisions on a weekly basis. He also proposed to marry the girl – a forbidden marriage. Neville proposed to the Police Commissioner that Akbar was committing a breach of Section 44 of the 1905 Aborigines Act. This Section stated that 'any person who entices or persuades an aboriginal or half-caste under the age of sixteen years to leave any school or aboriginal institution without the consent of a protector, or to leave any lawful service without the like consent, shall be guilty of an offence against this Act'[49].

Neville told Connell that when Jack Akbar had visited him in his office he had stated that he had her hidden in the bush about a mile (two kilometres) out of Linden. Rod Schenk of the Mount Margaret Mission had confirmed that location in a report. Neville added that the police could acquire up-to-date information on the movements of Jack and Lallie from Schenk, as he received it directly from the 'natives'. The Schenks were willing to report what they could on Jack's movements because they were aware that the local Aborigines did not wish Lallie to 'consort with Afghans or whites'[50].

On returning to his district in the goldfields from Perth Akbar continued his carting and retail business. Now, in late March 1928, two years after the time Jack started to seek permission for their marriage from the appropriate authorities, he and Lallie faced more opposition than ever before. The missionaries could not offer any safe haven or protection to the girl and were collaborating with the police and the Aborigines Department by sending them regular reports on Jack and Lallie's activities[51]. Schenk got his information from the Wongai who were opposed to their girl's association with Akbar. If Jack and Lallie were to persist with their ambition to be married then they would not be able to be seen together by almost anyone in Western Australia – no missionary, Wongai, pastoralist, farmer, miner or policeman. The only people he could turn to if he needed assistance were Afghans, and amongst those he had developed only a few friendships. Feeling that there was almost no one to whom to turn or to trust, Jack attempted to work out what option remained for Lallie and himself so that they could get married.

There was only one option left for him to take. If Lallie and he were to be free to marry, to be liberated from being pursued by the government's authorities, free of the police net, free of punishment by her people, they would have to find a set of laws elsewhere that would give them permission to be husband and wife and permit them to feel safe. They would have to leave the State of Western Australia entirely, telling no one of their departure, and find more sympathetic authorities and more tolerant laws regarding Aborigines and Asiatics.

It was not the solution Jack and Lallie would have taken if they had had a choice. It was a heartbreaking and dangerous choice to make. Jack understood how close the kinship of the Aborigines was, how binding the Aboriginal relationship to their tribal land was. It would make Lallie extremely unhappy to have to cut herself off from her people so completely, to leave her birthplace and for some years ahead deny herself any contact with her mother and her people. Her clandestine departure would hurt her mother deeply. The elders would be offended and would want to punish both their girl and the Afghan whom they had forbidden to be her husband and who now had dared to steal her away from them.

Probably the greatest danger Jack and Lallie would have to face in their flight from the goldfields would be the threat not just to the loss of her loved ones and their freedom, but to their lives. Lallie had been associating with Akbar against the orders of the elders, and after all their effort to keep her secluded from the police and to protect her, they would be incensed when they learned that she had left them without their consent. Their interpretation of the Afghan could be that he was acting as an adulterer because some still believed Lallie belonged with Burtville Jack. Lallie would have demonstrated that she had abused their trust and their laws. The elders would sit down to discuss what was the most appropriate discipline for her and the Afghan. The mission of the emufoot man whom they would send to track Lallie and Jack would be to pursue them until he encountered them and then to throw his spear. How close to death he would make his wound would be decided by the elders.

While Lallie continued to be cared for by her people the Afghan trader commenced putting plans together for their secret escape from Western Australia. He would have to calculate at what time of day or night and of the month they should depart, what they needed to take, what mode of transport and what direction were best, and at what speeds they would need to travel so that they could gain time on whoever would wish to pursue them. He would have to outwit the Wongai who were expert bush trackers. Her people would be able to sight her, even under the cover of the bush and the night. The spearman would be committed to pursue them relentlessly for many kilometres beyond the site where other pursuers would have halted in despair. Should he fail his mission he could in turn be dealt a painful punishment. Meanwhile Akbar would have to be seen to be living his usual lifestyle so that nothing seemed irregular or aroused suspicion about his movements and behaviour. The task that lay ahead would require very clever and thorough calculating. Their race to the east over the border would be frought with danger, the route sprinkled with spies. Jack would not now give up on their marriage. He was determined to be successful.

A.O. Neville was just as determined that the police and his own department be successful in capturing the two absconded women and in prosecuting Jack Akbar for his offences. The announcement that Rod Schenk made at this time through Constable Warren at Laverton was a totally unexpected twist of events to the Chief Protector. On 17 April 1928, Rod Schenk sent a short letter to Constable Warren in Laverton to inform him that the mission had learned from the local Wongai that Akbar had moved Lallie away from Linden. They believed he had taken her in the direction of Kalgoorlie, though the Wongai were not able to tell the missionary exactly where the Afghan had her secluded. The last statement made by Schenk may have alarmed the Chief Protector. He was under the impression that Akbar had finished his business altogether at this end[52] .

CHAPTER SEVEN

Escape into South Australia and marriage

The direction Jack chose for their escape into another State was east across the Nullabor Plain to the South Australian border. From the vicinity of Linden to the eastern border, a distance of nearly 900 kilometres, they would have to keep their identity hidden from police and their potential informants. Both the Wongai girl and the itinerant Afghan hawker were familiar with disused bush tracks, engraved originally on the bush landscape by immigrant prospectors and miners during the gold rushes of the 1890s. With the gold boom passed, and many miners gone to enlist in the armed forces of World War One, the number of travellers on these tracks were fewer. The advent of the motor vehicle required roads to be located in more open areas on flatter land, so traffic was further diverted from the original routes; thus there was less probability of the couple being sighted and recognised if they took the old tracks. Jack and Lallie knew where the police patrolled most frequently, where old miners still resident in the district were camped. They knew the location of the pastoralists' homesteads, the regular Wongai bush camps and larger meeting places. Akbar could plan a route to avoid all these sites and gain a good distance between themselves and their pursuers. Jack would have to be selective of the desolate tracks. Damage to the tyres of his truck could bring their flight to freedom to grief.

He had to avoid running out of petrol. His proposed escape route would take his truck through country parallel to Lake Carey, country in which he would thread his way carefully through hilly and sandy sections of the terrain. There were a few places beyond Morgans, like

Pinjin and Yarri, where petrol pumps were installed. From there Akbar could fill up his tank and some spare drums that he had lifted onto the back of his truck. The Moslem hawker would be familiar with the distribution and location of the numerous government water tanks, the bores and dams on pastoral or Crown property, and gnamma holes and soaks all through this district.

The route also presented the threat of exposure. The vegetation of the goldfields landscape was mainly mulga bush, jam wattles and eucalypt trees which provided irregular seclusion. East of that region the taller vegetation was replaced with more open grassland interpersed with flat dried lake beds with a mixture of ground-level swamp plants and barren salt patches. The transition out of cover meant that not only would the fugitives increase their visibility, but they would have to also be on the alert for areas with less firm surfaces.

Akbar calculated that their escape out of the Morgans-Linden district should be undertaken at night. They had to cover as much distance as possible in the initial stage, to get beyond Lallie's tribal area. Once they began their journey east they could not allow any delays to put them at risk. They were both anxious to gain and maintain distance on any potential pursuers and to be free finally of all in Western Australia that had worked against their union. They knew that what they were doing now would add to the number of offences against the 1905 Aborigines Act of Western Australia. There was no turning back once they had started their bid for freedom. It would become a flight for their lives. If anyone was likely to accurately estimate the speed of Jack's movement, or the direction he was most likely to take, it would be someone in the Morgans-Linden district.

The railway line that ran from Perth to Kalgoorlie and was extended in 1917 across the Western Australian-South Australian border to Port Augusta and on to Adelaide was called the Transcontinental (or Trans Australian) Line. A telegraph line was installed along this line. Akbar would have assessed what advantage there might be of them boarding the train in their bid to outmanoeuvre their pursuers across the open Nullabor Plain. Jack realised that once the police discovered that he and Lallie had quit the goldfields and were travelling east, they would expect the fleeing couple to board the train at some stage. The police would use the telegraph line to wire all the police outposts ahead and to alert the attendants at the rail sidings to be on the watch for an Asiatic man and a part-Aboriginal girl. The police would pass a basic description of the couple along the telegraph line transversing the continent. Jack concluded that it would be in their favour to avoid the train altogether.

Jack had to minimise the visibility of Lallie. He had to devise some means of keeping her out of sight so that people would not see a couple travelling together who fitted a police description. In the first part of the journey, from around Linden and south-eastward to the rail siding of Karonie on the eastern fringe of the goldfields, Jack would hide Lallie in a trunk secured to the back of his truck. He estimated that by Karonie, a place where no-one knew them, they should have gained enough distance between their pursuers and themselves so that Lallie could come out of her dark confinement and cease her extreme physical discomfort in the trunk. She could then sit up in front, in the cabin of the truck, beside him. However, they would be driving through settlements and rail sidings and past pastoral stations which could have received the police bulletin to be on the lookout for an unusual couple on the run. When she sat beside Jack she would have to be disguised. The solution was to dress her in male attire so that Aborigines and other local settlers might think that what they perceived was an Afghan male travelling with an Aboriginal male[1].

By mid-April of 1928 Jack Akbar was finalising the preparations for their clandestine departure. He would use the nature of his business to disguise his preparations. The procedure included doing a few more trips of hawking and carting so as to demonstrate business as usual. His last genuine business trip would be a journey to Linden where he had a contract to pick up a load of sand from the Devon Mine. He would transport that sand load to Messrs Allsop and Don's Treatment Plant in Forrest Street, Kalgoorlie. After unloading it he would park his truck near the rail goods shed in Sammy Noas's backyard in Duggan Street where he would leave it hidden overnight while he made his last call on his solicitor, Cook. Though Jack would make arrangements with Mr Cook to have all his outstanding accounts brought up to date, he would not leave a forwarding address with his solicitor, as this could indicate an intention of leaving the district. Akbar had arranged privately for an Afghan friend named Mahomet to manage his shop in Morgans for a while. Mahomet's presence there would create the impression that it was 'business as usual' there also[2]. After his visit to the solicitor Jack would return to his truck and depart from Kalgoorlie for the Morgans-Linden area.

The night came finally that would cover their escape. Lallie knew these were her last moments with her mother and people and this would have brought her deep concern. Her life was about to take a dramatic change once again. After being forcibly removed from Mount Margaret mission then risking so much by making three attempts to escape from the Moore River Native Settlement to be back with her own mother and people, she was now about to leave them again, to go to a place that was further than she had ever been before, for a very long time perhaps, and she was departing by her own choice. She could not turn to any one of them to say goodbye or to tell them where they could find her one day. She had felt before the hurt and grief of a separation that had also shocked her people. This voluntary departure would shock them, and perhaps offend them. It was a very high price to pay for the type of happiness that for any Caucasian was a normal human right. In Lallie's life it may have been her only chance for happiness.

During April 1928 those who learned that Jack Akbar had discontinued taking on delivery contracts in the Morgans area had assumed that he was transferring his carting business to elsewhere in the goldfields. The thought apparently had not occurred to any of them that the Afghan storekeeper might decamp permanently well beyond the goldfields. The change in his regular patterns of movement had been so subtle that it was quite some time before the constabulary would sense any need for alarm[3]. The gradual realisation that the girl Lallie was not being seen about with her own people might not have been alarming initially to the police. They had been informed that she was spending some time away from her mother travelling about in Jack's company, and he kept her secluded at times to hide her from the police. The police were confident that they were in receipt of most current and reliable information from the missionary to whom the Wongai communicated. The constabulary thought that it was only a matter of days before the order would be sent from their District Inspector at police headquarters in Kalgoorlie for the arrest of the Moslem storekeeper as well as the Linden girl. The police perspective of the situation was that the Afghan was almost in their grasp rather than slipping out of it.

This absence of visionary thinking aided Akbar and Lallie's chance to escape. It was supplemented by subsequent police reports that reflected their self-assuredness that when the Morgans Afghan travelled the countryside he did not go beyond his field of regular customers and income. Constable Perks at his Gwalia police station near Leonora learned that Jack Akbar had closed his store at Morgans. His information was that the Afghan was trailing around mining centres in his motor truck, and had his goods and perishables consigned to him at different railway stations to which he would go to collect orders for those mining and other settlements. Due to his current itinerant activity

Akbar's home was transferred to Comet Vale, a railway town[4].

Subsequent to Perks's report from Gwalia, District Inspector Spedding Smith in Kalgoorlie ordered a trace to be kept on the Afghan. He instructed Sergeant McGuiniss to contact clerks at various railway stations to check on the current whereabouts of 'that Akbar and Lallie Matbar'[5]. Neither the District Inspector nor the constabulary posted out in the bush seemed to have yet hit upon Jack and Lallie's flight. They may not have considered that the couple were capable of such courage.

The first person to realise that Akbar and Lallie were attempting to flee was Rod Schenk. The thought occurred to him a short while after he had learned that Jack Akbar had 'finished business altogether in Morgans'. As he was also aware that Lallie had not been seen very much lately in her people's company he extended his suspicion to include the thought that perhaps Jack had gone with Lallie. When he came to realise what it was that Akbar had finally schemed to do, Schenk was faced with a dilemma.

His correspondence reflected how his duties and loyalties were committed in two directions. He signed all his letters and reports that went to the police or the Chief Protector of the Aborigines with, 'Yours in Christ and the aborigines'. In the case of Jack Akbar fleeing the goldfields and perhaps having Lallie with him, Schenk had to once again decide to whom he should give his loyalty. He had to choose between the Aborigines and the Police Departments on the one hand, or the Afghan who had with him the Aboriginal girl who was a member of the people whose souls he believed he had come out here to save for Christ. As a Christian he worked and lived for those in need of help and love. However, because his work was with the Aborigines who were the wards of the Chief Protector, to serve the Aborigines he had to serve their Chief Protector. Rod Schenk was a man of the law and preached and practised respect for authority. The Christian Church and the government, both fundamental to Schenk's life and existence, were now pulling at him in a mental tug of war. He needed to be true to both without doing a disservice to either.

The missionary made a decision. With the assistance of two probationary missionaries and some Wongai who were skilled at tracking, Rod Schenk formed a posse which would go in pursuit of Jack and Lallie. Schenk may have hoped that if his group could catch up with the fleeing couple before the police did, then perhaps he could think of some way in which he could make things a little easier for the couple. By now his ration depot was up and running. Perhaps he could persuade the police and the Chief Protector to let him keep Lallie at his mission, so that she was under their supervision but not removed from this district nor imprisoned. Hopefully, Schenk could convince Neville that on being returned to the mission Lallie would get the appropriate care and training she needed and that he would work with her people to find her a husband who Neville would consider met the criteria of an appropriate choice.

Rod Schenk and his company gave chase but they lasted only about half a day. When Rod got back to the settlement he said to his wife Mysie that 'it was no use continuing to give chase to Akbar because they would never catch him'[6].

The missionary had not persisted for very long in the chase partly because Jack was in a truck and the transport available to Schenk at the time was a light spring-cart. Some of his possee had to track the couple on foot. Rod Schenk could have had an underlying motive for the timing of his return. By collecting a group of people together and going in pursuit of the Afghan and the Aborigine Rod Schenk was able to demonstrate to the police that he was just as concerned as they were in attempting to stop some runaways. Schenk's action that day may have been an attempt to cover what privately he and his wife Mysie were truly feeling. They were 'aiding and abetting in their hearts'[7].

Not long after Rod Schenk's return with his posse it was confirmed that Lallie Matbar and Jack Akbar had departed from the district. As a consequence, the missionary soon received a visit from Constable Warren of Laverton who came to interview the Schenks about the matter. Warren believed that because of their direct association with the local Wongai the missionaries may have heard rumours or information of which the police were not yet in possession. Warren's responsibilities included reporting on any movements that occurred in his district subsequent to the confirmation that Akbar and his Aboriginal girl had fled the area. Depending on what he learned from his enquiries in the Morgans-Mount Margaret area and what he stated in his reports, Constable Warren could influence the District Inspector to decide to order a police posse to track the absconded couple.

During the interview at Mount Margaret mission Constable Warren asked Rod Schenk for whatever clues or specific details he may have collected from the Aborigines about the precise direction the couple may have taken and how long ago they may have left. Rod Schenk told the Constable that they were no wiser for their efforts. After completing his investigation and concluding all formalities with Schenk, the Constable said he was eager to get on to Morgans that night and left Mount Margaret[8].

The outcome of the interview was disappointing for the officer. When writing up his subsequent report Warren could not see a reason to enthusiastically recommend to his superior that a search party should be formed promptly. There was no theory about the direction to take, and there was doubt about how successful a police search party could be in locating and seizing the couple when the Aborigines who were expert at reading signs in the bush had no clues.

Akbar's thoughts would have been focused on what might lie ahead. He was propelled onward by his single-minded determination to cross the border of Western Australia, and by the thought that a message of their disappearance had by now filtered throughout the goldfields and had triggered off a number of pursuers. Akbar would not have been aware of Schenk's posse, though he would have suspected some activity to have occurred by now. Lallie's people would be very angry and offended. They would be considering the type of punishment Jack Akbar and their girl Lallie deserved and would most likely be arranging for a spearman to commence tracking them down. The police would be acting under instructions to search out evidence of their whereabouts and would send wires on ahead to alert their outposts. The police order would be that the couple were to be apprehended on sight.

Of all those in pursuit the one causing the most concern to Jack and Lallie would be the Wongai spearman. The pursuer most likely to deduce which way Jack would be travelling with Lallie and the least likely to quit would be the emufoot man bearing the potentially lethal spear. If and when he caught up with the fleeing couple there would be no preliminary legal debate in a courtroom before the sentence was served for the crime they had been accused of by the Wongai. He would spear either Lallie or each of them in a most injurious or lethal way.

Constable Warren's unproductive visit to Mount Margaret mission was followed up with further investigations. The reports the police at various stations in the goldfields wrote and sent as an outcome of further investigations were characteristically unsynchronised, delayed by 'red tape' and thus not very conducive to prompt police action. The reports that came into police district headquarters in Kalgoorlie and forwarded to Messrs Connell and Neville in Perth did not agree even on which direction the constabulary in the field thought Jack and Lallie were heading. After reading the rather confusing reports of the 'present whereabouts' of Lallie and Jack, the Chief Protector of Aborigines may have become concerned that the police might lag behind in their own pursuit so much as to fail totally at catching up with the couple or apprehending them. Some were still expecting their search for Jack Akbar and Lallie Matbar to take them to Laura and her three children. In order to give the constabulary some stimulus to maintain their vigilance and pursuit, and a more constructive direction in which to pursue their fugitives, on 23 April Neville sent a telegram to Inspector Spedding Smith at Kalgoorlie. He advised the Inspector that he was very certain that Akbar was endeavouring to remove Lallie 'to Kalgoorlie thence east'[9].

The contents of the telegram Inspector Spedding Smith sent the next day to the Chief Protector reflected the lack of decision making and direction afflicting the police at this time. The Police Inspector stated that the two Constables he had out after Lallie Matbar, Akbar, Laura and the three children had not yet returned and added the vague comment that careful inquiries were being made still about the whereabouts of Akbar[10]. There was not yet verification about which direction Akbar had taken, or that Akbar had gone in an easterly direction.

From 24 April, the police continued to focus their work around their stations in the goldfields, from Southern Cross to Kalgoorlie to Linden, from Burtville to Laverton to Leonora. They interviewed colonists, missionaries, Aborigines either at Mt Margaret or in the bush, and Afghans. Their summary reports, all coming into police headquarters in Kalgoorlie for collating, continued to contain confusing and dissimilar information. It was realised eventually that there had been some individuals who were sympathetic to Jack and Lallie's case and that these people had been deliberately supplying the police with misleading information.

Just after 24 April, Sergeant McGuiniss received at his desk in the Kalgoorlie office a very detailed report from one of the Constables out in the goldfields who had made extensive enquiries about Jack Akbar's location. The details in his report reflect some of the misleading information self-chosen collaborators of Jack and Lallie gave to police. The Constable declared that he could not find any trace of Lallie Matbar, Laura Quince or Jack Akbar either around Kalgoorlie or in the vicinity of Linden. He had tracked down and interviewed in Kalgoorlie Mrs Forrest and Mrs Tucker who were two 'half-caste women' from Laverton. They stated that they had not recently seen Lallie Matbar and had no knowledge of her present whereabouts[11].

The details that the Constable had collected on Akbar were vague. He had been informed that Akbar sent a telegram from Leonora to an Afghan named Mahomet at Linden, asking him to look after his interests. By the time the Constable acquired this information it was estimated that Akbar had already gone overland to South Australia.

The policeman apparently did not follow up the potentially significant reference to Mahomet, though he did conduct interviews with a number of other Afghans including one named 'Abbebullah' who recently travelled with Jack Akbar on his visit to the Aborigines Department in Perth. Abbebullah informed the Constable that he was under the impression that Akbar had gone to Meekatharra, a settlement in the opposite direction from the eastern border, but he had no knowledge of whether or not Lallie was with him or of the whereabouts of Lallie Matbar. Neither did he see her during the time Akbar was in Kalgoorlie[12].

Mining people who had haulage contracts with Akbar were interviewed. Both Mr Norton, owner of the Devon gold mine in Linden, and Mr Hill, manager of the same, informed the police that Akbar did not return to Linden after he collected a load of sand from them to take to Kalgoorlie on 10 April[13].

The police were still not clear whether or not Laura and her children were in the company of Lallie and Akbar. Their information remained unreliable and inconsistent until they encountered a brick wall of silence and ignorance. Overall, they received little information of substance and little cooperation in their efforts to do their duty.

The piece of information that finally diverted the attention of the police to the possibility of the couple having fled to South Australia had to be reported twice before being seriously noted, and these details came some time after the couple had been present in that state. The brief information that Police Constable F. Woodfin provided on 28 April 1928 to his Inspector proposed that from the number of people he had interviewed he concluded that if the police did not find Akbar to the west on the Murchison then it was possible that he had gone to South Australia[14].

Woodfin's report was given a higher priority for the Police Commissioner in Perth by a subsequent wire from the District Inspector in Kalgoorlie. The latter advised the Police Commissioner that informants were saying that Jack and Lallie had made for the Murchison via Leonora-Wiluna, or may have gone to the eastern States[15].

Another explanation for the lack of success by the constabulary, and for their tardiness in verifying conflicting information, was that other duties called. Most police stations out in the field were manned by one Constable, and the area for which they were responsible could be a few hundred square kilometres. They preferred not to venture too far afield in their investigations or patrols at any one time, as they could not leave their stations unattended for too long. Their motivation to travel great distances, alone, over many hours in pursuit of missing persons waned, particularly when they considered the quality of their quarry. Some of the police officers considered that the characters of the quarry they were now under direction to locate were that of a 'rebellious, recalcitrant Mohammedan' and 'one or two half-caste women who were experienced absconders'[16]. Such categories of persons did not deserve too excessive a waste of time, money or energy.

Constable Warren at Laverton police station was one of the Police Department's most relentless and resourceful sources of information on the Akbar-Matbar case during the months from March to May. In his goal to learn of the exact location of Lallie, Laura and her three children or Akbar he chased up leads and interviewed residents and Wongai. When he had received information that Lallie was suspected of being at Greenhills, a gold mine near Linden, he followed up that lead and attempted to locate her between there and Morgans, expecting to find her in the company of Laura and the children and perhaps Akbar. His pursuit was to no avail. He made inquiries amongst the Afghans in the district and was at least able to ascertain that Akbar went through to Eucla taking the girl with him dressed in male attire.

Constable Warren obtained knowledge that soon a large number of Aborigines were to gather around Morgans from all different parts of the district. When that occurred he visited those people and questioned them about Lallie Matbar. All those with whom he spoke informed him that they did not know where she was, though some conjectured that she may have been with Akbar. Warren was not given any further clue in being able to locate his quarry or get a charge against Akbar[17].

During that May the police achieved some success for all their persistence. At least they did find Laura Quince and her three children. By that time Laura had a tribal husband to provide for her and the three children. This normally would have satisfied the Chief Protector in considering that his wards were satisfactorily being cared for. However, the seriousness of Laura's offences made this information inconsequential at this time. She and the children would not be allowed their freedom and would be pursued until recapture by the police. The success of the constabulary in this case was due largely to the assistance of an informant, a local pastoralist, who may have considered his action as being dutiful and supportive, rather than informing and betrayal. Mr Green, manager of Edjudina station, provided the valuable assistance that helped the police encounter and take into custody Laura Quince and her three children. The family were separated from the tribal man caring for them and were sent to the Moore River Native Settlement where they were interned for some time. It is known that Laura's youngest child eventually became a resident at Mount Margaret mission where she went to school and grew up. Green's cooperation was acknowledged by Inspector Spedding Smith who praised him to the Police Commissioner in Perth[18].

While the police focused their search for Lallie and Jack in the goldfields the couple had managed to make their getaway without any obstruction. On quitting the goldfields Akbar drove his truck down towards the Transcontinental Line. When he reached the safety of Karonie rail siding Lallie emerged out of her confinement in the trunk. She changed into male attire and resumed her seat in the cabin next to Jack.

The next phase of Akbar's plan was that from Karonie they would motor, travelling parallel to the railway line, into South Australia. At the rail siding settlement of Rawlinna they would alter their path, moving away from the proximity of the railway line and travelling south-east then east. They would use the main dirt road which would take them past the large sheep station named Balladonia. That homestead which was in a remote location had a telegraph station and Jack realised that if the police suspected that he and Lallie were travelling that way a message to alert the manager there could be transmitted very quickly along the wire. Akbar hoped that once getting south of Balladonia he could drive on to join up with the main road that connected Kalgoorlie with Adelaide. With two forty-four gallon petrol drums filled to capacity on the back of his truck he and Lallie could travel as far as Eucla without wasting time. Another telegraph station existed there, so having extra petrol did not require them to pull into the town and refuel, thus avoiding contact with people who might have heard the police description and be able to recognise them. Passing Eucla Jack and Lallie crossed the border and drove across the Eyre Peninsula on to Ceduna and then to Port Augusta.

Once across the South Australian border Jack did not waste any time in getting Lallie to the capital city. There was a possibility of a threat to their safety there in that Adelaide had a police headquarters and word of their escape may have been wired ahead from Western Australia. The fleeing couple could not take much time for respite. Once in Adelaide Jack would have to make enquiries about where to procure lodgings, a marriage certificate and achieve the goal of their long journey. In May

1928 Jack and Lallie motored safely and without any impediment into Adelaide, the capital city of South Australia.

On arriving in Adelaide Akbar found some temporary accommodation for them amongst some familiar company. He had learned from camelmen in the goldfields who had travelled the crescent shaped route between Adelaide, the far north of South Australia and westward over the State border into the goldfields that some of the original immigrant Afghans had built in Adelaide a large, solid white mosque with four tall turrets. It was located in Little Gilbert Street in the south-west corner of the square mile of the city and the grounds included some rooms for temporary lodging. As the couple intended to establish their married life in Adelaide Akbar and Lallie stayed there while Akbar made further enquiries about rental accomodation available in the vicinity of the city or the suburbs.

Another task for the caring Jack Akbar was to familiarise himself with the laws and regulations of this State regarding Aborigines and mixed marriages. As he had done in Kalgoorlie, he sought the advice and counsel of a solicitor. He took on the services of Mr Kevin McEntee, a 'law clerk' in the company owned by Messrs. Joseph Nelligan and Joseph McCarthy of Scottish House, Numbers 9,10 and 11 Waymouth Street, Adelaide. McEntee became a crucial legal adviser to Jack Akbar during the next several months.

On 23 May 1928, Jack Akbar married Lallie Matbar at the Registry Office of Births, Deaths and Marriages in Flinders Street, Adelaide, in the State of South Australia. Whereas the marriage certificate stated the father of Jack Akbar to be 'Dilber Akbar', Lallie did not provide a name for her father. Jack stated his age to be 48, and Lallie claimed hers to be 23. Their marital residence would be in the near northern suburb of Enfield, which was on the rural-urban fringe of the city. Mr K. McEntee, who resided at St Ann's Estate, New Glenelg, was one of the two witnesses of the marriage. The second witness was Sheik Abdul Kader, an 'Oriental Interpreter' who was a prominent businessman in the large Afghan camel town of Marree in the far north of South Australia[19]. This man was more educated than many of the camel drivers around Marree and was often requested to read their letters from home, to write letters or business papers for them, and to interpret for those camelmen whose English was not very accomplished[20]. When he travelled down to Adelaide he took accommodation in Gouger Street which was in close proximity to the mosque.

Mr and Mrs Akbar now resided in South Australia where the laws

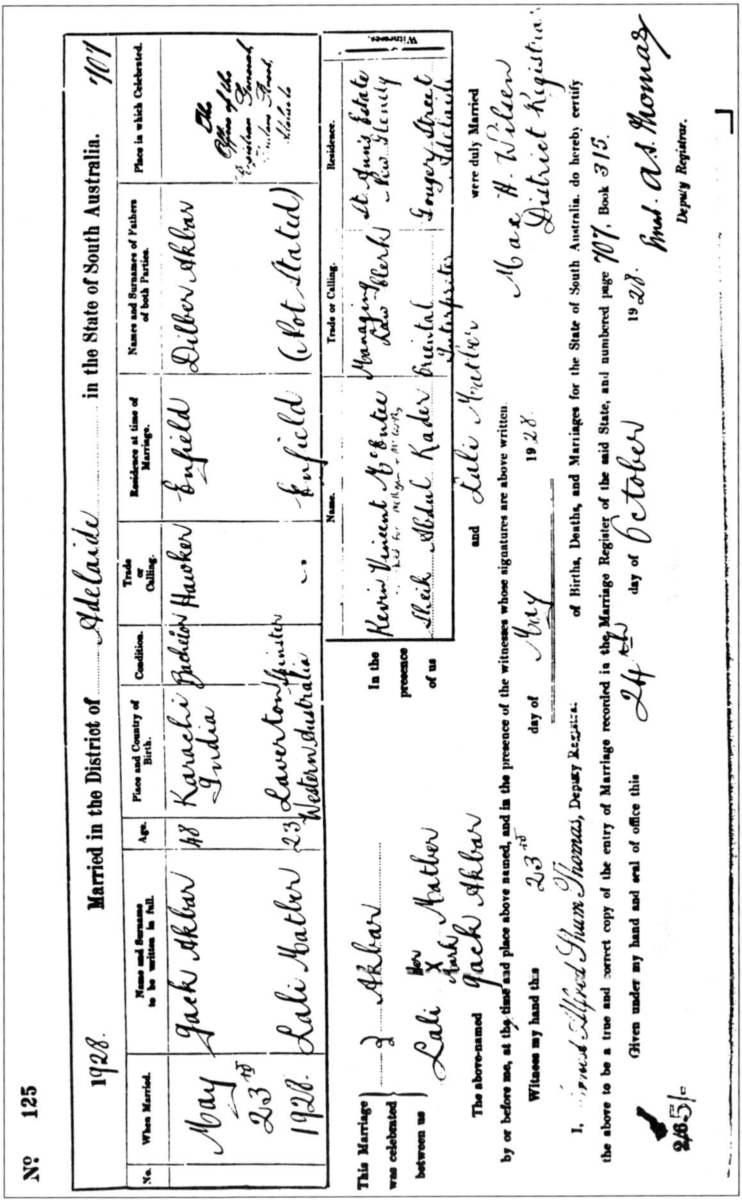

No. 125

1928. Married in the District of Adelaide in the State of South Australia. 707

No.	When Married.	Name and Surname to be written in full.	Age.	Place and Country of Birth.	Condition.	Trade or Calling.	Residence at time of Marriage.	Names and Surnames of Fathers of both Parties.	Place in which Celebrated.
	May 23rd 1928.	Jack Akbar	48	Karachi India	Bachelor	Hawker	Enfield	Dilber Akbar	The Office of the Registrar General Flinders Street Adelaide
		Lali Matber	23	Laverton Western Australia	Spinster	"	Enfield	(Not Stated)	

This Marriage was celebrated between us: J Akbar; Lali her X mark Matber; Jack Akbar

In the presence of us:

Name.	Trade or Calling.	Residence.
Kevin Vincent McEntee	Managing Law Clerk	St. Ann's Estate New Glenelg
Sheik Abdul Kader	Oriental Interpreter	Gouger Street Adelaide

The above-named Jack Akbar and Lali Matber were duly Married by or before me, at the time and place above named, and in the presence of the witnesses whose signatures are above written.

Witness my hand this 23rd day of May 1928. Max H. Wilson District Registrar

I, Ernest Alfred Shum Thomas, Deputy Registrar of Births, Deaths, and Marriages for the State of South Australia, do hereby certify the above to be a true and correct copy of the entry of Marriage recorded in the Marriage Register of the said State, and numbered page 707, Book 315.

Given under my hand and seal of office this 24th day of October 1928. Ernst. A.S. Thomas Deputy Registrar.

2/6 5/-

The marriage certificate of Lallie, spelled 'Lali Matber' and Jack Akbar, 23/5/1928, Adelaide, South Australia.

were more tolerant. Their new life had not commenced in the happiest of circumstances but they had the determination to make the best of what was available for them in their new freedom. Their past was in another State of Australia and would not confine their future. Perhaps now in their own home in Enfield Jack and Lallie could feel safe, secure, free and independent of rules and regulations that wanted to separate them. Lallie was given a life now in which she would not have to run or hide, would not have to fear the forced removal of herself or any of the children she and Jack might have together. Though Jack's income would be very meagre for a while, she would no longer be expected to participate in the undesirable ways she had had to resort to in Western Australia. Jack and Lallie could feel assured that if they had any daughters of their own they would not be faced with that way of life as an option. Jack and Lallie hoped that the police of South Australia would not learn of her time in and abscondments from Moore River Native Settlement, nor how since May 1927 Lallie had lived as a fugitive, nor how since mid-April until late May Jack and Lallie had eluded the Western Australian Police and Aborigines Departments, the missionary and the Wongai spearman in order to be married.

Jack and Lallie had finally found peace, a freedom to live their life the way they wanted to and a chance for their own happiness. In their quiet, private, relaxed moments Jack and Lallie may have seen their situation from the point of view of a kind of personal victory. Had the unjustly treated couple been more successful than the senior administrator of Aboriginal affairs in Perth?

From their home in the northern suburb of Enfield Akbar maintained his contact with members of the South Australian Moslem community. Many of the men with whom he talked were camel drivers from the Ghan communities of the far north South Australian railhead towns of Marree, Farina and Port Augusta. Through the Moslem men who came down from the northern towns to pray at the Adelaide mosque Jack renewed communication with a friend he had known in Coolgardie in the goldfields but who was now living in Farina. To get away from the city and their proximity to the police headquarters, Akbar made arrangements to travel north and visit his friend Gool Mahomet and family at home.

Gool Mahomet's family was the single, established Afghan family in Farina. There was no regular Ghan camp like the one about seventy kilometres up the road at Marree. Afghans who lead camel strings loaded with wool from the large pastoral properties along the Strezlecki and Innaminka tracks came into the railway yards at Farina to drop their load off so that the wool could be railed south to the capital city from which it was distributed to distant markets. The camelmen would camp a while near the railyards and visit Gool Mahomet.

Gool Mahomet had made his permanent home in Farina with his wife Desire (pronounced 'Des-e-rey'), who he married in Coolgardie where she was believed to be a French governess. Their four children were Sallay, Sherali, Sayira and Marjan. Two other children, Payrosa and Willie, had died at very young ages. By the time that Jack and Lallie Akbar visited this family in Farina Gool had given his wife the Moslem names of Miriam Bebe[21]. The Farina couple offered their guests hospitality, friendship and peace.

It was not an uncommon practice for the Afghans who had settled in the far northern Ghan towns of South Australia to legally marry young women of Anglo-Saxon descent. They often had two marriage ceremonies, the second with a Moslem priest the 'mullah', presiding[22]. Mona, the eldest daughter of Jack and Lallie Akbar, was told many years after her parents visited Farina that her father and mother were married by the Afghan mullah also[23].

On returning to their home in Enfield, Adelaide, Mr and Mrs Akbar considered making a home for the family expected in the near future. They wanted to start a married life just as most couples had. Their income would be erratic until Jack had found a regular kind of job or established a business. They began to settle into living the life they had wanted to live in the goldfields but could not at any price.

It was not until August 1928, three months after Jack and Lallie had fled to Adelaide, that confirmation of their whereabouts reached Connell and Neville. On 21 August, as an outcome of persistence together with several interviews, Constable Warren was able to advise the District Police Inspector that he had definite information regarding the exact whereabouts of Jack Akbar and 'the gin'[24] Lallie Matbar. The couple were at this time in Farina, South Australia, receiving the assistance of an Afghan named Gool Mahomet who lived there. Constable Warren aslo informed Inspector Spedding Smith that Akbar had married the girl at the Registry Office in Adelaide by special licence, for which he paid thirty pounds[25]. By the time this information reached A.O. Neville, Jack and Lallie had been husband and wife for about three months.

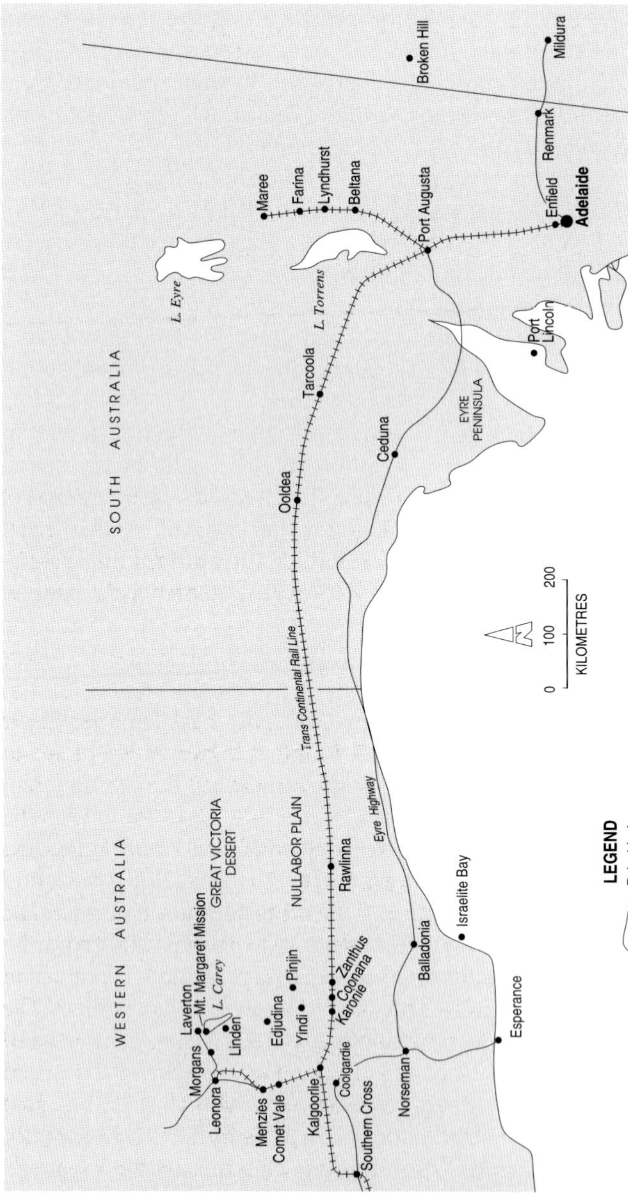

Escape into South Australia followed the rail line.

C H A P T E R   E I G H T

Extradition

The defiant couple who had dared to run the gauntlet for the trophy of freedom had not managed to run beyond the thoughts of the Chief Protector of Aborigines in Perth. That exacting and virtuous administrator was most unlikely to dismiss the fact that a disagreeable Afghan immigrant and an Aboriginal ward had been more successful than the Chief Protector in combination with the Aborigines and Police Departments of Western Australia.

The occasional public criticism of his treatment of Aboriginal people did not distract him from taking a case to its end. He would prefer to ignore criticism, to defer a response to it, or respond only when required, with his usual diplomatic yet non-committal style. Not long after the deputation of Aboriginal men led by William Harris approached the Premier of Western Australia regarding the treatment of Aboriginal people by the Chief Protector's office, more criticism was directed to the Premier of Neville's administration. At their 1927 annual conference the Western Australian National Council of Women produced a number of resolutions aimed at supporting the need for better protection of the Aboriginal people, as well as the establishment of proper reserves and patrols by the Western Australian Government. The Secretary conveyed their resolutions to the Honourable Premier who, in turn, on 19 August 1927, passed them to the Secretary of his Department L.E. Shapcott. By 29 August the despatch with the resolutions, prepared by the Premier's Secretary, was on its way to the administrator most appropriate to provide a response, the Chief Protector of Aborigines A.O. Neville. It was not until nearly a year later, in August 1928, that Neville provided a response, and it was worded in a manner that cleared him of any intentional maltreatment. It was his opinion that no action was necessary in this connection: 'This Department is doing all that is possible for it to do with the means at its disposal and the matter of reserves has received special attention'[1].

The timing of public criticism and of events in the Akbar-Matbar case could have been a concern to Neville. The media was willing to publish any story they encountered about Neville's administration that contained controversial matter which could direct more criticism at him. Should they learn of the Akbar-Matbar case with its range of issues they could present the facts in a way that suggested there was reason for the public to be concerned about the Chief Protector's administration of the Aboriginal people. Neville would not want the media to give publicity to the Akbar-Matbar case so soon after the Premier had read the proposals of Harris and his deputation and the resolutions of the Western Australian National Council of Women.

At the same time Auber Neville would have been mindful of possible repercussions from the combined success of Akbar and Lallie of escaping from Western Australia and marrying. Such flaunting of authority could provoke the Aboriginal population between Morgans and Laverton to become unsettled and even insurgent. Through her insubordinate behaviour, her successful escape from Moore River Native Settlement, her outrunning of the police and regaining of freedom, all without being held accountable or punished, Lallie had the potential to catalyse her people into rebellion against the police and the Aborigines Department. The Aborigines could be less willing to be compliant with the regulations of the Aborigines Act and with the orders of the police. The police and the Chief Protector of Aborigines classified Lallie as a serious offender and fugitive, but to her people she could be percieved as a heroine, as someone successful in opposing the system that they considered suppressed their lives. With the ration depot now located at Mount Margaret mission the police had lost a means of intimidating the local Aborigines. With some settlements and ration depots in the eastern goldfields being closed during late 1927 there were fewer police staff on hand to rally quickly at a site of Aboriginal insurgence or conflict with the police. In such a potentially volatile atmosphere the indigenous folk would be difficult to intimidate, to catch, to arrest or to contain once arrested.

Neville was concerned further that it could appear to the public that the small Aborigines Department in Perth did not have much authoritative clout or control over its charges. The populace and media, quick to criticise any new incidences of apparent failures by any of the politicians or government administrators, were accordingly ever watchful of Neville's treatment of his wards. Neville may have thought that public exposure of the Akbar-Matbar escape to South Australia and subsequent marriage, and the potential for disorder in the eastern goldfileds this could create, would be detrimental to the reputation and public image of his administrative post, which was already considered insignificant[2].

Though the couple seemed to be beyond the extent of the jurisdiction of the Western Australian authorities, Neville did not close the file on Lallie Matbar. From his point of view, regarding the enforcing of regulations of the 1905 Aborigines Act, the business with Jack and Lallie Akbar was not finished, nor could be. As repeat offenders who had evaded punishment, the Morgans Afghan and the Linden Wongai ought not to have been at liberty. He most probably believed they had no right to a normal and liberal life until they had been made to pay for their offences. Neville had emphasized the point to Police Commissioner Connell earlier that their departments together needed to be perceived as the 'all powerful ones'. The public and the eastern goldfields Aborigines needed to know that the result of those two departments combining their forces was the recapture of even the most insignificant or insolent individual absconders. So far, the newspapers had not continued an interest in this case. Neville would have been preoccupied with suppressing published information that demonstrated that the active association of two disciplinarian government departments and a Christian mission had been unsuccessful in tracking and seizing one defiant couple. Should the public be made aware of this case the Chief Protector would prefer that the impression made on them, government peers and indigenous population, be that Messrs Neville and Connell were able to make an example of Jack and Lallie.

In his next move in dealing with the Akbar Matbar case Neville focused on extending the influence of his office, his Department and the Western Australian Police Department into territory in which these had no jurisdiction. To gain the collaboration of the Aborigines Protection Board in Adelaide, the South Australian Police Department and the South Australian Crown Law system, Neville would have to include the weight of an authority that represented the law. He would commence with attempting to convince Police Commissioner Connell of the importance of persisting in tracking the absconded couple.

On 14 August 1928, Neville wrote a letter to Connell to impress upon him the gravity of staying with the Akbar-Matbar case. He proposed that if Connell had not done so already, he should make enquiries of the Police Department in Adelaide about Jack and Lallie Akbar. Neville added that he would make similar enquiries of the Chief Protector of Aborigines in Adelaide. The grounds the Chief Protector gave to Connell for pursuing such enquiries was that as Akbar had removed this girl from the state he had committed a breach of Section 9 of the 1905 Aborigines Act. This Section stated that:

> Any person who, without the authority, in writing, of a protector, removes or causes to be removed any aboriginal...or a female half-caste from one district to another, or to any place beyond the State, shall be guilty of an offence against this Act.
>
> Before such authority is given the person desiring such removal shall enter into a recognisance with a surety or sureties, at the discretion of the protector, in a sum which the protector considers sufficient to defray the expenses of the return of such aboriginal or half-caste female to the place from which such aboriginal or half-caste is to be removed[3].

His job required him to seek assistance in having Akbar dealt with accordingly[4].

After instigating the proposal to the Police Commissioner, Neville commenced to approach the representative of the law, the Under Secretary for Law in the Crown Law Department, the Honorable Charles Vickery. He informed him of the possibility that Jack Akbar had committed several breaches of the 1905 Aborigines Act and that the guilty parties were now out of the state and unpunished. By providing a summary background of the culprits and listing Section 9, Section 42 and Section 44 of the Aborigines Act as all probably being contravened by the Akbars, Neville hoped to impress upon the administrator of the Crown Law Department the gravity of their escape and thus provoke him to beseech the collusion of the authorities in South Australia. Neville left Vickery with the notion that if the matter was not dealt with promptly the parties would become increasingly difficult to trace at a later date[5].

While Vickery read Neville's correspondence the Western Australian Police Department took action on the Chief Protector's recent proposal. Police Commissioner Connell was able to persuade the Police Commissioner of South Australia to cooperate in the Akbar case. By 31 August, the Plain Clothes Branch of the Metropolitan Police Station were conducting enquiries into the whereabouts of Jack Akbar and his wife

Lallie whom they presumed were still residing in Adelaide.

The Adelaide detectives were able to report to their superior, Inspector Horseman, that an Indian named Jack Akbar was located at Olive Street, Prospect, that he was a hawker and had arrived recently from Western Australia. He was residing at that address with 'Lala Matber'[6]. The Inspector arranged for a copy of this report to be sent to the Police Commissioner in Perth, who in turn informed Chief Protector Neville. The involvement and productivity of the South Australian Police Department must have confirmed for Neville his anticipation that their involvement would move the case against the Akbars more quickly.

Now that Jack Akbar's present whereabouts had been confirmed, the Crown Law Department agreed to support the Police Department of Western Australia by promptly drawing up a warrant for his arrest. This warrant could be transferred to the Police Department in South Australia. To serve it there on Jack would necessitate his extradition to Western Australia. When Jack Akbar would be taken into custody they would have Lallie also.

The warrant for the arrest of Jack Akbar was typed up by the Police Department, authorised by the Crown Law Department on 2 September 1928, and a copy was sent to Neville's office for his files. The despatch prepared for Adelaide containing the warrant for Akbar's arrest was stamped 'Urgent'[7]. Neville would have been pleased and relieved by the two departments' response to his appeal for their assistance with the Akbar-Matbar case, and by their active collaboration with authorities in a state beyond his influence.

However, the Chief Protector would have been caught by surprise when he noted that the Crown Law Department had made an amendment to the number of offences Jack Akbar could be charged with. The details on the warrant recorded that Akbar was to be charged with only one offence, that against Section 9, which was removing a ward of the State beyond the relevant boundaries without authorisation. The Crown Law Department considered that the evidence relevant to the other two Sections was not substantial enough. Also, the same Department pointed out to the Chief Protector that his office would be expected to finance the extradition expenses[8].

This process by the Crown Law Department to verify what charges could be made against the Afghan may have reduced their number on the warrant, but in Neville's view the behaviour of Jack and Lallie remained serious. With the cooperation of the two Western Australian departments and the South Australian police Neville may have felt that he was getting closer to achieving his goal — the arrest, then discipline of Jack and Lallie Akbar. He sought to impart the seriousness of the Akbars' case by taking it up with the Under Secretary, now Mr Hampton. The Chief Protector insisted that apart from committing a breach of Section 9 Akbar had committed other breaches. This recalcitrant Afghan was outdoing himself in that the Aborigines and the Police Departments had to deal with a man who, as a paramour, had removed one of Neville's wards, who was part-Aborignal, from the State without permission. It was important that this couple did not set a precedent for others who might consider similar action. Neville needed to have all part-Aborigines under his control, confined to Western Australia, and marrying appropriately so as to maintain the pace of assimilation.

Another point of concern Neville wished Hampton to be aware of in this case was that the marriage between these parties had been outlawed by the Aborigines Department from the first time Akbar had ever mentioned it[9]. Since it was the Chief Protector who had requested the support of other government departments in obtaining the return of the Akbars to Western Australia, Neville confirmed to the Under Secretary that his department would bear the costs associated with the extradition.

The Under Secretary for Law took note of the arguments in this most persuasive recent correspondence from A.O. Neville. He saw to it that the Police Department was undertaking without delay the paperwork for the extradition of Jack Akbar. By 2 October the Police Department was completing the Form of Indemnity for Jack Akbar's extradition. Detective Sergeant Doyle took the papers to the Chief Protector of Aborigines for completing and signing. This legal form was then transferred to two South Australian Departments, that of Crown Law and of the Police. It would give them the authority to take Jack Akbar and his wife into custody in preparation for an extradition exercise[10].

In Adelaide Mr and Mrs Akbar would have been unaware of the mounting collusion between the Western Australian and South Australian authorities, who altogether were arranging for their arrest and extradition. They were most probably certain that they were safe, anonymous and free of their past. They had been in Adelaide for about five months when the South Australian police were given the order to move in on them.

On the Wednesday night of 3 October 1928, Jack answered a knock on his front door. The result of his answering that knock was to once again change their lives. Three men who were total strangers to him stood in the doorway. The first man to speak introduced himself as Senior Detective Ferguson and his two colleagues as Detective Sergeant McMahon and Police Constable Miller who was from the Plain Clothes Branch. The Senior Detective asked Jack to acknowledge his identity and enquired if his wife was at home. Jack replied, 'Yes, Lallie is with me. I have married her since I have come to Adelaide.' The man in charge then took a folded white paper from his jacket pocket and holding it up in front of the resident informed him that 'he had a provisional warrant for his arrest for removing a half-caste girl from Western Australia'[11]. One can imagine what Jack Akbar must have felt and thought at this declaration.

Having confirmed that both of his quarry were present Senior Detective Ferguson informed Jack and Lallie Akbar that the three law officers were there to escort them to the Adelaide lock-up where they would spend the rest of the night. On the following day Jack would have to appear in the Adelaide Police Court. After that they were very likely to be kept in custody until an escort arrived in Adelaide from Western Australia to take custody of them. They were then to be taken back to Perth.

On the next day, 4 October, Jack Akbar appeared in the Adelaide Police Court. Those present included the magistrate Mr E.M. Sabine, and Jack Akbar's legal representative Kevin McEntee. The charge put forward by the Crown's representative was that Jack Akbar had removed 'the native girl Lallie Matbar' unlawfully from Western Australia between 1 May and 31 August 1928, thus breaching Section 9 of the 1905 Aborigines Act of Western Australia. The case of the Afghan and his Aboriginal wife from interstate, and the offence of which they were accused, seemed enough out of the ordinary for it to be given a small amount of publicity by the local newspaper[12], which at the time did not consider it controversial enough to follow up.

In defence of the accused McEntee proposed that hc would bring in evidence that would demonstrate that Akbar did not commit the offences read out in court. He intended to prove that the warrant for the return to the west of the accused Jack and his wife should not be issued. Also in Akbar's favour was the realisation by the magistrate that this court could not continue to try and judge the Afghan on a matter that was not an offence against the laws of South Australia. Eventually, the solicitor appearing for the prosecution, Mr H. Allchurch, asked the magistrate for an adjournment of this case until Friday week, October 12. This amount of time would allow for a police escort to arrive from

Western Australia. So that his client and his wife were not kept in the lock-up all that time, McEntee made a request to the magistrate that bail for his client might be granted, and it was[13].

The adjournment gave Kevin McEntee time in which to assemble evidence so as to compile a thorough case in his client's defence. He may be able yet to convince the Western Australian authorities to cease the process of the extradition and altogether prevent the relocation of the couple and the possible ruin of their marriage and life. The Adelaide law clerk set about dissecting accusations that had been raised in the court. McEntee trusted and believed in the goldfields couple and knew they were no villains, that their plight and their desire to be together were genuine, that their hearts were honest and their consciences free of guilt.

From his conversation with Jack Akbar Kevin McEntee could see the irony of this case. If the Afghan had wanted simply to live 'in sin' out of wedlock with the young Aboriginal woman and then be rid of her once desires were satisfied, as long as the police did not know of the Afghan's behaviour, the law would have left them alone. Many of the male Anglo-Saxon population in the western goldfields were doing precisely that with Aboriginal girls, even though the Aborigines Act made it unlawful. As long as these men remained anonymous to the local police they were left unpunished. If Jack Akbar had not asked the Chief Protector for permission to marry Lallie, Neville may never have sent any order to have Lallie removed from her people and taken to Moore River. However, Jack had insisted on marrying Lallie, and as a result of his persistent morality, had drawn much attention to themselves. They had gone through so much adversity just to be able to live as any normal, average couple. They had been hounded by police, threatened with the loss of their lives, and now they were being prosecuted by the law.

Kevin McEntee hoped to deter the Western Australian Government from going through with the extradition by persuading the Chief Protector of the relative insignificance of the case. He also believed that there was doubt that the senior administrator in Perth had a strong legal case. On Monday, 8 October 1928, in his office at the solicitors' firm Nelligan and McCarthy, Kevin McEntee composed a letter to A.O. Neville. The Adelaide solicitor assured the administrator of the Aborigines Act that the South Australian courts sought the enforcement of justice in the case of Jack Akbar and Lallie Matbar. However, these courts would prefer that justice was done in the matter that did not result in divorcing these people from each other and did not need Akbar to be returned to Western Australia to stand a trial. He pointed out to

Neville that the Crown Law Department in Western Australia may not be able to win in court because his examination in Adelaide of the details of the case indicated that there could be an error in the claim that Akbar had breached Section 9. McEntee understood that Lallie had always held an intense affection for Akbar, and on several occasions when she ran away from the Native Settlement in Western Australia she did so entirely on her own volition because she was dissatisfied with the living conditions there. McEntee further stated that Lallie had genuinely fallen in love with Akbar and desired to marry him. Subsequently, when Akbar came to Adelaide the girl came across from Western Australia entirely of her own free will. There is no suggestion of anything approaching abduction and the marriage had eventuated as a result of the girl's desire to live with him.

The Adelaide 'law clerk' (the title of McEntee's position according to Lallie's DCS file) also put it to Neville that there was not a case for neglect of the girl. The parties, who were presently living at Prospect, were happy and settled. The girl was well clothed and excellently cared for.

McEntee concluded his letter by encouraging the Chief Protector in Perth to take pressure off the case of Jack and Lallie Akbar. He requested him to impress upon the Western Australian police authorities that it would be ethically inappropriate and unjust to proceed with the charge against Akbar, particularly in view of their present happy life together. It would be the wisest thing for the Chief Protector to call for the withdrawal of the Indemnity Form and terminate the extradition[14].

In his Perth office Neville may have been elated to hear that Jack and Lallie had been finally placed in police custody and that Jack Akbar had appeared in the Adelaide Police Court. It would now be only a matter of days before he could expect to see Jack and Lallie standing before him before going to court for their offences. He could be seen then to be the final victor.

However, it was not to be as simple as anticipated. A few days after Jack Akbar made his court appearance in Adelaide, the Chief Protector of Aborigines of Western Australia received two letters that originated in McEntee's office in Adelaide. One letter was the comprehensive one composed by McEntee himself, as legal counsel for Jack Akbar. The second letter represented an Adelaide resident who was a client of McEntee. Miss A. Smith lived with her mother Mrs J. Smith at Leicester Street, Parkside, an inner suburb of Adelaide. She had learned of Jack Akbar's presence in Adelaide and his legal problem when she had read the article referring to the illegal removal of a half-caste in the Adelaide newspaper. She knew of Jack and Lallie. Becoming very concerned for their situation Miss Smith contacted the office of the Afghan's legal representative and made an appointment to come and talk with him.

Smith informed McEntee that she had done some voluntary work at Mount Margaret mission in 1927 and in that time had seen Jack and Lallie around the mission. Of what she knew of them, she was sure that Lallie had not been enticed, lured or abducted across the state border by the Moslem. This claim by Smith strengthened McEntee's suggestion that it was inappropriate to accuse Jack Akbar of breaching Section 9 of the Western Australian 1905 Aborigines Act. To strengthen the defence of Jack Akbar McEntee invited Smith to put what she knew in writing and then he would send that letter off to the Chief Protector in Perth.

In the letter she composed for Neville, Smith informed him that in correspondence she had received recently from Mount Margaret mission she had learned that Lallie had been very unhappy at Moore River Native Settlement. When Lallie learned that others had run away from that place she attempted the same. Later Akbar talked with her about going to Adelaide. Akbar recognised that in Adelaide he would have to act in an honourable way and marry Lallie. Smith was aware that they were now living together very happily. Akbar had provided his wife with a nice, comfortable home and was feeding and clothing her.

Further down in her letter Smith proposed to the Chief Protector that Mr and Mrs Akbar would be model citizens if they were left in peace to build their lives. They were currently living lives as self-respecting citizens in one of Adelaide's suburbs, and because of the nature of their characters she believed they both had a good future with productive lives ahead of them. Lallie could speak English very well and the training she had received at the mission and the native settlement would now stand her in good stead as a wife. From her knowledge of Akbar, gained during her stay at Mount Margaret, she had known him to have always acted in an upright and honourable way and be always very willing to help, not only missionaries, but anyone else. Here in Adelaide she knew him to be working as a trader and to be willing to live quietly and respectably. She believed that Jack did what he thought best, not wanting to do anything wrong, and acted honourably all along for Lallie's sake.

So as not to antagonise the Chief Protector by inferring that he had made an error in making the decisions that he had, or that he had misguided other authorities in initiating the arrangement of the Indemnity Form and extradition, Miss Smith employed some diplomacy. She put her case to the Chief Protector from a Christian perspective. She commented that she appreciated that in his capacity as the protector of the indigenous people he was striving to do what he thought was best for those under his charge from a Christian standpoint. However, in spite of all his care things had turned out not as he expected. So, it would seem best from all points of interest and from a Christian standpoint, to let Lallie and Jack live clean and happy civilised lives in South Australia, instead of sending them back again to the West. There also, it was most likely that Lallie would have to go back to her life of loose morals among those who would not care so much for 'the souls of our dear Natives'.

Smith concluded her case to Neville by claiming that if his prayers were united with those of Mr McEntee and herself in favour of ceasing the extradition of the couple, then 'perhaps out of this chaos, two souls might be led nearer to Christ'[15].

In his office in Murray Street, Perth, Neville read the two letters from Adelaide. This shrewd administrator recognised how they both insinuated that Jack and Lallie's actions did not warrant the accusation that Akbar had breached Section 9, that they argued that there was no real evidence for a case in court, that the extradition was not warranted, and that the standard of the present lives of the wanted couple should eliminate the need for any discpline to be dealt them relevant to their past behaviour. Neville's reaction to the two letters from Adelaide in October 1928 can only be guessed at. What is known is that they did not have the intended effect.

Instead, they alerted Neville to the fact that there were firm sympathisers in Adelaide for the wanted Western Australian couple. The voices of such people could be dangerous to his ambitions. Neville was aware that to make public the fact that the girl had followed Akbar to Adelaide, rather than was lured there by him, could crack the case at its foundation. If McEntee's words fell on amenable legal ears, then Neville's one main argument for having Jack extradited would no longer have any substance in either a South Australian or a Western Australian court of law.

Neville dwelled on the letters. He did not want any doubt raised in Perth about the charge made against Jack Akbar of breaching Section 9, or of the necessity of the extradition of Jack. It would serve his purposes more if the letters appeared to be intending to interfere with the process of the law, as well as to be creations of fictitious, emotive pieces of reporting. Lurking behind their contents, nevertheless, was the fact, noted by Neville, that there was a need to obtain some evidence that demonstrated absolutely and irrefutably that Lallie was taken out of the

State by the Afghan. In order to raise doubt about the motives and the integrity of the Adelaide writers and to find the piece of infallible evidence, the Chief Protector would need the further cooperation of the Police Department.

On 12 October, Auber Neville sent the two letters from Kevin McEntee's Adelaide office to Police Commissioner Connell. In the personal note he attached to them Neville conveyed to Connell how important it was that if the evidence implied the girl followed Akbar to Adelaide, when as a matter of fact it is understood that such was not the case, the whole case would break down[16]. He proposed to Connell that McEntee's letters were obstructing the process of justice and that they be filed by his staff as incriminating evidence.

Neville then attended to uncovering that piece of missing evidence. It would not be easy. A few days later in Adelaide its absence was to provide a snag also in Neville's extradition plans.

On the 12 October, the police escort sent from Western Australia to extradite Jack and Lallie Akbar arrived in Adelaide. Neville would pay the Police Department 50 pounds to cover the expenses associated with the return journey of Detective Alfred Henry Parker, despatched from Kalgoorlie police headquarters [17]. The officer had left from Kalgoorlie by train on the Saturday and arrived in Adelaide on Sunday 14 October. While the Transcontinental Line transported the detective eastward across the Nullabor Plain six months after Jack and Lallie had travelled that same direction, a Perth newspaper called the *Mirror* published a sympathetic story on this couple. The title of the article was, 'Not allowed to love'[18]. This was the second time that the Akbar-Matbar case was given media exposure. As the reporter was not given a by-line it has not been possible to trace his career so as to find out what attracted that person, or that paper's editor, to this unusual case. It was not possible to verify if the Adelaide newspaper article had caught this journalist's attention, or if the case of the Akbars had stirred up interest in its own state because it was another attempt to direct criticism at Neville's administration.

In Adelaide, the procedure for carrying out the extradition did not go as smoothly as Detective Parker was assured. When he met with the South Australian Crown Prosecutor Albert A. Wolff at his office he showed him the papers he had brought from Western Australia. One was the authorisation for the extradition of Jack Akbar. The others were a set of copies of some papers from the file on Lallie Matbar that was kept in the Kalgoorlie police headquarters.

NOT ALLOWED TO LOVE!

Because He Was an Afghan and She a Half-Caste

Perth Officialdom Seeks to Separate Wedded Pair

ADELAIDE, To-day.

An almost unbelievable story of the persistency and expenditure of time and money on the part of Western Australian officialdom in order to separate a dark-skinned husband from his dusky wife was brought to light by "Mirror" investigations here to-day.

The story began when Akbar, a well-known Afghan on the W.A. Goldfields, wooed, loved and hoped to marry Lalla Matbar, a half-caste aboriginal maid.

To live with Lalla without entering the state of matrimony, as many of his less honorable countrymen and white men have done, was against Akbar's code of honor, and when Lallah said "Yes" to the impressive question Akbar applied to the W.A. Aborigines Dept. to wed his lady love on her nineteenth birthday.

The department gave a stern negative, but

LOVE WILL FIND A WAY

so when all his importunities to officialdom failed Akbar and his maid made other plans.

Mr. A. O. Neville, Protector of Aborigines

With a motor truck the couple set out across the Nullabor Plains, much the same as Akbar's ancestors' crossed the wastes of his country for many centuries.

There was more broad humanity in the laws of the Southern State and the ceremony was performed at Farina, where the couple settled down in their love nest.

They might have been forgotten by Western officials if Akbar had not openly written West for the reference necessary for a hawker's license. This reminder of his existence caused the Aborogines Dept. to set the ponderous and expensive machinery of law into motion.

Under some section of the Aborigine Act the department ordered the arrest of the Hindoo and his wife. Some days ago the couple were taken from their home to the Adelaide lock-up, where they are held pending the arrival of Detective Parker on Sunday's express.

The expenses of the escort and the accused's fares will probably be £150, all of which Akbar might have saved the country if he had been content to live with the girl without an honorable desire to go through the marriage ceremony.

The law's anxiety in this case is a striking contrast to that of the two thieves who stole a motor car at Kalgoorlie, which they abandoned half way between Port Augusta and Kalgoorlie owing to engine trouble, continuing the journey by rail. When the culprits were located officials decided that escort and transport expenses were too costly, so no action was taken.

Yet good Government time and a lot of good money is being spent and an escort is sent half way across the continent to separate two dusky lovers. Little wonder that the white man's law is often an enigma to those who are not of our color.

("The Mirror" believes that it is not yet too late to end this ridiculous application of the law, and we suggest that the Protector of Aborigines (Mr. A. O. Neville) acts to that end immediately. Otherwise the Minister should intervene.—Ed. "Mirror.")

The story of Jack and Lallie was given precedence in the daily newspaper, the Mirror, *13 October, 1928. Note that the comment of the editor at the bottom of the article calls for ministerial intervention if A.O. Neville did not act to 'end a ridiculous application of the law... immediately'.*

Wolff perused the papers thoughtfully, as a matter of procedure, before giving the visiting detective the authority to serve his order on the couple in Adelaide. The absence of the highly sought after, critical evidence was now picked up by Wolff. Though the file papers viewed by the Adelaide Crown Law prosecutor contained relevant records from both the Aborigines and the Police Departments in Western Australia, Wolff pointed out that they did not contain any interviews with Jack or Lallie since their departure from the goldfields. Constable Warren's entries had led to the belief that there was evidence which stated soundly that Jack took Lallie across the state line. However, Wolff divulged to the detective that he could not cite any such evidence amongst the papers, nor any paper that had the admission by either absconders of their part in breaching Section 9.

Wolff did not want to seem disagreeble or to be hindering the process of the law. His outlook was to see that it was just. The detective was welcome to serve the order for Jack Akbar's extradition. However, Wolff imparted to the detective that as he saw it, the charge against Akbar would fail in court. The legal system in Western Australia would find it difficult to convict Akbar unless 'evidence could be obtained of him having had the girl with him when he called at the stations en route to Eucla'.

The detective comprehended the logic of the Crown Prosecutor and responded by attempting to convey to him the frustration he had experienced since coming to Adelaide at not being able to meet the absconders so as to be able to conduct an interview with them. Lallie's DCS file relates that as the Akbars were out on bail there was some reason why they were not available to the detective. Wolff offered advice that could ease the work of the Kalgoorlie visitor. He suggested that in order to obtain the fundamental missing evidence that would secure success in court for the Chief Protector, it might be useful to send a wire to the Constable who was based out in the district from which Mr and Mrs Akbar had come. This Constable Warren at Laverton could perhaps obtain evidence from any of the local Afghans that would ascertain that Akbar left with Lallie for Eucla. Meanwhile, Wolff would communicate to the South Australian Police Department that it was satisfactory to cooperate with Detective Parker and that Jack and Lallie Akbar should be taken into custody in preparation for their extradition.

Detective Parker left this meeting with the advice offered by Prosecutor Wolff in his mind. He would mention Wolff's advice to Neville when he returned to Perth. Meanwhile, he had a purpose in coming to Adelaide – an extradition to carry out. Once the South Australian police had collected Lallie and Jack Akbar and placed them in Detective Parker's custody, the Kalgoorlie officer booked himself and the two people in his custody on a steamer bound for Fremantle, the port of Perth. They arrived there at 7 a.m. on 1 November 1928. Detective Parker travelled first class paying ten pounds for his ticket, and the two prisoners were placed in third class with a cost of eleven pounds and twelve shillings for the pair. From Fremantle the trio took the train into Perth[19].

On his return to Perth the detective went to the Aborigines Department to meet with Chief Protector Neville. In his conversation with the administrator Parker passed on Wolff's advice that the lack of concrete evidence would make it difficult to prove there had been an abduction; and the suggestion that Constable Warren was in the position to make enquiries that might find the missing information.

This was essentially a victorious moment for the Chief Protector. Jack and Lallie Akbar were back in his state finally, in police custody, and their court case was pending. The Chief Protector did not want this couple to get away from him a second time. Their capture, their return and the trial of their case could be used ultimately to demonstrate to the citizens, his peers and senior colleagues, the public and the goldfields Aborigines how his small Aborigines Department could assemble so much authority, manpower and influence, even beyond its own state. The populace would see how indispensible was the small Department, and how it and the Police Department had ultimately won. One wonders, though, at the significance of the victory when one considers the total size of the pursuing party and the amount of bureaucratic energy, time and paperwork, compared to the status of and the real crime committed by those captured. It could be compared to a 'Pyrrhic victory'[20].

While rallying a lot of human effort and time to persist with the Akbar-Matbar case Neville had attracted more public criticism of his activities and goals. For some politicians some of the things Neville did in his official capacity appeared to be extravagant and the Perth newspapers echoed their comments. On 3 November 1928 strong criticism was made of the Chief Protector of Aborigines A.O. Neville in the Legislative Assembly during the debate of the Estimates of Expenditure of the Chief Secretary's Department. Some members believed that what Neville had put up for viewing was excessive, in spite of the fact that the Aborigines Department had a small budget. The 149 regulations that A.O. Neville gazetted that week further stirred the government which suspected that this administrator was attempting to exceed his authority. Mr Marshall (Labour representative for Murchison) proposed that the current regulations under the Aborigines Act already intended to place the Australian Aborigine in chattel slavery. Some of these new regulations were 'childish, frivolous and inhuman and others were drastic'. The remarks provoked by the combination of the excessive expenditure and the extraordinary number of regulations, the quality of some being a debate in itself, lead to questioning Neville's character and reviewing his qualifications: 'Where had Mr Neville come from, anyhow? His appointment came to him because he was in the public service and there was no other position for him'.

Mr Mann (from the political district of Beverley) suggested that Mr Neville had not been a success in the administration of native affairs. 'To put forward regulations like he had and ask Parliament to agree to them was disgusting. If proper action was to be taken he should be discharged and an officer appointed who would be capable of doing the job properly'.

Another member of the Assembly, Mr Lathan, added that the present Chief Protector 'desires to extend his powers considerably beyond what was ever intended by the [1905 Aborigines] Act'. The result was an amended set of regulations[21].

In the face of this recent criticism Neville did not want to confirm for those who doubted him that he could expend so much in extraditing two people back to Western Australia and then still could not bring them to court. He took Mr Wolff's advice, followed his suggestion, and requested Detective Parker to send a wire to Constable Warren to instruct him to interview Laura Quince who was now at Mt Margaret mission. Perhaps she could give evidence against Akbar[22].

By 2 November 1928, Detective Parker had received the report of Constable Warren's interview with Laura Quince. Laura had stated that when she left Lallie Matbar outside of Linden, 'Akbar was associating with Lallie and they were going to go away to Adelaide by motor truck'[23].

The detective passed on Warren's details to the Chief Protector and to the Crown Law prosecutor. Laura's evidence did not assist the State in giving it a watertight case that could convict the Afghan of abduction. She had not made it clear in her interview whether Jack had tricked or forced Lallie to go with him, whether Lallie had chosen to go with Jack of her own free will, or had followed him against his wishes. The concrete evidence that proved beyond a doubt that Jack had removed the Aboriginal girl against her will from their State and so had breached Section 9 still did not exist. The available evidence stipulated that Lallie had gone interstate willingly, and had planned to do so, with Jack Akbar. She had not been abducted, nor enticed to leave a reserve beyond her free choice. The Police Commissioner advised Neville that, 'According to the information now obtained, there is no evidence to show that Akbar removed the girl from the State, and the charge must fail, so far as Akbar is concerned'[24].

Another factor weakened the case that Neville had the authority to keep Lallie interned. According to her marriage certificate her age was given to be about 23 years of age. According to the progression of details in her DCS file, Lallie's age would be estimated to be around nineteen or twenty. Whichever number is accepted, Lallie was no longer legally a ward of the Chief Protector. She was also legally married and thus in the care of her husband.

Neville on his own could not deduce any overlooked legal measure to which he could resort to keep Lallie and Jack Akbar confined. In his search to find the single unnoticed technicality, the Chief Protector sought the counsel of the government's legal officer. On 6 November Mr C. Greif, the Crown Law solicitor whose office was in Warwick House, St George's Terrace, Perth, visited Neville in his office. It was most likely that he would be the prosecutor for Jack and Lallie Akbar in court.

Greif was given the opportunity to read through the file on Lallie and was informed of the details of the case against Akbar the defendant. It was evident to Greif that the sole basis of the case against the Afghan was that he was accused of breaching Section 9. Greif was made aware of the new evidence provided by Laura Quince. The Crown solicitor came to the same conclusion as had Mr Wolff in Adelaide, that as far as the evidence stood there was no case against Akbar. The solicitor asked the Chief Protector if it would be possible for the charges to be withdrawn[25].

With Jack and Lallie finally confined in a police cell in Perth, Greif's suggestion must have sounded absurd to the Chief Protector. Now that his department was finally in the position to bring Jack and Lallie to court so that punishment for their offences could be decided on and served, a man of the law was suggesting that they be given their freedom. The Chief Protector was aware that without that crucial piece of evidence he would have to agree with the suggestion of the government's legal representative, and with the consequent proposal that the charges against the Afghan husband and the Wongai wife be withdrawn. However, Neville could not abandon the whole episode without some form of retribution being levelled against the returned absconders.

He was mindful of the possible range of consequences to be faced if Jack and Lallie Akbar went free and undisciplined after all the manpower, money and authority had been collated by him to bring them back. Certain questions may have been going through Auber Neville's mind at this time regarding how he would appear to his peers and superiors: What impact would their dismissal from custody have on his public image and his career? Though Neville had attempted to discredit Jack Akbar in the past, who now would the public perceive as the buffoon? What would be the effect on the Aborigines in the goldfields? Would the Aborigines see Lallie as a heroine around whom they could actively rally?

The Chief Protector pursued the case of the Akbars a little further with the government's legal representative Greif, hoping that in their conversation a means by which Neville could maintain some influence in their lives would become obvious to him. Then he could demonstrate that he was a public servant who was ultimately not to be outmanoeuvred. Greif provided the Chief Protector with that means.

The Crown solicitor drew the Chief Protector's attention to the second part of Section 9 which implied that persons released from police custody could be expected to enter into a Bond with the government. Greif pointed out to Neville that Jack Akbar had not entered into any recognisance with any protector before leaving Western Australia so as to arrange 'a surety or sureties in a sum which would be sufficient to defray the expense of' that half-caste girl returning to the place from which she had left. Also, there had been much expense incurred already regarding the retrieval of Lallie. It would be better that the Aborigines Department was seen to be attempting to show an awareness of the girl's cost to them and that she would not incur any further costs, time and inconvenience. So, the surety could be a substantial figure. The fact that Jack Akbar was legally her husband and guardian was relevant. In getting to the point, Greif proposed that one option remaining to Neville was to commit Jack Akbar to enter into a Bond with the Government of Western Australia for taking full responsibility of Lallie. The purpose of the Bond would be to oblige Akbar to ensure that the girl was well provided for and would not become a charge of the State in which they resided, which most likely would be South Australia. This would be the means by which Neville could have some influence or control in the Akbars' lives. The Bond would bind Akbar to him legally. If Akbar broke any conditions of the Bond he could be disciplined[26].

What Greif suggested was the solution to the dilemma in which

Neville had found himself. The Bond could also take away some of the public criticism directed recently at the Chief Protector of Aborigines and his Department. The legal system in two different states had declared there was no case against the Afghan. The dedication and single-mindedness with which Auber Neville had applied himself all this time to this case in order to demonstrate his competency in dealing with its indigenous wards had not imprinted the image on the minds of the public that he had hoped for. His outspoken political critics considered that with regard to this case the application of the law had been stretched ridiculously in trying to make a point. The cumbersome, overwhelming intricacies of officialdom set in motion by this bureaucrat seemed to the public observers to have been drawn out for too long and consequently any rational reasoning and semblance of humanity or Christianity had been swept aside[27].

The Chief Protector was determined still to maintain his credibility as a professional and senior servant of the government. The exercising of the Bond over Jack Akbar may have been an accessory to this. If Jack Akbar was at any time to break the conditions attached to the Bond, then he would be breaking the law. Should such an incident occur then perhaps the State could proceed successfully with the arrest of the couple and finally the government could outwit them and score a sound and final victory.

Neville was most agreeable to having the Bond drawn up. However, perhaps contemplating recent public criticism and his public image in the future, he considered that one more step should be taken in the procedure of drawing up the Bond. He did not want to leave it to chance that he could lose face, or that he had to give in, should something go wrong with the exercising of the Bond. He did not want to be seen as the official who did not really know his own regulations, who set up a process of the law and the involvement of the Police Department so as to have the charges against Jack Akbar made, then was made to release him because he had apparently mismanaged the case and had not seen soon enough that the charges were not backed up by sufficient evidence. If he was the one who gave the authority for the Bond then should anything be erroneous he would be held as the one accountable. Neville would rather have it appear that any decision he may have made was overridden by a higher authority. At this time the Chief Protector advised Greif that the decision to go ahead with the Bond should rest with Mr Kitson, the Minister controlling the Aborigines Department.

Greif arranged for the papers of the Bond to be drawn up then submitted to Minister Kitson for his approval and signature[28]. Detective Parker arranged for the release from police custody of Jack and Lallie Akbar and they found temporary accomodation at the Perth mosque. This was located on the corner of William and Robinson Streets, just north of the city centre, and within walking distance of the Aborigines Department and the legal counsel's office[29].

The next task for Greif was to inform Jack Akbar of the Bond and explain its conditions. When Greif visited Jack Akbar at the mosque he was able to inform him that he could be hopeful about taking his wife out of Western Australia and that they could be free of the Police and Aborigines Departments. They could retain their freedom and residence in South Australia permanently. Once the Bond was signed by Jack the warrant for the girl and the case against himself would be dropped. They would be free citizens with no criminal record[30]. All Jack needed to do was to agree with the arrangement about and the conditions of the Bond. The solicitor made it clear to Jack that the fundamental condition of the Bond was that he would be expected to pay five hundred pounds to the Aborigines Department if Lallie ever attempted to leave him and to return to Western Australia.

However, being told that they were able to leave the state and travel east again as free persons with reputations saved did not evoke the expressions of delight in Akbar that the solicitor had anticipated. Akbar explained to Greif a concern that was preoccupying him. Though he was Lallie's provider Jack did not have money with which to back up the guarantee that he would be agreeing to once he signed the Bond papers. At the moment Jack Akbar had no money whatsoever. He had money owing to him, but was not in the position to collect it. He also owed his countrymen so much money that he dared not ask to borrow any more. Though he was very pleased to know that he could take Lallie to their home in Adelaide he could not do so because of his penniless situation.

The only way Jack and Lallie could leave Western Australia was with financial assistance. Greif took to Neville the proposition that arose in their conversation at the mosque. If the Aborigines Department was prepared to pay the steerage fares for himself and Lallie back to Adelaide, then Jack would leave with her as soon as it could be arranged. Without this assistance Jack and Lallie would have to stay in Western Australia until he earned sufficient money to pay the fares. The Crown solicitor informed Neville that he supported this idea[31].

While waiting for the return of the Bond papers from Minister

Kitson's office, Greif visited Jack Akbar again in the mosque to further analyse the Afghan's financial situation. The Moslem priest, the mullah, was present at times to assist Jack with language difficulties or with any financial or practical queries that were raised in conversation and that needed clarification by Akbar.

Jack had also had more time to think about the implications of the Bond in their lives and had more points to raise with the legal adviser. This time Jack stated that he was reluctant to take on the condition of the Bond which could eventuate in owing the Aborigines Department a large amount of money, and attempted to avoid that agreement. Akbar argued that there would not be any need for a Bond if they were to stay in Western Australia. He explained to the solicitor that if he stayed in Western Australia, where he was 'very well known', he could get work and earn the money to keep Lallie cared for properly. It was necessary for Jack to consider where he was most likely to get work and could keep Lallie safe. If they went to the goldfields where Jack was known and likely to get some work the Wongai spearman might still be waiting to complete his task. If he took Lallie to South Australia where they would be safe from tribal reprisal he would be a stranger there and find it difficult to get work.

Even though going to South Australia by steamer was cheaper than even travelling by train, Jack made the point that even the cheapest fare was too much for his means at this time. He was not able to tie himself down to repaying the fare for him and Lallie to travel interstate to restart their own lives.

Akbar had also given some thought to what his financial and legal position would be if one day Lallie chose to leave him. He raised the issue of his wife being Aboriginal and thus very close to her family and people. Jack would do all he possibly could to maintain and protect his wife. He would never dessert her or leave her neglected. However, in spite of his efforts she could still leave him one day to come back to her people. Jack made the point to Greif that Lallie might run away from him as she had already done from the native settlement, not so much because he was not good to her but because she missed her own people so much. Though this would not be of Jack's doing this would still be a breach of the conditions of the Bond. He suggested to Greif that it would not be reasonable to expect anyone to go surety under those circumstances.

The various issues Akbar raised about the conditions of the Bond made an impression on the legal adviser. Greif came to think that there was something worthwhile in what the Afghan said. Later that day the solicitor reported to Neville on his further discussion with Jack Akbar. The solicitor suggested to the Chief Protector that the Afghan's reasoning had some merit. He was compelled to agree with Akbar's contention that it would be very difficult to force Lallie to stay with him if she did not want to. Looking at the case from all angles Greif felt sure that it would be a very difficult thing to expect anyone to enter into a bond under these circumstances. He proposed to Neville that a condition of the Bond be amended to take into account the Aboriginal character of Jack's wife. A Bond could be entered into the effect that so long as Lallie lived with Akbar he would maintain and properly care for her. The condition that she must stay away for ever from any particular district needed to be amended. Greif advised that it would be wiser to state that so long as Lallie of her own accord lived with Akbar she would not go near any Aborigines[32].

Both Greif and Neville continued to see that there was some concern in permitting Jack and Lallie to remain in Western Australia. Lallie's DCS file records that he and Neville were mindful that Lallie's own people still wanted to settle a score with her and the man they had forbidden her to marry[33]. The emufoot man had never caught up with them when they fled to the east, but the punishment still had to be meted out. If Lallie and Jack stayed here a serious crime – murder – could be committed. Both Neville and Greif agreed that it would be best all round for the Akbars to leave for South Australia.

On 9 November 1928 the Bond papers arrived at Greif's office. They were signed by the Honorable Mr Kitson and now required the signature of Jack Akbar. The contents of the papers included the amendments that were an outcome of Greif's discussion with Akbar at the mosque. The terms also stated that Jack Akbar should take his wife Lallie Matbar out of Western Australia within fourteen days, and after their departure that Jack Akbar should do everything in his power to prevent Lallie Matbar from returning to this state. However, if Lallie were to leave Akbar without his consent then the above written Bond or obligation would be void. At the mosque Jack Akbar viewed the papers and, most probably pleased about the amendment, signed them agreeably in the presence of Greif who also signed them[34].

The condition in the terms of the Bond that released Akbar from repaying the Aborigines Department five hundred pounds if Lallie left him may have been privately another disappointment for Mr Neville. Should she ever carry out that act she would be free of Neville, and Jack would not be in debt for that substantial sum of money. There seemed to be only one minor means left by which Neville might still have some influence in the lives of the Akbars.

On the occasion that Jack Akbar signed the Bond papers Greif requested him to sign another paper. It acknowledged that the Chief Protector of Aborigines had made a loan to Akbar to cover the cost of the steerage fares for the couple to go to South Australia. Jack Akbar agreed to have that loan paid off within six months from 17 November, 1928[35].

Now that the future of Jack and Lallie Matbar was decided, the Police Department was no longer required to provide assistance in the case. To finish his involvement in this case, Detective A. Parker prepared his final paper work which included a page titled, 'Expenses incurred in the return of Jack Akbar and Lallie Matbar, from Adelaide, South Australia, to Perth, Western Australia'. He had to account for how he had spent the fifty pounds given to him by the Chief Protector's office[36]. On 9 November, Detective Parker boarded the train in Perth that returned him to his home station, the District Police Office in Kalgoorlie.

Something impelled Auber Neville to resist closing the case of Lallie Matbar and Jack Akbar. He had left the final decision about conditions of the Bond to his superior the Honorable Mr Kitson, Minister in charge of the 1905 Aborigines Act. Yet for Neville there remained some unfinished business. If a decision could be made at this late moment to impinge on the freedom given to the Akbars, the authority to implement that action rested at ministerial level. Neville was aware that the couple had from the 9 November, the day Akbar and Greif signed the Bond papers, to the 23 November in which to depart the state. Perhaps Neville could uncover in these final two weeks some transgression that could bring this couple back into custody.

After a few days of contemplating what course he could take, Neville came to a decision. On 14 November he put himself to the labour of composing a lengthy and comprehensive letter. He planned to document in it all the issues relevant to the Akbars' case and to use their combined weight to at least raise doubt in the mind of his superior and the higher levels of government about how correct their decision was to allow the Akbars to go free and to leave Western Australia without any degree of punishment. Perhaps then they may rescind their decision and hold the Akbars back for punishment.

One issue the Chief Protector raised early in his long letter was that the freeing of repeat offenders without giving them a trial when they were in police custody was a poor role model of appropriate behaviour for the indigenous population of Western Australia. Such success by one of their women could have encouraged them to galvanise their dissatisfaction and energy and to move to rebellion. This was reason enough for the constabulary to take measures against the Akbars.

Neville incorporated in the letter the implication that the characters of Lallie and Jack were dubious. At least three charges had been brought against Akbar. Two had been dropped and the surviving one, that he breached Section 9, was withdrawn because the police evidence could not be substantiated. Though this brought about their release from police custody Neville wanted Mr Kitson to appreciate the wider implications of the Akbars' actions.

The Chief Protector attempted to portray a defiant Moslem to the Minister. When Constable Perks repeatedly told Akbar that his marriage to an Aboriginal girl was prohibited and he would not be granted an exemption, the Afghan went beyond the Police Department and the acceptable channel of communication and approached a solicitor to represent him. Mr Kitson should be aware that there were wider implications for the community if the couple were allowed to go entirely free of any control or punishment and remain in this state. The Chief Protector divulged to his Minister that after Lallie escaped successfully from Moore River Native Settlement a certain number of civilians defied the police by rallying to her support. Her whereabouts were concealed from the police for some time by Akbar, the Wongai and 'certain whites conniving to this end'.

There was the issue of the girl's morality to be taken into account. At the time her case came to Neville's attention he learned that Lallie had had two children and was about to give birth to her third. It was alleged that 'white men' had been responsible for her condition formerly, and Neville declared that Lallie was always running after white men and cohabiting with them continuously. At one time it had been reported that both Lallie and Akbar were reported to be suffering from venereal disease. Though Neville did not have any reliable evidence to support these last two claims, he inferred to Kitson that such immoral behaviour would be what one would expect from a bush girl. To embed in the Minister's mind that Lallie was most assuredly a girl of highly questionable character Neville mentioned there was a strong suspicion that in the case of her three children, who had all died, she 'most likely connived to this end'.

Neville included the issue that the quest by Akbar to marry this 'native girl' aggravated the 'natives' of the Linden-Morgans area. As Lallie was not with the tribal husband to whom she had been promised there was potential for tribal reprisal. The Aborigines Department decided that if she was removed from her surroundings and kept at Moore River Native Settlement for a period of time, it might then be able to hand her over by arrangement to her tribal husband, who would see that she behaved herself in future. If Akbar and Lallie stayed in the Linden district 'the natives might have speared not only Matbar but also her husband'.

The outcome of interning Lallie in Moore River Native Settlement showed more defiance by Lallie and Akbar. She attempted several abscondments and made it back to Linden to be reunited with her people. Akbar became involved in her life again and there was no doubt that she was hidden and fed by this man. Neville pointed out to Kitson that bringing the girl back and showing her to be accountable would indicate to the 350 inmates of the Moore River Native Settlement that the government must be obeyed so far as absconding was concerned.

Not only did Neville emphasise to the Minister how the Afghan and the Aboriginal girl breached regulations and conducted themselves 'immorally'. He compounded the gravity of it all by a reference to the cultural and the biological inappropriateness of Asiatics mixing with Aborigines. He declared to the Minister that it had always been part of the practice of the Aborigines Department to try to prevent association between Asiatics and Aborigines. The belief was that Indians and Afghans had 'a particularly baneful influence' on the natives, and had resorted to 'all sorts of subterfuge to obtain their women'. Lallie Matbar, though half-caste, was deemed to be an Aboriginal, and was one to all intents and purposes. There had been serious trouble in the past with some such associations and they could expect no less with the coupling of Jack Akbar and Lallie Matbar. According to Neville's experience and awareness of mixed marriages, permitting Jack Akbar to marry the girl would not have been sufficient guarantee that this man would have, more than any other, taken good care of her. The Chief Protector could mention two or three cases in which Aborigines had been taken to the eastern states, and then abandoned and stranded there. The Aborigines Department had to arrange for them to be brought back.

Neville incorporated an ethnological reason for preventing 'Asiatics, negroes and other coloured races from associating with the aborigine'. He stated that the Aborigine was not subject to atavism so far as colour was concerned, and so their association with 'whites' could possibly result in 'the elimination of the black'. Neville continued the rationale that when the 'Asiatic and the negro element' came into the matter not

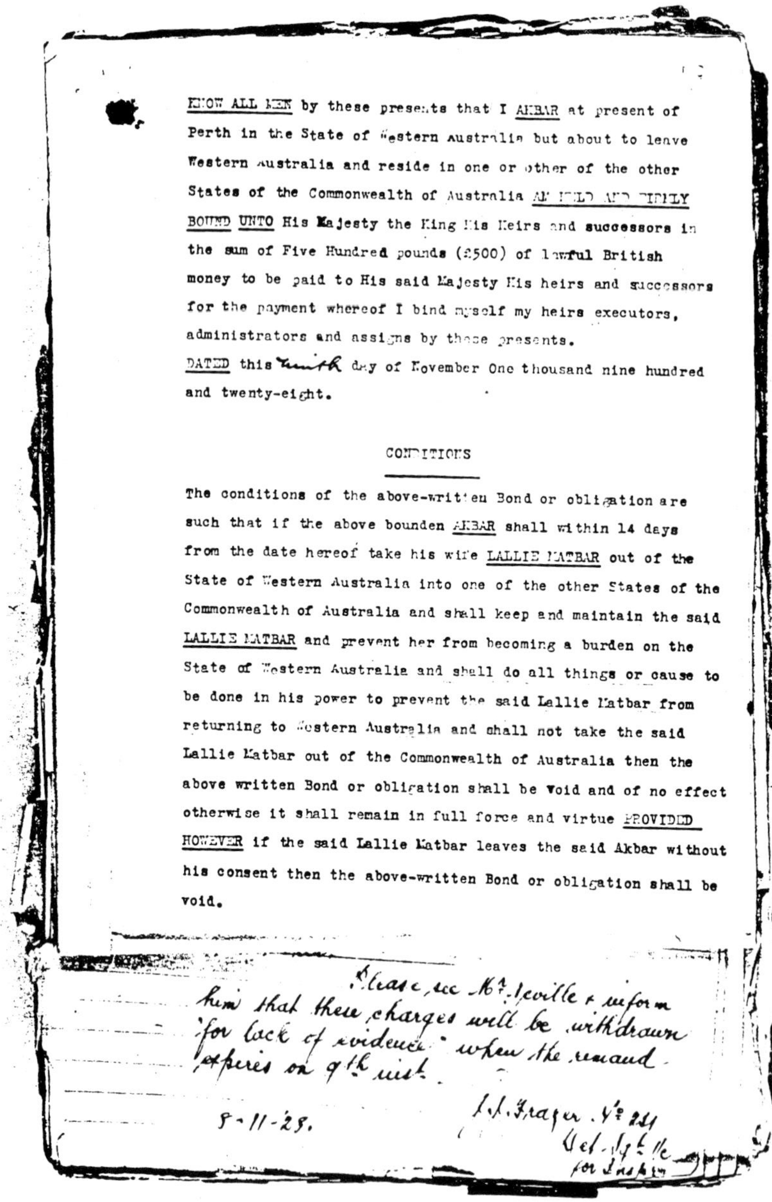

KNOW ALL MEN by these presents that I AKBAR at present of Perth in the State of Western Australia but about to leave Western Australia and reside in one or other of the other States of the Commonwealth of Australia AM HELD AND FIRMLY BOUND UNTO His Majesty the King His Heirs and successors in the sum of Five Hundred pounds (£500) of lawful British money to be paid to His said Majesty His heirs and successors for the payment whereof I bind myself my heirs executors, administrators and assigns by these presents.

DATED this tenth day of November One thousand nine hundred and twenty-eight.

CONDITIONS

The conditions of the above-written Bond or obligation are such that if the above bounden AKBAR shall within 14 days from the date hereof take his wife LALLIE MATBAR out of the State of Western Australia into one of the other States of the Commonwealth of Australia and shall keep and maintain the said LALLIE MATBAR and prevent her from becoming a burden on the State of Western Australia and shall do all things or cause to be done in his power to prevent the said Lallie Matbar from returning to Western Australia and shall not take the said Lallie Matbar out of the Commonwealth of Australia then the above written Bond or obligation shall be void and of no effect otherwise it shall remain in full force and virtue PROVIDED HOWEVER if the said Lallie Matbar leaves the said Akbar without his consent then the above-written Bond or obligation shall be void.

Please see Mr. Neville & inform him that these charges will be withdrawn for lack of evidence when the remand expires on 9th inst.

8-11-28.

J.J. Fraser. No 2[illegible]
Det. Sgt. [illegible]
for Insp.

A copy of the bond of Jack Akbar, 8/11/1928.

SIGNED SEALED AND DELIVERED by the said AKBAR at Perth in the State Aforesaid this 9th day of November 1928,

before me

[illegible signature]

A Commissioner for Affidavits

AKBAR

for lack of evidence when the remand expires on 9th inst.

8-11-28.

J. J. Frazer. No 281
Det-Sgt. No
for [illegible]

only did the colour appear to be perpetuated, but also 'the characteristics of some of these cross connections are deplorable'[37].

Upon receiving this lengthy documentation from the Chief Protector, Minister Kitson may have appreciated why the guardian of the Aborigines was preoccupied by Jack and Lallie Akbar's case. He may have considered that Neville was quite astute in pointing out all its implications and possible consequences. However, Kitson did not respond as promptly as Neville had hoped, and there was only a number of days before the couple's departure from the state.

Some time passed before the Minister responded to the Chief Protector's long letter. For all Neville's labour Kitson's response was a very brief note. He informed Neville that he would submit his letter for further consideration to another higher source of authority, the Honourable the Premier of the State P. Collier whose Labour Party was in government.

The delay in getting a response from either the Minister of Aborigines Kitson or the Western Australian Premier Collier had allowed for the departure of Jack and Lallie Akbar to go ahead without any impediment. By 17 November Mr and Mrs Akbar left Fremantle on an Adelaide-bound steamer. They had begun their second departure from the state that had tried to keep them apart, and which would have interned them in an institution or prison if it had found a case convincing enough to do so. By the end of November the couple were again settled in Adelaide, the address this time being Olive Farm, Beaven Avenue, Enfield.

The only link that Jack Akbar had now with the western state and its authorities was a seemingly minor one, his signature on two papers. One was a Bond that put Lallie in Jack Akbar's charge, and discouraged Lallie's return to the land of her birth and her people. She was where they both wanted to be, so Jack saw no need to be concerned about the dishonouring of that paper's terms. The second was a promise in writing to repay the Aborigines Department the eleven pounds it cost the couple for their steerage fares to leave Western Australia. That debt seemed amenable to repayment in installments.

Perhaps now, cleared by the law of any crimes or need for custody, and without an order from Minister Kitson to reverse any decision regarding their freedom, Jack and Lallie were free completely of the Chief Protector, the Aborigines Department's regulations and both the Western Australian and the South Australian Police Departments. It is not certain to what degree A.O. Neville was resigned to defeat and what level of interest he had in further involvement in their lives. Perhaps the file in Perth that had been maintained most conscientiously on the movements of Lallie Matbar might be closed now for good.

It was a message from the accountant in the Aborigines Department in May 1929 that reignited the Chief Protector's interest in the Akbars' case. The first installment from Jack Akbar in repaying his loan was about six months overdue[38]. The repayment of the loan of eleven pounds came to have a significance in the life of the Akbars that was greater than the amount of the loan.

CHAPTER NINE

Settlement in South Australia

On their second entry into South Australia Jack and Lallie Akbar could feel more assured that they had made a clean break from their past lives in Western Australia, from colonists' authorities such as the Aborigines and Police Departments, and from the emufoot man and the elders who opposed their marriage. There were people they, particularly Lallie, would have wanted to maintain contact with, such as Lallie's mother and Mr and Mrs Schenk. Lallie may have wished to know that once her people found out she had fled with Jack Akbar they did not divert the emufoot man on to Tjirrgulu. Though the Schenks had expressed their dissatisfaction with Akbar's association with Lallie they were still two of the very few European settlers that Lallie could ever turn to for support.

It may have been more in Jack's heart to start life afresh without any communication with people in Western Australia. He did not have immediate family from which to cut off communications. Lallie was his family. Her DCS file does not contain any details of the events of the Akbars' life in Adelaide from the time they arrived on 14 November. Information about the Akbars' life from that date until they left Adelaide, and the reason for their departure from that city, is derived from the oral depositions of the Akbars' two daughters Mona and Shirley. In South Australia Jack would have set about to provide his young wife with a safe and secure home and a peaceful future. He would have been prepared to work as hard as was necessary to be a good provider and to re-establish a regular income and, eventually a successful business. Though there is no mention of the outcome of the truck in Lallie's DCS file, Jack's daughter believes that he may have sold the truck in Adelaide when they needed money to pay for their fares to Farina to visit Gool Mahomet and his family. Without his truck for conveying any goods, one of his first jobs was to go from door to door selling small goods. He renewed his marine store collector's license which gave him a permit to collect empty bottles from houses and yards, and saved what money he could until he was able to purchase the horse and cart that would be his means of transport for bottle collecting[1].

Jack most probably gave some thought to the best direction in which to move within South Australia so as to establish a successful enterprise. In their new lives Jack and Lallie would have wanted to be situated geographically and financially in such a position that their children would be as free as possible of the influence or memory of the Western Australian Aborigines and Police Departments. They would want their children to have the opportunity to live normal lives without the appearance of police or the need to keep moving, with the chance to have an education, and to be raised in a complete, stable and happy family unit.

Their survival for their first several months in this state was uppermost in Jack's mind. Any pennies Jack could gather for himself and his wife would have to go to their food, amenities, rent and transport, then into savings for a horse and cart. In these months it may have been Jack Akbar's view that repayments to the Aborigines Department in Perth were a lower priority. The expectancy of the accountancy section of that department was that the repayment of the eleven pounds in installments would start promptly. Bookkeeping entries in Perth showed that J. Akbar was behind paying his first installment due on 17 November.

This fact eventually reached the attention of Mr Neville. The senior administrator of the Aborigines Department would not let the matter lapse, but before he could focus on this issue another matter regarding the Akbars in South Australia came to his attention.

Though living a life of freedom and peace with an absence of harassment the extent of which she may never have experienced before, Lallie could not so readily dismiss the memory of her mother, brother and people from her thoughts, particularly because of the manner in which she and Jack left the goldfields. Lallie may have been concerned about how her people were reacting to Tjirrgulu because of her daughter's unacceptable relationship with Akbar. Lallie would have wanted to know if an emufoot man, who had never caught up with her and Jack, had speared her mother instead. It may have also preyed on her mind that they did not know where she was or whether or not she was safe and well. Within less than one month of their return to South Australia

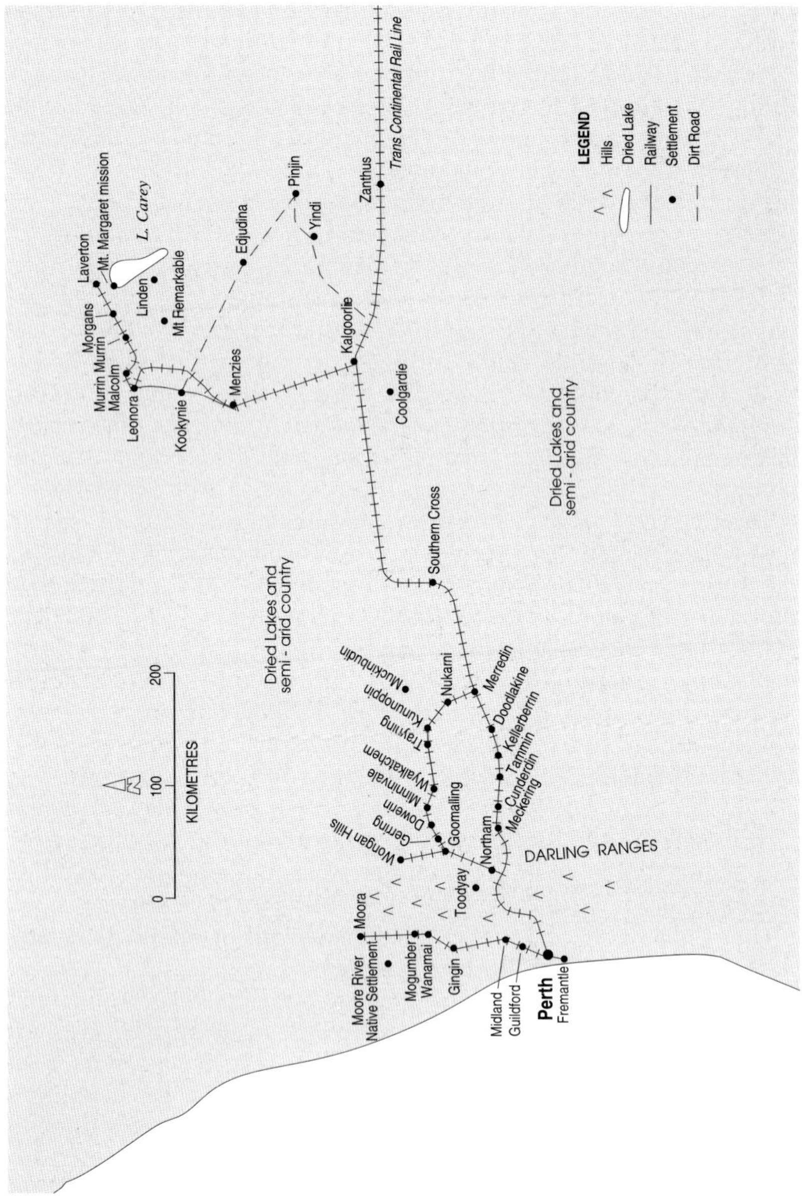

Lallie, Laura and three children escaped from Moore River Native Settlement to Linden.

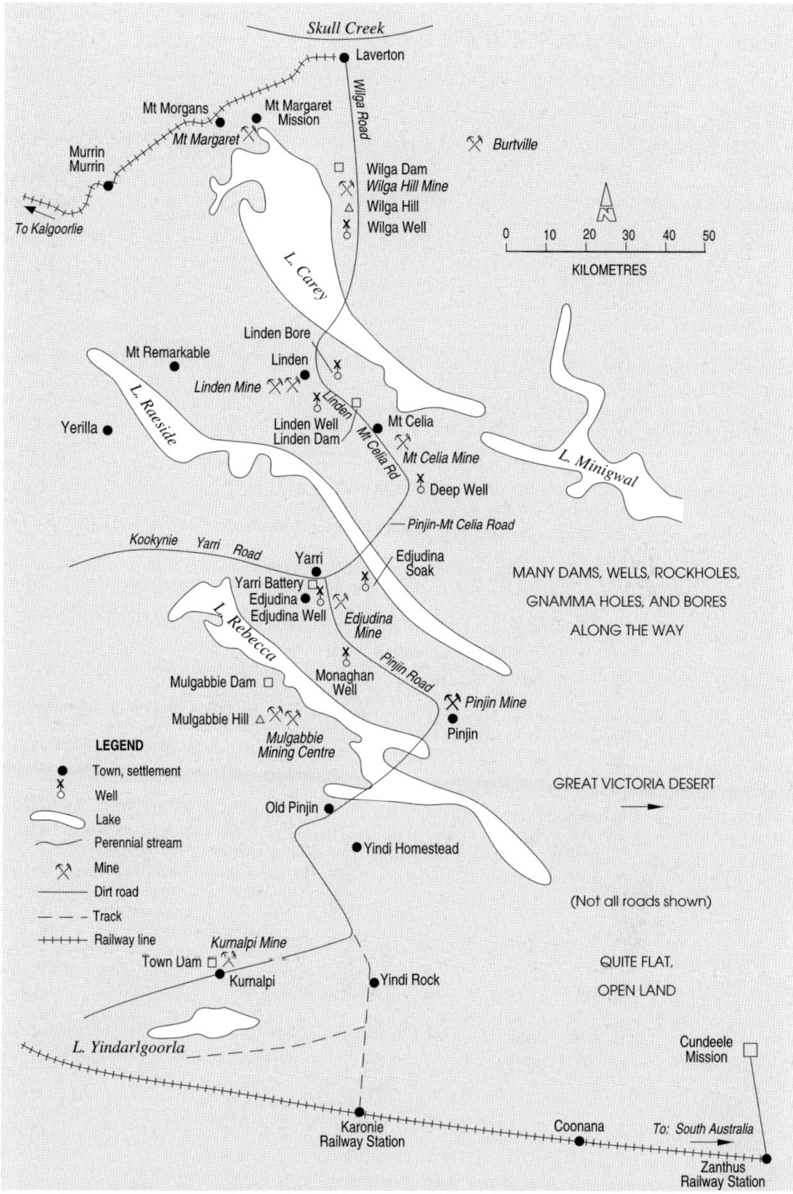

The eastern goldfields of Western Australia where Lallie was born and from where she escaped with Jack Akbar in 1928.

Lallie had confided in her husband that she was missing her mother. She was able to convince Jack that she needed to make some contact with her people. She discussed with him the idea of sending some news and some presents to her mother.

Neither Lallie's DCS file nor any of the depositions describe the contents of the presents. In considering his wife's wishes Jack would have had to consider how much they could spare of their meagre income to buy presents, and by what means the presents could be transferred from Adelaide to Lallie's people around Linden without the authorities finding out. None of her people, who were still semi-nomadic, used the convenience of a post office box. The only person they knew who had direct contact with the Linden Wongai and who could get a message to Tjirrgulu about the existence of the presents was Rod Schenk. However, the Akbars' experience of the Schenks' relationship with the police made them now very cautious about communicating with and involving him. Renewing communication with the missionary could again bring the police either down onto Lallie's people or into Jack and Lallie's peaceful home in Adelaide.

The couple resorted finally to a human channel of communication not related in any way to the Police Department, the Aborigines Department or the mission, yet that knew the goldfields bush country and many of the Aborigines there quite well. Jack's visits to the Adelaide mosque had kept him in touch with the Afghan camelmen's community and these traders and transporters traversed the interior outback country between the major Ghan towns of northern South Australia and of inland Western Australia. Akbar negotiated with some of his fellow countrymen to take the presents across the South Australian border into Western Australia and eventually to his wife's family in the Laverton-Linden area. The Afghans were a discreet migrant community and Jack and Lallie could trust them to be their allies and to maintain confidentiality.

Nevertheless, word about the existence of the presents and Lallie's effort to re-establish a connection with her people again did reach Mr Neville. Due to Rod Schenk's close relationship with the Linden Wongai conversations with those coming into his mission from the bush informed him of Lallie's initiative. Rather than be in sympathy with the girl who he realised was absent from the people and home she loved very much, Rod Schenk took another view of the situation.

The missionary was preoccupied by the potential the arrival of the presents had to unsettle the Aboriginal people. Since the success of Lallie and Jack in outwitting the police, leaving the state twice as free people and being cleared of her alleged offences against the Aborigines Act, Rod Schenk was concerned about the impact such achievements might have on some non-Anglo-Saxon communities in his district. Not only might the local Aborigines rally to inciteful behaviour. Perhaps the Afghans, whose presence in the colonies had been resented since the 1880s, might find a cause to become uncooperative with the law. If there was to be any misconduct or any insurgence, Rod Schenk would prefer that the Chief Protector and the police were prepared for it and ready to deal with it.

Thus the missionary set about following through with his regular duty to the Aborigines Department. By 7 December 1928 the missionary commenced the report he would pass to the local protector Constable Warren so as to update Mr Neville on Lallie Akbar's movements. Rod Schenk informed Neville that 'Lallie has sent presents to her mother through an Afghan at Murrin Murrin'. Rod could not obtain the name of that Afghan but he did know that 'Chilgaloo alias Polly [Lallie's mother] has gone down to him to receive these presents'. Rod continued in his report to enlighten the authorities to the possible civil disorder these presents, and the relationship between the Afghans and the Aborigines, could provoke in the district:

> As we know the chaos that generally ensues by the mixture of Chinese and Afghans with the natives in other States, [he and Mysie] stood pat against Akbar even talking to Lallie when she was here...His success lately has impressed our natives in a wrong way and we have no doubt it will encourage other Afghans in a wrong way. We...intend to dig a little deeper into the conduct of other Afghans. The natives protect them by their silence... Akbar will no doubt be sending more presents and we ask you to take measures to have them sent through us or the police and thus prevent this being an excuse and an incentive to gather native women around the Afghans[2].

After closing his letter with his regular signature, Rod Schenk added, '70,000 Heathen Need saving Light and Liberty'.

This notification received by Auber Neville from Mount Margaret mission, now called, The Gospel Mission to the Australian Aborigines, may have evoked some ire in that administrator for a few reasons. The Afghan and the Aborigine were once again demonstrating a disinclination to be intimidated by his authority. Also, Neville had been informed by the accounts section that Jack Akbar had not yet begun to repay any of the eleven pounds the Aborigines Department had leant him to pay for the passage of himself and his wife to Adelaide and freedom. The

Afghan who had been able to persuade the Chief Protector and a Crown Law solicitor that he was in a state of impoverishment was able apparently to find sufficient spare finance to purchase some gifts!

Of most concern to Neville, as well as to the police and the missionary, was that the Akbars, now settled in another state far from the goldfields, could still possibly have an unsettling influence on the Aborigines and the Afghans in the Laverton-Mount Margaret districts. The sending of the presents may have been motivated by love and the most honourable and dutiful of intentions, but they initiated another unexpected twist of fate in Jack and Lallie's lives. As far as the Chief Protector was concerned, those few simple items were justification for his department to reopen the dormant file on Lallie Matbar. On 14 December, Neville sent a reply to the missionary at the Gospel Mission near Morgans. He encouraged Schenk to keep him acquainted with anything further he learned in regard to Lallie and Jack Akbar. He informed Schenk that it appeared the Afghan had been treacherous and deceitful. Akbar had been attempting to convince the Aborigines and Police Departments that he was a very poor person, but it occurred to Neville that by his sending of presents he indicated that 'he has more money than he makes out'[3].

In the way that bureaucratic process slows down at the end of one year and is slow to gain pace in the beginning of a new one, it took a further length of time for the paper work in the accounts section to be collated and updated. It was a while before the accountant of the Aborigines Department realised that Jack Akbar had still not yet sent to Perth one penny towards paying off his loan and he was nearly six months behind in doing so. On 17 May 1929, the accountant sent a brief note to the Chief Protector of Aborigines informing him that Jack Akbar had not yet made any repayments on his loan. The accountant added a hand written comment at the bottom of his letter to Neville asking him if he was able to ascertain Akbar's present whereabouts[4].

This latest correspondence from the accountant implied to the Chief Protector that Jack Akbar was continuing not to comply with regulations imposed on him by a government department and was adamant in going about things disagreeably. He was persistent in demonstrating a disregard and disrespect for the importance of the position of the Chief Protector and the Aborigines Department. The Afghan was still not intimidated by the power of the Chief Protector, nor that of the Police Department. Neville believed it was time once again to act, to have the police investigate the location of Jack Akbar, then to approach him to have him pay up. The day after the arrival of the accountant's note Neville sent him a response. He advised that the best course would be to ask the Commissioner of Police to ascertain from the South Australian Police the present whereabouts of Akbar. There was a possibility of getting the Crown Law Department also to communicate with him[5]. The paperwork involved in attempting to have Jack Akbar make payments on his loan kept Lallie's file open.

Neville himself eventually sent the letter which would involve the police once again in tracking down Jack and Lallie Akbar. He advised his peer, Police Commissioner Connell, of the matter of Jack Akbar neglecting to commence repayments to meet his debts, and of the need for contact with Akbar so as to be able to collect arrears concerning refund of passage money for himself and his wife. He requested the Police Commissioner to make enquiries to the South Australian police as to the present whereabouts of Akbar[6].

The participation of the manpower provided by the South Australian Police Department once again proved productive. On 18 July 1929 Mr Neville received notification from the Police Commissioner's Office in Perth that Jack Akbar was at this time residing at Beaven Avenue, Olive Farm, Enfield, South Australia[7].

With the knowledge of Akbar's current address Neville took the step to make contact with the Afghan himself. He was anxious to remind the immigrant that the agreement he had made to repay a sum of money to the Aborigines Department was legally binding. On 25 July 1929 Jack and Lallie Akbar received their first correspondence from a man they must have thought was a part of their past. Neville was personally reminding the couple that 'remittances for the amount owing' were still expected[8].

A personal reminder from the Chief Protector himself did not evoke the reaction in Jack Akbar that Neville anticipated. Two months passed and the Aborigines Department did not receive the first repayment on eleven pounds from Jack. The Akbars had now been in South Australia for about ten months.

On 20 September the Chief Protector sent a second reminder letter to Jack Akbar at the Enfield address. After reminding the Afghan that he had written to him on the 25 July last, he warned Jack that unless he received satisfaction from him in the near future he would 'be forced to take more drastic action for the recovery of same'[9].

Peace had not yet come to Jack and Lallie's lives. The Chief Protector in Perth had found reason to continue to keep Lallie's file open. The correspondence from Neville must have been alarming for Jack and Lallie. The surviving evidence, such as Lallie's DCS file and the depositions, does not reveal the reason for Akbar not promptly commencing repayment of his debt of eleven pounds. Certainly to have repaid the debt promptly could have guaranteed that Neville would have kept his Department and the police out of the Akbars' lives forever. Akbar's lack of repayments may not have been deliberate. One main reason for not resuming repayments may have been their financial circumstances. Within the first ten months of their residence in South Australia Jack Akbar had not been able to establish a regular income or viable enterprise that made it possible for the couple to pay all bills as well as send money to Western Australia, even though doing so would contribute to their disconnection totally with the authorities in Western Australia. The Great Depression had commenced by 1929 and work and income were hard to find for many people. At the time of the arrival of the second letter from the Chief Protector Lallie was pregnant with their first child. Their personal economic circumstances were not conducive to long-term saving or paying off debts. It is possible that Jack may have decided, once in South Australia again and feeling safe from and beyond the legal jurisdiction of the Aborigines Department, to defy the obligation to repay the eleven pounds to the Aborigines Department. However, it was not a characteristic of Jack Akbar to be deliberately and calculatedly defiant. The Chief Protector was not interested in knowing or understanding the circumstances of the lives of the debtors. The Department did not have a place for including compassion in its interpretation of its policies. It would not consider closing the Akbars' account in light of their personal circumstances.

The second, curt letter with a comment that was intended to intimidate the couple still did not extract the first payment from Jack Akbar. Neville heard nothing from Jack Akbar for some time. Eventually, the Chief Protector considered action consequent to his threat. On 4 November the Chief Protector requested Police Commissioner Connell to arrange with the South Australian Police to visit Jack Akbar and interview that man on the subject of his making repayments on the loan. He advised the Commissioner that he would also consider taking further action through the Commonwealth Crown Law Department[10].

Commissioner Connell complied with the official request of his colleague and approached the Police Department in Adelaide. About three weeks later Neville received a response from Connell's office. The details in the report from the South Australian police were not what Neville had anticipated. The Chief Protector was informed that Jack Akbar 'is camped at Renmark, South Australia. He is destitute and drawing government rations for himself and wife'[11].

Because of Jack Akbar's poverty the Chief Protector had to give some thought to his next move. Neville would not cease his pursuit of having the loan repaid. However, how could he continue to harangue Akbar for money, even with the police force in another state supporting him, when that same man was penniless and in dire circumstances? If Neville persisted in chasing the Afghan for the eleven pounds, his public and media critics could see him as inhumane, a man obsessed rather than an administrator reasonable and dutiful. They would influence his public image with the accusation that he was not just following up but hounding, not just prosecuting but persecuting the Akbars in South Australia. With such destructive criticism directed at the Chief Protector rather than at the Afghan, the police in either state may not want to aid the Chief Protector in pursuing this particular case.

The Chief Protector would not succumb totally to criticism. He would just tread more cautiously. When he received a typed police letter enquiring of the 'C.P.A.' if he would like the matter of attempting to get repayments out of Akbar to be paused for six months, Neville sensed a welling of sympathy for the Akbars. Rather than stir it to a cause, the Chief Protector compromised and replied with a personal scribble at the bottom of the letter, 'Say 3 months'[12].

There may have been a combination of factors that caused Jack and Lallie to leave Adelaide and establish their future in another South Australian town. The two letters from Neville himself and the police interview would have unnerved them. Lallie was pregnant with their first child. They may have hoped for more children in the future, and to be able to live a life with peace and stability in which to raise their family. They may have feared that if the authorities discovered their identity they would be separated, or taken back to Western Australia, and either way their infant given to welfare. Founding a small business of his own so as to have a regular income for his future family may have been difficult in the capital city during the Depression. There was an increasing number of people such as some local police and court staff who were now aware of their past lives.

Perhaps with a combination of very frugal living, some self-denial, disciplined budgeting, plus some assistance from their supporters at the Adelaide mosque, Jack managed to buy eventually the horse and cart that he needed for both business and family transport. When they were ready to leave Adelaide Jack and his pregnant wife packed what they had and commenced to travel as far east in the state, as far from the west as they could get. Jack would have wanted to go to a place where job opportunities were more likely and where there was a more recently established substantial community that could make selling wares door to door a viable proposition.

The couple arrived eventually in the eastern region of South Australia called the Riverland. This area was very near the eastern South Australian border, and its spine was a wide and perennial river named the Murray. There were many new settlements based on orchard irrigation springing up in the Murray River valley, and there were jobs available in them and in the newly established fruit blocks scattered between them. These growing centres would need the provision of a variety of services. It must have appeared an opportune place in which Jack Akbar could start a new career for himself and provide a home for his family.

Having travelled several hundred kilometres from Adelaide through the farm belt into semi-arid country, and spending many nights camped in the bush or grass not far from the edge of the road, Jack and Lallie had arrived in a district that would have compared to an oasis. The reflection of sunlight off the wide, long, deep flowing river shimmering through trees would have been refreshing for the weary travellers and uplifting to their spirits. Jack and Lallie followed the River Murray a little further eastward for a few more days until they came to the last settlement along it before the border with the State of Victoria. This town was called Renmark.

Jack and Lallie found a sheltered clearing along the banks of the river and made a camp for themselves. Having to move once again, from one settlement to another, to avoid Neville's influence in their lives reduced the standard of their shelter to a primitive and impromptu abode — a tent — but in it they felt they had regained their freedom, anonymity and dignity. They were now in a peaceful place in which they would be left alone to get on with their own lives. They would not be found and hounded by the authorities from Perth this far away to the east. No-one knew them here, or why they had come here. No-one knew their past. They could be free again to choose where their home would be and where their children would be born, raised and educated. After the many years Jack had spent in the desert areas, living along the banks of this mighty Murray River was uplifting. Physically it was a beautiful and wonderful thing to fill his field of vision. Spiritually, it was refreshing and revitalising. Water meant life and for Lallie and Jack this river would be their life line. They would always be able to have food here and find some kind of work. Their children could have a safe and happy life here. No police would come and harass them or threaten to seize and relocate their children 'for their own good'.

The tent on the banks of the Murray was the Akbars' first abode in Renmark. In 1929 their humble dwelling would not have looked much out of place as there were a lot of itinerant unemployed men about the country who had been made jobless and homeless because of the Great Depression. It was not unusual to see strangers in a town setting up a temporary shelter for somewhere to sleep.

The discomfort Lallie was feeling because of her pregnant condition, the pain Jack's gammy leg still brought him, and their primitive facilities required Jack to seek medical assistance. Jack went to the town's centre where he found a chemist. In the discussion which ensued between Jack Akbar and the chemist Mr Hagley, the latter became concerned about the dire situation of the newly arrived couple who were expecting their first baby. He later discussed it with his own wife. The Renmark couple offered the Akbars accomodation in a workman's shed located in the far end of the backyard of their new home. They helped to take care of Lallie for some time and over the years remained very good friends of Jack and Lallie Akbar[13].

Lallie was admitted to the Renmark hospital where on 28 February 1930 she gave birth to a daughter they named Mona. During that year Jack's priorities were to find a house, to find regular work, and to provide for the needs of his family.

The Chief Protector wanted the South Australian police force to keep checking on the progress of Jack and Lallie Akbar in Renmark. The three months of pausing on the matter of expecting Akbar to make repayments on his loan had well passed. On 15 January 1931, Auber Neville sent yet another memo to the Police Commissioner in Perth requesting a copy of the latest South Australian police report on Jack Akbar.

Commissioner Connell sent Neville a copy of the most recent South Australian police report, dated 10 February 1931, that his office had. It came from a policeman who had interviewed Jack Akbar at his new home in Eighteenth Street Renmark where he now resided with his wife Lallie and six-month-old Mona[14]. After all this time, and after such an effort to be free of their past and start a new life without any harassment by any authorities, Jack Akbar was still opening his door to encounter uniformed men or police authorities who wanted to question him.

Lallie stands beside the pram in which her fourth child Johnny is sleeping, Shirley and Jimmy are in the foreground, Renmark, South Australia, 1939. Photo courtesy Mona Wilson.

The report from the South Australian police declared that, on 29 October 1930, Jack Akbar had signed an agreement to purchase from Joe Saidameer two allotments of land, one of which included an iron cabin. He had paid a deposit of five pounds and had agreed to pay the remainder of the ninety pound purchase price in weekly installments of ten shillings at seven per cent interest.

The remainder of the report summarised Akbar's present financial circumstances. Akbar worked steadily at making 'mats and baskets from palm leaves'. He told the policeman that he 'had no money in hand', though he managed to have his rent paid to date, and that he was drawing rations for himself and family. He had only 'one suit of clothes which [was] not too respectable' and 'Lallie Akbar dresses in clothes that are given to her by neighbours'. Akbar also held a marine stores collector's license, and in connection with his collecting business he kept a horse, which was always in good condition.

The policeman concluded his report by commenting that from his observations Akbar appeared to be a 'tryer' and that he worked 'long hours and travels long distances endeavouring to dispose of his goods and gather marine stores'[15].

To know that Jack Akbar was working very hard to maintain care of Neville's ex-ward, that he was providing accommodation, clothes and food for his family, having started with nothing, and that he and Lallie were living very moral lives, did not evoke any sympathy in the Chief Protector. Neville did not cease in making the occasional request to the Police Commissioner for further, current data on the circumstances and location of Jack and Lallie Akbar. In one report written in November 1930 the Police Commissioner informed the Chief Protector that Jack Akbar was 'still at Renmark but is about 20 pounds in arrears in rent and still owes 67 pounds, eleven shillings and 7 pence on the land previously mentioned. He is of sober habits and industrious but is not doing very well and as he is in receipt of relief it is impossible to collect anything from him'[16].

A.O. Neville never let go of his obsession with the Akbar-Matbar case. He believed the just thing to be done in this case was to continue to have the South Australian police maintain observation of Jack Akbar until the eleven pounds was paid in full.

The first part repayment on the loan of eleven pounds was extracted finally from Jack Akbar early in January 1934, just over five years from the time he was obliged to borrow the money. In a brief report Police Commissioner Connell informed the Chief Protector that an amount of one pound had been collected from Jack Akbar and paid into Revenue. Akbar promised also that from now on he would pay ten shillings per month direct to the Aborigines Department until the debt was cleared[17].

Akbar attempted to keep his promise. Within two weeks he provided a second part-payment. He sent a Postal Note for ten shillings to the Aborigines Department in Perth[18]. Neville must have begun to feel that he was being rewarded for all the years he had maintained this case, and for all the hours of labour and paper work contributed by two states. Finally he would be seen to be effective and in control.

However, by July of 1934, Jack Akbar was not able to mantain his rate of repayment. On 10 July a policeman at Renmark sent a note to the Aborigines Department in Perth that explained what was the cause of the cessation of repayments. On visiting Akbar at his home the policeman had found the Afghan to be 'sick in bed'. He had been 'ill for some time with bronchitis and will not be able to send the money as he is not earning any[19]. By now Jack and Lallie had three small children and themselves to feed and clothe.

Mr Neville did not let the case rest. By 16 November 1935 Akbar received another reminder of his dues from the Chief Protector. Neville pointed out that he had not made a payment in reduction of his account since 14 September, 'the balance of which stands at 30 shillings'. Neville concluded this very brief and curt letter by stating, 'I should be glad if you will let me have a remittance by return of post'[20].

The Chief Protector appears to have achieved a response within twenty-four hours. In Renmark on 19 November 1935 a letter, written on Jack Akbar's behalf, was sent to the Chief Protector in Western Australia and referred to Jack's next and last repayment. It stated that early in October thirty shillings had been sent by Akbar in final payment of his dues. It added that no receipt had yet arrived recording that final payment[21].

On 30 November 1935 Jack sent a letter of his own to the Aborigines Department in Perth. He requested that he be given a receipt so as to have 'clearance and a statement that this is my total indebtedness to your department'[22].

The Aborigines Department officially recorded that Jack Akbar was no longer in their debt in regard to that financial arrangement.

The Chief Protector no longer had a legitimate reason to pursue the Afghan. He had no further need to request the South Australian police force, through the Western Australian police force, to monitor Jack and Lallie Akbar. They could truly be left alone by all authorities.

After November 1935, however, the DCS file on Lallie Matbar was still not closed.

Jack Akbar photographed with his four children, from left, Jimmy, Mona, Shirley and Johnny, and showing a sample of the wares he was well-known for in Renmark, 1946. Photo courtesy of Mona Wilson.

E P I L O G U E

During the 1930s the size of the Akbar family was increased by the addition of three more children - Shirley was born on 17 March 1932, Jimmy was born on 3 May 1934, and Johnny was born on 5 March 1939. A fifth child, Jack, did not survive childhood and was buried in the Renmark cemetery[1]. By the late 1930s Jack and Lallie were well settled into the life for which they had outdone fate and risked everything. Jack had as his wife the woman with whom he wanted to establish a home and family, and their house resounded with the chatter and enthusiasm of their four handsome, healthy children.

During the years in which Lallie lived in Renmark with Jack Akbar her own people remained divided over the matter of who was Lallie's correct husband. The spearman had never caught up to Lallie and Jack when they fled from the goldfields in 1928 and so one faction of the Wongai believed that a punishment had not yet been served. The debate continued between the reactionary faction of the Linden mob who still believed that Lallie should be with Burtville Jack, and the more liberal folk who adhered to the decision that Burtville Jack's action had exempted Lallie and Tjirrgulu from a spearing. Though Lallie was well beyond the reach of an emufoot man Tjirrgulu was still with her people. Peace did not settle over the Linden mob for some time.

Jack Akbar continued to practise his religion. As a devout follower of the Islamic faith he maintained his contact with the Islamic and Afghan community by making a few trips each year to the mosque in Little Gilbert Street in Adelaide[2]. Because of his adherence to fundamentalist beliefs Jack Akbar developed into a strict father and husband, though never deviating in his commitment to his marriage. He was strict with his children though not unkind[3]. Shirley Wilson recalled that her father maintained a strong sense of morality, one of his favourite sayings being, 'You have to live by your principles. You have to do the right thing'[4]. One of Jack's more regular working companions in Renmark ascertained that Jack Akbar never lost sight of his ambition to provide a secure and fulfilling life for Lallie[5].

His attitudes about the roles of wives and mothers, of males and females, were more consistent with traditional Moslem customs and became more entrenched as his daughters grew up. His strictness about Mona and Shirley's upbringing and their movements beyond the house was in keeping with the traditional Afghan female experience[6]. Mona and Shirley were not supposed to go out of the house alone unless they were chaperoned by either one of their parents, or another adult who was a close and trusted friend of the family, or were accompanied by their brothers if there was no adult on whom to rely, or if they were in pairs. Their father preferred that his daughters did not go to the shops to buy their dresses, skirts or blouses, or other personal items. The store would be requested by the Akbar family to bring a range of garment samples to their home where the girls would try them on and decide which ones to buy[7]. It was an Islamic and an Afghan custom that no men were allowed inside a house to visit either the wife or daughters if the husband or father was not at home[8]. This was the practice in the Akbar household[9]. The reluctance that Jack expressed about Lallie going out on her own to shop or visit was also in keeping with Islamic attitudes.

When Lallie married Jack she would not have known what it was like to be the wife of a Moslem. According to the traditional ways of Moslem communities it was expected that much of the child rearing years of the women would be spent in the house, where the mother was the hub of family life. She would have given most of her time and energy to taking care of the children, keeping the house clean and tidy, and doing the washing and cooking. She would be expected to keep her personal appearance clean and tidy. Her social life beyond the house would be quite limited. It was more a custom that her grown-up children or relatives would visit her in her home[10].

It did not take Lallie and Jack very long to increase the number of acquaintances and establish a few more friendships. The local women who came to know Lallie considered her to be quiet, unassuming and retiring, yet quite approachable, gregarious and happy in company and delightful. They found her company to be very comfortable. Lallie liked to visit her female friends at home when she had the opportunity, and over time developed a number of acquaintances[11]. Bill Summerfield, whose main occupation for some time was a grave digger by night in Renmark but who also worked during the day alongside Jack Akbar for some time, described Lallie as a 'lovely lady'[12].

The Akbar children made their own friends during their primary school years. Other students found them very likeable and the Akbar children were quite popular[13]. Friendships were founded that have lasted into the 1990s.

As Jack Akbar was enterprising, resourceful and dutiful he eventually established himself as a local businessman. One major aspect of his business was based on the production of a range of woven mats and baskets. His raw materials were binder twine, bull rushes and palm leaves which he found growing abundantly along the banks of the River Murray. Jack was a very skilful weaver, adapting his items to suit individual requirements. To promote his wares he would either walk the streets carrying a range of samples, or drive around the town in his old truck carting and hawking his mats and baskets[14]. The Afghan hawker accrued over the years such a volume of orders for his mats and baskets that he found it difficult to keep up with demand[15].

The other major aspect of his business was a vegetable round which included the selling of fish, fruit and cool drinks. When he went to Adelaide, about twice a week, to fill up on stock for this service, he would stay overnight at the mosque. He had different days for different sections of the Renmark district. He took nine-year-old Mona with him in school holidays to be his legs, as he was still inconvenienced to a minor degree by his 'gammy leg'. Mona also did some of her father's bookwork[16].

To further supplement the family's income Jack did rounds to collect empty bottles. He renewed his marine collector's license regularly and in a horse and cart, often accompanied by Bill Summerfield, he would travel about Renmark, down to Berri and to other towns, as well as among the fruit blocks, calling out for empty bottles. The empty bottles were put into large hessian bags, brought back to Jack Akbar's back yard and Lallie and the children cleaned them out. The bottles were then filled with kerosene which was used by the local stores. Bill recalled how he and Jack would work week days bottle collecting, then all Saturday and Sunday Jack would concentrate on his weaving, sitting on his kitchen floor and producing mats and baskets. Jack took the opportunity to promote his woven wares while doing his bottle rounds[17].

Through the various aspects of his business Jack Akbar became a familiar figure to people in shops, in homes and on the blocks. He retained an air of privacy, not talking very much about himself or his family. Only a few of Jack's business associates came to his home. On rare occasions he had Afghan visitors. When 'Indian' hawkers came into

Renmark they seemed to know of the Afghan on Eighteenth Street and would camp at his place until they moved on. Mona could recall one older Afghan named Shergool who stayed with her family in Renmark a few times as a guest. He lived essentially in Adelaide. The only details Mona could remember about him were the odd things, like his gold teeth, and his laugh which sounded like the laugh of a kookaburra. For Akbar's children the name of that bird became their nickname for Shergool[18].

The citizens in the township saw Jack Akbar as a man with bearing who was courteous, diligent, dignifed and proud[19]. During World War Two when people had to dig trenches in the yards of their homes, even with his gammy leg he would not let anyone else dig tranches for his family. He insisted on digging them himself[20]. Because of his fine manner the Hagleys, the first friends Jack and Lallie made in Renmark, believed Jack Akbar to be of people of good breeding[21]. The community of Renmark came to have a high regard and respect for the Afghan trader who was frequently addressed as 'Mr Akbar'[22].

The introduction to Christianity that Lallie had experienced in the goldfields seemed to have provided her with an opportunity to establish a spiritual link in her community on the Riverland. She and Jack became friendly with the reverend of the Congregational church and sent their children off to church quite regularly. Jack believed his children should have a religious upbringing so that they would not grow up to be 'free thinkers'[23].

Within their home Jack Akbar made his Moslem religion apply so as to give his children some exposure to the religion of his own people. He wanted them to become familiar with the teachings of the prophet Mohammet and of his god Allah. Glen Locke, a local boy who grew up with the Akbar children and eventually became a pastor, commented that Jack Akbar was a unique man in Renmark in that he was the only practising Moslem in that municipality. Mr Akbar was very committed to his faith. In particular, he taught his boys some words of the Koran and Moslem prayer, and in some school holildays he would take his children to visit the mosque in Adelaide. The Reverend recalled seeing on several occasions Jack kneeling on his prayer mat both inside and outside his house[24].

Jack Akbar also maintained some of his cultural practices within their home. The family's meals included curries, quite hot curry Bill Summerfield recalled. The meat served at the Akbars' table had to be killed according to Islamic practice[25]. Mona recalled that she and her siblings were 'reared on goats'. The main sources of meat for the Akbars were goat and, less frequently, chicken. At home there was a goat yard with a wooden fence. The killing of a goat for a meal required that the throat of the animal be cut and the blood of the animal be allowed to drain while the Moslem recited over the animal three times 'Allah is great'. Then Jack's children helped their mother cook the goat meat the way he directed them to[26].

The first feelings of restlessness to come into the family that could threaten the cohesion and peace of Jack and Lallie's lives came from Lallie. After being in Renmark for about eight years Lallie revealed to her husband that for some time she had been pining for her people and her tribal land and she could no longer contain it. She had not forgotten the condition attached to the Bond which stated that while she stayed in the care of Jack Akbar she was forbidden to re-enter Western Australia or see her family and people. She understood what it could cost her husband financially and emotionally if she acted against that condition. However, the homesickness was increasingly preoccupying her thoughts and gnawing at her heart and mind[27]. She discussed with her husband her need to find out if there was a means of getting back to the eastern goldfields.

By June 1939 Jack was apparently prepared to be lenient with his wife's request. He was tied by the conditions of the Bond and could not himself take her back home for a visit. They decided to seek the advice and assistance of the Schenks at Mount Margaret mission and Lallie wrote them a letter. Jack advised Lallie to convey to the missionary's wife the understanding that Lallie was in a good home and was being cared for as he had told them she would be. Lallie could then express for herself how important it was for her that she be allowed to return home for a month's holiday to see her mother and her people. Lallie commenced her letter, which she addressed to Mrs Schenk, with, 'You will be surprised to get a letter from me', then explained to the Schenks that she was writing to them to ask them to do a favour for her. 'I am here got a good home but would like to go over to my people for a change. I would like a month holiday I am sure it would do me good to be among my people. My children are good children but I feel for and like to go home sweet home.' Lallie added that should she return to the goldfields for this brief visit she would be bringing her youngest child, her three-month-old baby Johnny. She assured Mrs Schenk that her husband Jack was agreeable to her going home for a while. Lallie signed off the letter with 'Your's Homesick'[28].

Nearly sixty years after Jack's arrival in Australia he continued to don his turban in the traditional manner - early 1950s, Renmark, South Australia. Photo courtesy Mona Wilson.

Rod and Mysie Schenk had retained fond memories of Lallie and were willing to support the earnest appeals of any one of their indigenous congregation. The missionary couple put Lallie's appeal to the Chief Protector of Aborigines, who was now titled the Commissioner of Native Affairs[29], for written permission for Lallie to re-enter Western Australia. Rod Schenk assured the Commissioner that Lallie understood that her stay could be for only one month, just sufficient time to visit her family and friends[30].

Though the title of office had changed the person occupying that position had not. The Commissioner of Native Affairs in 1939 was Auber Octavius Neville. On receiving Schenk's letter he immediately recognised Lallie's name. He had not forgotten the case of Jack and Lallie Akbar. He was an implementer of legislation and an upholder of the official written word. This prohibited any consideration of appeal or making an exemption of a case. In his response to the missionary at Mount Margaret Neville stated that the conditions of the Bond that had been drawn up eleven years previously were still in force and were to be observed. Neville added that the granting of permission by his office for Lallie to come home was unthinkable as that reversal might encourage Akbar to think that the undertakings of the Bond no longer needed to be maintained. To make sure that Schenk appreciated the gravity of the situation should Lallie ever return, the Commissioner added in his conclusion that there was still a possibility of tribal repercussion on Lallie arising out of her marriage to Akbar, even though it was eleven years since Lallie and Jack had left[31].

Rod and Mysie Schenk could not so easily dismiss Lallie's case. Driven by their consciences and Christian duty they gave Lallie's situation further consideration. They believed that her request was a reasonable one and that it deserved a humane response. They would attempt to employ an amount of reasoning with Neville in a second letter. Schenk proposed to the Commissioner that it seemed quite hard that Jack and his wife should never be allowed ever again to re-enter the State of Western Australia. In the eleven years that Jack and Lallie lived in South Australia they had proved their worthiness by maintaining a stable marriage, raising a good family and living a wholesome and productive life. The Schenks considered that Neville was holding the Akbars to the Bond, 'like the law of the Medes and the Persians'. The missionary suggested that as Lallie herself expressed that she wished to stay for only one month, such dogmatic observation of the law might be put aside temporarily[32].

Jack displaying some of the raw materials he collected along the river Murray with which to make his baskets and mats during the early 1950s. Photo courtesy Mona Wilson.

The Commissioner remained resolute in his decision. He reminded the Schenks of the fundamental importance of maintaining the status quo of the law. The obligation to follow the law bound both himself and Schenk, and 'the terms of the bond enforce observance and I do not draw any conclusions favourable to Akbar because he appears to have observed its terms'. The Commissioner reminded Schenk that 'Akbar gravely offended against our laws for the protection of our natives, and personally I think he was a lucky man to escape punishment and retaliation from the natives at the time'. A.O. Neville concluded the letter by raising the point that there was still a very strong chance that 'the memory may remain with them still' and these same people may still wish to deal a punishment on Lallie or the Afghan[33].

After some time Lallie and Jack received correspondence on the outcome of her appeal to seek permission to re-enter Western Australia. The details provided very disappointing news for Lallie. It is most likely that the Akbars decided to cease for a while actively seeking permission for Lallie to be allowed to go home. However, the feeling to see her mother and her people continued to smoulder in Lallie's heart. It was an ambition that never left her.

The time came once again when Lallie raised the matter of her homesickness. Two years after her first official attempt to return home, in September 1941, Lallie wrote once again to the Schenks at Mount Margaret to appeal for their assistance in gaining permission for her to visit her people. Schenk wrote again on Lallie Akbar's behalf to the Commissioner of Native Affairs, who responded with the same rigidity and with the same practical reasons why Lallie should never come home again[34]. Lallie once again had to allow the matter to lapse, though privately she hung onto the hope of one day 'going home'.

The exact year in which Lallie lost her mother has not been recorded. Tjirrgulu apparently died in those years during which Lallie was attempting to return home. It is remembered that her death was due not to natural causes but to an act of violence served in justice, a spearing. It is understood that those of the Linden people who had not accepted Lallie's marriage to Akbar believed she should be with her tribe-given husband and did not acquiesce over time. They maintained that discipline had to be served on the girl whose actions may have been seen to be comparable to that of adultery and to offending traditional customs. As Lallie now lived very far away the punishment was to be served on her mother[35].

During the years of the Second World War Lallie's brother Snowy

Bradley made his way from the goldfields to Renmark to visit his sister. The four Akbar children met one of their mother's relatives for the first time and Snowy stayed with his sister's family for six months. When he returned to the West Snowy joined the Home Guards. He was in the Australian Army from 1942 to 1944[36]. Snowy's DCS file states that by 1940 it was estimated that he was 40 years of age, and Lallie would have been about 32 years old.

After his brief time at Mount Margaret mission Snowy earned an income by doing casual work around mines and some prospecting for himself. After the Second World War Snowy continued to work in mines such as those at Gwalia near Leonora and around Laverton. By 1962, Snowy was given the pension. He had settled at Menzies where he did some casual work and prospecting[37].

By the mid-1940s, when Jack was about 68 years old and Lallie was estimated to be 34 years old, Jack Akbar took upon himself one of the duties an Islamic father was expected to pursue. He had to consider the arrangement of the marriage of his eldest daughter. Mona was about 15, a pubescent virgin, and in traditional Moslem society of a marrying age. It was a custom that such young women be wed to a husband who was usually chosen for her and was much older than her. Jack wanted to find a suitable husband among the Afghan camelmen who inhabited the communities of the far northern towns of South Australia. Mona's recollection about this incident is vague. Islamic men did not discuss business or important decisions with their women, and the matter of selecting a suitable husband for a daughter was discussed mainly by the men who had eligible sons.

The man Mona believes her father selected for her was to be one of the two surviving sons of Gool Mahomet of Farina. Mona could recall on one occasion an older man coming from Farina. As Jack was not at home when the traveller arrived in Renmark he had to sit outside the house until Jack came home. Mona added that 'we were the only family in the town that did this'. This Afghan, who her father said was named Gool Mahomet, had a son there and her father and this man were considering matching that man's son with Mona. As Gool and Jack were very close friends and Gool's sons were well respected and well known members of the Afghan camelmen's wider community of the far north of South Australia, the two fathers may have been quite optimistic about the marriage they were attempting to arrange[38]. By the mid-1940s Gool's two sons Sherali and Sallay were in their late thirties and worked with their father in their family business of camel carrying and dam sinking

Snowy Bradley visited his sister and her family in South Australia in the early 1940s. He is pictured in jocular mood with his niece, Mona, the eldest of the Akbar children. Photo courtesy Mona Wilson.

with camels. They practised their father's faith regularly at home, made regular trips to the district mosque in Marree and occasional visits to the major one in Adelaide[39]. Jack Akbar most likely believed that the marriage of a good young woman and a financially secure, diligent and devout man would be a most prestigious, solid and blessed one.

Before the marriage plans could be consolidated the Akbar family was to learn of news which would have a shattering impact. Mona had been seeing a lad in Renmark without her parents' knowledge, and was pregnant.

Lallie was sympathetic to her daughter's situation. She herself knew what it felt like to be an unmarried teenager who was pregnant to a man who did not want to take care of that child. When Jack had decided to seek permission to marry Lallie she had been pregnant. If it had not been for him she could have been a single mother of fatherless children likely to be living in hiding and in danger and staving off starvation. Tjirrgulu had cared for her daughter when she had become pregnant and was abandoned by the biological father. Lallie wanted now to do the same for her own daughter, to give Mona support and care, to look after her and her child and make sure they both had shelter, a family and love.

For Jack the news of Mona's pregnancy was devastating. He believed that Mona's behaviour was against almost everything he believed in and upheld. Within the framework of his religion and culture he felt that his daughter had brought shame on him, and on his house. The behaviour of his daughter was too much shame for him to bear.

Lallie attempted to reason with her husband. Over the years in their marriage he had become a very strict and stern man and over this matter, to do with his own daughter, she could not persuade him to be flexible in his attitude or to diffuse his anger. Mona, Shirley and Jimmy could recall the extreme conflict their parents experienced over this situation. Jack had not forgotten how hard life had been for his wife before he had married her. He remembered that when he wanted to marry her she was pregnant and unmarried and he had been prepared to love her and the baby if it survived. However, his point was that such behaviour could be understood in circumstances such as the bush but could not be condoned in this different circumstance. He declared that Mona would have to leave their house and be sent away from Renmark. She would have to go to a home in Adelaide where she could deliver her baby in secret. Jack did not want her to come home until she had given it away[40].

Lallie could not tolerate such a solution to Mona's condition. It was the belief of her people that mothers especially should look after their children with unconditional love, and support them with care, protection and compassion. Jack's way of handling this situation may have evoked her own memories of the injustices that she had experienced at the hands of the authorities back in Western Australia. Lallie's unhappiness about the way Jack was reacting to Mona's pregnancy combined with her homesickness for her own mother's people. It is very probable that she felt that if Jack insisted on sending Mona away from home to relinquish her baby then she would have to leave this home also.

Mona left Renmark to spend the remaining time of her pregnancy in the McBride Home for Girls in Adelaide. She gave birth to a healthy infant girl whom she named Janice (pronounced 'Janeece'). For the first six weeks of Janice's life she was held, cuddled and breastfed by her birth mother. A bond had been established between the two. Finally the South Australian 'Welfare Department' came to take the baby from her mother as they had found foster parents eager to receive a child. By the time Mona returned to her home in Renmark her mother had gone[41].

Early in 1946 the Commissioner of Native Affairs received a letter from Schenk at the Mount Margaret mission that informed him Lallie Akbar had re-entered Western Australia and was back in the goldfields visiting her relatives. She was accompanied by her second oldest child, fourteen-year-old Shirley. Also, though still married, Lallie had found a new partner. This knowledge was confirmed for the missionary by a 'half-caste' man named Arthur Victor Newland. This man had come to Mount Margaret mission with his 'full-blood' woman Norah. He informed the Schenks that he wanted to leave her there as he no longer wished to care for her. There was another woman with whom he wanted to live. He was going to start a new life with Lallie Akbar[42].

Auber Neville, whose position had been retitled in 1937 as 'Commissioner of Native Affairs' retired after twenty years in that position on 20 March 1940. He was succeeded by Mr F. Bray who had been the Deputy Commissioner. Commissioner Bray reviewed Lallie's case before responding to Rod Schenk. He suggested to the missionary that at this time it would not be appropriate to take any action against Lallie's presence in the goldfields. She was well beyond the age of being a ward of the Department of Native Affairs and so it was no longer a practical solution to remove her to a native settlement or mission. However, the Commissioner had noted that Lallie had brought her daughter Shirley from South Australia and he was more anxious about the future welfare of the teenager. He was disturbed to learn that Shirley's parents had separated. The bureaucrat was concerned about the instability in her own home in Renmark and about the company she would be exposed to in the goldfields. She was involved in her mother's association with a 'half-caste' man who was not tribally responsible for Lallie or her children. The Commissioner assessed that it would be most expedient to contemplate taking action in the case of Shirley and arranging for her removal from her mother. Shirley could be placed into an institution for her own good and her protection. The Commissioner asked Rod Schenk what his thoughts were on having Shirley relocated to his mission, or removed to be interned in one of the department's native settlements.

The Commissioner passed these comments to the missionary with some caution. He was aware that Shirley Akbar, though of ward age, had grown up in a prosperous town, in an established home with two parents and had completed a primary school education in a state school. He was concerned that it was very probable that Shirley might be 'too sophisticated' for living in the welfare institutions he had in mind[43]. Before the Commissioner made a decision on what action to take regarding the welfare of Lallie's daughter he was informed that Shirley Akbar had departed from Western Australia and returned to her home in Renmark.

Arthur Newland was born in Kanowna. His main occupation was as a woodcutter so he and Lallie went wherever he could find employment. From 1945 to 1946 Arthur was employed chopping wood at Bulong, which was originally the site of a mining town[44]. It is calculated that Arthur met Lallie during this job.

Lallie Akbar took on Newland's surname[45] and he was her partner for the rest of her life. They had children of their own. On 26 April 1948 Lallie, now aged between 38 and 40, gave birth to their first child and her fifth surviving child, Ann Joyce Newland, in the Leonora hospital[46].

During 1948 Lallie returned to Renmark for a short time to visit her family. Photographs taken of this occasion indicate that Lallie left her baby girl Ann Joyce in the goldfields with her husband's family. When Mona returned to Renmark after the birth of her baby girl she had resumed the responsibility of looking after her father and siblings. By 1948 three of the Akbar children were teenagers and Mona was married to Ray Wilson. The first of the Wilson children met their grandmother for the first time. Mona and Ray Wilson had four boys and a daughter, all much loved by their grandparents.

Upon returning to Western Australia Lallie and Arthur moved a little way out of Leonora and for a while lived with their daughter at the Woodline camp 38 miles (61 kilometres) south of Gwalia. During 1950 the family moved to Coolgardie where Arthur got work at the State gold battery. In Coolgardie their second child, Marjorie May Newland, was born on 29 January[47].

From Coolgardie the Newland family moved to Laverton. In January 1956 Lallie Akbar applied for the Certificate of Citizenship. The Natives Citizenship Rights Act passed in 1944 offered a citizenship with limited rights to the Aboriginal people and it could be withdrawn at any time. A condition of this limited citizenship was that the Aboriginal person had to once again prove, among other things, that he or she had adopted a

Lallie Akbar with her defacto husband, Arthur Newland, and their two daughters Ann and Marjorie in Western Australia. Photo courtesy of Shirley Wilson.

'civilised life' and did not associate with Aboriginal people who did not have citizenship rights. At that time and until 1967 Aboriginal and part-Aboriginal persons did not become citizens of Australia from the moment of their birth[48]. Granting citizenship to people of Aboriginal descent meant that they were accepted as citizens of the country in which their ancestors had lived for forty thousand years. With citizenship they then had access to most things that people of Anglo-Saxon and European descent had automatically. Lallie was granted her Certificate of Citizenship on 21 March 1956[49]. In 1967 all Aboriginal people were given citizenship rights from birth. This meant that all the Akbar children were granted citizenship in the country of their birth and ancestry. Shirley Wilson still has possession of her citizenship card which contains her photo and personal details, all stamped by a government official. In her later years Lallie finally settled in Menzies, where a number of her mother's people had already congregated over the years. The settlements that the Wongai regularly visited in the eastern goldfields around Lake Carey became deserted and from the late 1940s many of her people moved towards Menzies which was on a main road and rail transport network.

In 1954 Jack Akbar became seriously ill. He was admitted to the Renmark hospital where he eventually died on 29 September of that year. With no mullah or wife nearby it became the responsibility of Mona as his oldest child to arrange his funeral service and burial. After his funeral service at St Augustine's Church he was buried in the Renmark cemetery near his young son Jack[50]. His death initiated the exodus of the Akbar children from the town in which they had been born, raised and educated.

In 1989, after a period of separation of 43 years, Mona was reunited with her first born child, called Jan all her life. It was a happy occasion which has given both Mona and Jan a feeling of 'completeness' in their lives.

Shirley was married and lived in Adelaide. Jimmy and Johnny Akbar went to live at Lyndhurst, a town on the fringe of the desert country in the far north of South Australia. They were able to find work on the dingo fence and on pastoral stations. They married women from that area and have families of their own.

From the four Akbar children there are 22 grandchildren and 28 great-grandchildren. Though the descendants of Jack and Lallie Akbar are scattered across the continent of Australia between Melbourne and Inglewood in the east, Perth and Armadale in the west, they are spiritually close. Each one knows where they can contact anyone at any time and there is a strong and tenacious fibre of affection and respect holding them all together. The meaning of family is very significant to the Akbar descendants who have all established lives for themselves and in the 1990s experienced two reunions. The family have come to learn and understand a lot more about their heritage since the family gained possession of a copy of their Lallie's DCS file.

Lallie became a prominent figure in her community around Menzies,

Lallie Akbar lived in Menzies,Western Australia, in the 1950s and 60s. She is pictured here with her brother Snowy Bradley. Photo courtesy Shirly Wilson.

where she lived her last years close to her brother Snowy. For many Aboriginal people she was a strong character who seemed to understand what her people needed. More and more she became a spokesperson for her people and by the 1960s the locals came to perceive her as being equivalent to one of their 'elders'. She was called 'aunty' by even the older women[51]. People went to her for help and advice. She was respected as a wise person and as an anchor to her people[52].

Lallie's position amongst her people around Menzies was prestigious: 'When the train pulled in at Menzies and the big corroborees were on, Lallie would know two-thirds of those wild bush boys who got off the train and who still had bones through their noses. High-ranking Aboriginal males with scarring on their chest that denoted their importance to their tribes would come and see her'[53].

Lallie had a strong will and was respected by Aboriginal and non-

Aboriginal people. The police would go to her to ask her to help them stop the drunk Aborigines from fighting out on the flat. A lot of drinking was done by some of the women too. Lallie would take care of these women. She would make them undress and wash and then put on clean clothes. She made sure they were safe and clean[54].

Lallie was 65 years old and living with Arthur in Kalgoorlie when in 1970 she became so unwell that she required a doctor's attention. The doctor's diagnosis was that Lallie had the 'flu and that seemed to develop into pleurisy. Once it was realised that her condition was throat and lung cancer Lallie was admitted to the Kalgoorlie Regional hospital from which she was sent to a hospital in Perth. During her time in Perth Lallie stayed on a farm at Armadale where she was kept medicated and comfortable by her daughter Shirley, her son Jimmy who had come over from Lyndhurst in South Australia to help take care of their mother, and by Shirley's son Richard. When her health improved she returned to the Kalgoorlie hospital[55].

As the oldest child, Mona was once again expected to see to the needs and unfinished business of her parent. Mona had to come from Inglewood in Victoria to conduct her duties. She and Lallie's other children and Arthur Newland took turns holding Lallie's hand and comforting her, helping her to try to consume what liquid nourishment she could manage. Even in her dying days Lallie thought of her people as well as her family. From her hospital bed Lallie 'laid it down the line to her community that there was not to be drinking, stone throwing or fighting'[56]. Before she died Lallie was allowed to go home for a while where Mona and other relatives helped take care of her. Shirley and her husband came from Perth as often as possible.

Just before she died Lallie asked Mona to make sure that she had a Wongai funeral. Seeing to her mother's peace of mind Mona asked her 'if she wouldn't mind the Christian praying done for her'. Lallie replied that she didn't[57].

The widely respected Lallie Akbar passed away surrounded by much love on 1 June 1970. Her body was taken from the hospital for her funeral service at the Eastern Goldfields Native Centre in Cassidy Street, Kalgoorlie[58]. The car cavalcade that commenced from the Native Centre consisted of 38 vehicles which travelled at about ten miles per hour through Kalgoorlie's streets to the cemetery. At the cemetery entrance people in 10 more cars waited to join the cavalcade that would drive to the site of Lallie's grave, located in the Anglican portion of the Kalgoorlie cemetery. Mona, Arthur and family arranged for the hymns that Lallie sung all her life to be sung at her funeral service, at the church and at the grave[59].

When the funeral service conducted by the Church's representative was over Mona and other immediate family members returned home, changed their clothes, then returned to Lallie's grave for a Wongai service, just as Lallie requested[60].

The DCS file kept on Lallie Matbar was kept open and updated until the year 1970. It was not closed any earlier, not as a matter of justice, of civil or human rights, of fairness, by virtue of the absence of crime or offences, or her reputable life making it unnecessary to monitor her. When all Aboriginal people were granted citizenship in 1967, at a time when no such files ought to have been necessary, Lallie's was one of those that was updated. It was finally closed only by her death.

APPENDIX

LALLIE'S MOB

The winds they blew, the Spirits they moaned.
Throughout the eons they've moved and sowed.
Such was an occasion when they moved in the birth
Of the woman called **Jirrgulu**, lived upon this earth.
Not much is known of this woman with Spirit,
All that we have is written by missionaries–
A Drop In A Bucket.
Jirrgulu had two children, of this I've read,
Raised them in desert, the place of the **Tjukurpa**.
These children of the Dreaming came into the Mission,
Jirrgulu seeked safety for her two offspring.
Lallie and Snowy were the names they had,
To the mission they came in the years of their teens.
Our Lallie was captured, sent off to Moore River,
Mixed breed child was meant to forget
That she had black blood, that she had the Spirit.
Away did she run, fear and strength propelled her home,
Across the vastness of desert and stone,
Returned to her country... the Tjukurpa moaned.
Time moved along, and life turned around,
Jirrgulu met the end of her days,
Innocently killed through vendetta... pay-back.
Lallie grew on, wore the cross of her lot.
At some time unsure, into her life came **Jack**.
This man was an alien, an Afghan by birth.
With his ships of the desert, moving through the outback.
Accused of kidnap, away they did flee,
Over the border into South Aussie,

Hounded and persecuted for years to come,
This man and woman had broken white-fella's law.
The trials and torments that they had to bear,
Have been recorded, from state archives the facts do glare.
It is my belief that in love they were,
They settled on the Murray, four children they birthed.
Lallie, I'm told, left after many years,
Returned to her birthplace, no longer fighting tears,
The spirit of Jirrgulu, insisting she die there.
Jack died alone, in the place he made home,
Buried near water, a town called Renmark.
Their children grew, experiences unique,
Mixed-breed children, many trials to defeat.
Each one carried the seed, the Spirit still spread.
Passed on to their children, of which I am one.
Now we're here, all cousins we are,
Across this land, scattered wide and far.
Across this great country we live our own lives.
Some of us claiming the role of not knowing,
Who were our ancestors, our blood, our seeding.
Yet some of us do realise the deeper meaning,
What it is to be part of an ancestral Dreaming.
The land and its spirit runs thick in our veins,
Lallie still lives, helps wipe away our pain.
We are the children of a long, strong breathing,
The breath of life, the Tjukurpa, the Dreaming.
Know now my family and friends,
That no matter what turmoil, no matter our lot,
We are the one's who are... we are Lallie's Mob.

D. J. Akbar
December 1992

ENDNOTES

INTRODUCTION

1. Rajkowski, P., *In the Tracks of the Camelmen*, Angus and Robertson, Australia, 1987, pp. 52, 125-6.
2. Letter from Mona Wilson (nee Akbar), Inglewood, Victoria, 5 September 1988.
3. 'Brief Chronology of Aboriginal Affairs Planning Authority (AAPA) in Western Australia', AAPA, Perth, W.A., February 1993.
4. Harry Taylor, Department of Community Services (DCS), Perth, to Rajkowski, October 1993.
5. Jacobs, P., *Mister Neville; A Biography*, Fremantle Arts Centre Press, W.A., 1990, p. 126.
6. Haebich, A., *For their own good; Aborigines and Government in the South-west of Western Australia, 1900-1940*, University of Western Australia Press, W.A., 1988.
7. John Priestley, Department of Community Services (DCS),Perth, Western Australia, to Rajkowski, 1989.
8. Laurel Cooper, (nee Johnston) Kalgoorlie, W.A., to Rajkowski, 5 January 1994.
9. Robert Rigney, Aboriginal Studies Coordinator, Aboriginal Education Unit, Education Department of South Australia, October 1993, 'Sensitive Terms and Issues', Aboriginal Education Unit, S.A. Education Department,1992.
10. Wilf Douglas, retired missionary, Kalgoorlie, W.A., to Rajkowski, 21 January 1989.
11. Dr John Stanton, Department of Anthropology, University of Western Australia, to Rajkowski, 24 May 1989.

CHAPTER ONE

1. Ranji McIntyre, Kurrawang Mission via Kalgoorlie, to Rajkowski, 18 January 1989.
2. Davis, Jack, 'The First 150 Years', in Berndt R.M. and C.H. (eds), *Aborigines of the West; Their Past and Present*, University of Western Australia, 1979, pp. 56, 57 Also, Margaret Morgan (nee Schenk) to Rajkowski, Perth, 25 May, 1989.
3. See Introduction for reference to use of the term 'tribal'.
4. 'Half Caste Lallie Matbar - Marriage to Jack Akbar',ACC 993, File 379/26, 1926-70, Chief Secretary of the Colonial Secretary's Department. This file, along with all the others, was initiated by the Aborigines Department, which from 1936 was retitled the Department of Native Affairs (D.N.A.). Later that department was reorganised and the files went to the Department of Native Welfare, and from there to Department of Community Services

(D.C.S.), where they are currently housed. Files from this department are referred to in this text as DCS files, e.g. Lallie's DCS file.

5. See Introduction for reference to use of 'full blood' in section on terminology.
6. Lallie's DCS File, ACC 993, file 379/26, p.3.
7. Ranji McIntyre to Rajkowski, op. cit.
8. Shirley Wilson (nee Akbar) to Rajkowski, Armadale, Western Australia, 25 May 1989.
9. Biskup, P., *Not Slaves Not Citizens; The Aboriginal People in Western Australia 1898-1954*, University of Queensland Press, 1973, pp. 111-2.
10. 'Half Caste - Snowy Bradley @ Lowe - Mt. Magnet', ACC 993, File No 74/34; now with the Dept of Community Services (DCS), Perth
11. See Introduction for reference to use of 'part-Aboriginal' in section on terminology.
12. Morgan, M., *A Drop in a Bucket; the Mount Margaret Story*, United Aborigines Mission, Melbourne, Vic., 1986, p. 44, plus map.
13. Letter from Police Constable (P.C.) Perks to District Inspector of Police (D.I.P.) Duncan, 31 May 1923, DCS File 379/26.
14. Letter from Inspector E. Mitchell Aborigines Department, 29 September 1927, DCS File 379/26.
15. Ibid.
16. Biskup, P., op.cit., p. 77-79.
17. Morgan, M., op. cit., p. 44.
18. See Introduction for reference to use of 'half-caste' in section on terminology.
19. Letter from P.C. Perks to D.I.P. Duncan, 31 May 1923, File 379/26.
20. Biskup, P., op. cit., p. 41. Also, see Introduction for reference to use of 'native' in section on terminology.
21. Biskup, P., op. cit., p. 42.
22. Morgan, M., *A Drop in a Bucket*, op.cit.
23. Letter from Rodolphe Samuel Schenk to police, 7 October 1926, p. 76, DCS File 379/26.
24. 'Information Re Half Castes, Mount Margaret District, 5 March 1928', from Police Files transferred to DCS File 379/26.
25. 'Information Re Half Castes, Mt Margaret District', op. cit.
26. Davis, Jack, 'The First 150 years', op.cit., p. 57.
27. Morgan, M., op. cit., p. 12.
28. Davis, Jack, 'The First 150 Years', op. cit., p. 57.
29. 'Maternity Allowance', 13 May 1948, p. 8, and 23 June 1967, p. 40, was File 138/46, Colonial Secretary's Office , now in DCS File 379/26.
30. 'Half caste - Snowy Bradley @ Lowe - Mt. Magnet', DCS File 74/34.
31. John Priestley to Rajkowski, Dept. of Commmunity Services, Perth, W.A., 10 January 1989.
32. 'Half Caste Lallie Matbar, marriage to Jack Akbar, DCS File 379/26.
33. Gordon and Jennifer Leaney to Rajkowski, Esperance, Western Australia, 17 January 1989.
34. Smith, H.P. (ed.), *The First Ten Years of Mount Margaret Mission, Western Australia*, United Aborigines Mission, Melbourne, Australia, p. 58.
35. 'Information Re Half Castes, Mt Margaret District, op. cit.
36. Ranji McIntyre to Rajkowski, op. cit.
37. Wilf Douglas to Rajkowski, Kalgoorlie, W.A., 21 January 1989.
38. See Introduction for reference to use of the term 'mixed blood' in section on terminology.
39. The reference to the distinction among Aborigines between 'full-blood' and 'half-caste' females particularly was common to the interviews conducted by myself, and by Verna Vos, a lecturer at Edith Cowan University, of Aboriginal

women of the eastern goldfields.

40. Howard, Michael C., 'Aboriginal society in south-western Australia', in Berndt R.M. and C.H. (eds) 1979, op. cit., p. 34. The names of the elders of the Linden mob, so often referred to in the text, were never recorded by police or the Aborigines Department.
41. Marks, S.R., 'Mission Policy in Western Australia 1846-1959', *University Studies in Western Australian History*, Vol. 3 (4), 1960, p. 61.
42. Margaret Morgan to Rajkowski, op. cit.
43. Colburg, Ken, 'On being an Aboriginal: a personal statement', in Berndt R.M. and C.H. (eds), 1979, op. cit., p. 103.
44. Berndt, Catherine H., 'Aboriginal women and the notion of "the marginal man"', in Berndt R.M. and C.H. (eds), op. cit., p. 34.
45. Morgan, M., op. cit., p. 107.
46. Ibid
47. Berndt R.M. and C.H, *The World of the First Australians*, Ure Smith, Sydney, 1964, p. 124.Also, Herb Basedow, *The Australian Aboriginal*, F.W. Preece and Sons, Adelaide, 1925, A M S Press, New York, U.S.A., 1979, p. 64.
48. Neville, A.O., 'Contributing Causes of Aboriginal Depopulation in Western Australia', in *Mankind*, Anthropological Journal, Vol. 4,No.1, September, 1948, Battye Library, W.A.
49. Laurel Cooper (nee Johnson), Kalgoorlie, W.A., to Rajkowski, 5 January 1994.
50. Verna Vos, Australian Aboriginal Planning Authority (AAPA), Perth, W.A., to Rajkowski, 22 May 1989.
51. Laurel Cooper to Rajkowski, Kalgoorlie, W.A., 21 January 1989.
52. Biskup, P., op. cit., p. 65. Also, 1905 Aborigines Act, The Statutes of Western Australia, 1904-5.
53. The term 'catch' is used by the police in their reports, which are contained in Lallie's DCS File 379/26, to refer to the apprehension of the Aboriginal children.
54. Biskup, P., op. cit., p. 156.
55. Haebich, A., 'On the Inside: Moore River Native Settlement inthe 1930s', in Bill Gammage, and A. Markus, (eds.), *All That Dirt: Aborigines 1938*; an Australia 1938 monograph, Canberra, 1982, p. 54.
56. Letter from P.C. Perks to D.I.P. Spedding Smith, 26 August 1926, DCS File 379/26.
57. Laurel and Norm Cooper, Kalgoorlie, W.A. to Rajkowski, 20 January 1989.
58. Dr John Stanton, Anthropological Research Museum, University of W.A., Perth, W.A., to Rajkowski, 24 May 1989.
59. Laurel and Norm Cooper to Rajkowski, op. cit.
60. Laurel Cooper to Rajkowski, Kalgoorlie, W.A., 21 January 1989.
61. Laurel and Norm Cooper to Rajkowski, op. cit.
62. Shirley Wilson to Rajkowski, op. cit.
63. Laurel and Norm Cooper to Rajkowski, op. cit.
64. Ibid.
65. Morgan, M., op cit., p. 83.
66. Shirley Wilson to Rajkowski, 8 January 1989, op. cit.
67. Laurel Cooper to Rajkowski, op. cit.
68. Laurel and Norm Cooper to Rajkowski, op cit.
69. Gale, Fay (ed.), *Women's Role in Aboriginal Society*, Australian Institute of Aboriginal Studies, Canberra, 1978, p. 29.
70. Elkin, A., *The Australian Aborigines*, Angus and Robertson, N.S.W., 1986, pp. 156-7. Also, Neville A.O., 'Contributing Causes of Aboriginal Depopulation in Western Australia',

op. cit.,pp. 3-13.
71. Elkin, A., op. cit., p. 158.
72. Neville, A.O., 1948, op. cit.
73. Basedow, H., op. cit., p. 222.
74. Neville, A.O., op. cit.
75. Smith, H.P. (ed.), op cit., p. 77.
76. Basedow, H., op. cit., p. 221.
77. Schenk, R.S., 1936, op. cit., p. 41.
78. Gale, F., op. cit., p. 37. Also, Morgan, M., op. cit., p. 120.
79. Basedow, H., op. cit., p. 224.
80. Morgan, M., op. cit., p. 120.
81. Basedow, H., op. cit., p. 223. Also, Smith, H.P., op. cit., p. 77; and Margaret Morgan to Rajkowski, op. cit.
82. Sharpe, W. and M., *What an Experience*, Boolarong Publications, Queensland, 1989, p. 30.
83. Basedow, H., op. cit., p. 223.
84. Morgan, M., op. cit., p. 76.
85. Ibid, p. 20.
86. Ibid, p. 77.
87. Bennett, M. M., 'Teaching the Aborigines: Data from Mount Margaret Mission, W.A.', Perth, 1935, p. 28.
88. Margaret Morgan to Rajkowski, op cit.
89. Biskup, P., op. cit., p. 92.
90. Morgan, M., op. cit., p. 21.
91. Bennett, M. M., *The Australian Aboriginal as a Human Being*, London, 1930. In Battye Library, W.A.
92. Elkin, A., op. cit., p. 159.
93. Margaret Morgan to Rajkowski, op. cit.
94. In the use of official language referring to sexual acts between colonists and Aboriginal girls the term 'prostitution' was not used. The use of the word 'cohabitation' in Lallie's DCS file was in keeping with the terminology of the 1905 Aborigines Act.
95. Shirley Wilson to Rajkowski, op. cit.
96. 'The Treatment of Native Women', *West Australian*, 24 August, 1935, p. 22.
97. Section 42 of the W.A. 1905 Aborigines Act; 'No marriage of a female aboriginal with any person other than an aboriginal shall be celebrated without the permission, in writing, of the Chief Protector'.
98. Bennett, M.M., *The Australian Aborigine as a Human Being*, op. cit.
99. Verna Vos to Rajkowski, op. cit.
100. Section 34, 1905 Aborigines Act, op. cit.
101. Letter from P.C. Perks to D.I.P. Spedding Smith, 19 September 1926, DCS File 379/26.
102. Battye, J., *Western Australia, A History from its discovery to the Inauguration of the Commonwealth* (facsimile edition), 1978, University of Western Australia Press.
103. Rajkowski, P., *In the Tracks of the Camelmen*, Angus and Robertson, Sydney, 1986, pp. 15-18.
104. *Inquirer*, 26 October 1887, p. 4.
105. *Western Australian Gold Fields (W.A.G.F.) Courier*, 30 October 1897.
106. 'Minutes of Evidence', in W.A. Votes and Proceedings of Parliament Third Session, Third Parliament 1898, Vol. One, Premier's Dept., p. 247, File 572/1900.
107. 'Immigration Restriction Act - 1903: Petition from Hindoos', Australian Archives, S.A., CSR A 1, Item 03/5781.
108. 'Islam' is the word introduced in the twentieth century to replace the traditional words 'Mohammedan' or 'Moslem'. The traditional words are used in this text so as to be in context of the time of this story.
109. Rajkowski, P., op. cit., pp. 86-7.
110. Letter from P.C. Perks to D.I.P. Spedding Smith, 5 August 1926, p. 7, DCS File 379/26.
111. Letter from R.F. Cook, solicitor, to Chief Protector of Aborigines (C.P.A.) Neville, 4 August 1926, p. 6, DCS File 379/26.

112. Rajkowski, P., op. cit., pp. 15-17.
113. Letter from R.C. Cook to C.P.A., 4 August 1926, op. cit.
114. Mona Wilson (nee Akbar) to Rajkowski, Inglewood, Victoria, 8 January 1988.
115. Letter from R.C. Cook to C.P.A., 4 August 1926, op.cit.
116. Photograph of Jack Akbar in possession of Mrs Mona Wilson, Inglewood, Victoria.
117. For details of what aspects of thc Afghan community antagonised the wider community of the colonists see newspaper references (a) to (g) below;
(a) The *Queenslander*, 14 October 1899, p. 746, col. b.
(b) *Western Argus*, W.A., 3 September 1901.
(c) *Western Argus*, W.A., 10 September 1901.
(d) 'Notes and Notices', *Australasian*, 1 February 1902, p., 269.
(e) *Coolgardie Miner*, W.A., 18 December 1994.
(f) 'The Afghan Question', *W.A.G.F. Courier*, 30 October 1897; also, 24/2/1897, 2/4/1897, 14/10/1897.
(g) *Coolgardie Miner*, W.A., 30 June 1894.
118. Farwell, G., *Land of Mirage*, Cassell and Co., Australia, 1950, p. 23.
119. For example, court case of Shannaway (or Shannawaz) and Miss Gibson, *Western Argus*, W.A., 11 May 1899 and *Coolgardie Pioneer*, W.A., 27 May 1899; court case of Abdul Hannat and Sarah Simpson, Adelaide Observer, S.A., 18 October 1902, p. 724.
120. *Coolgardie Miner*, W.A., 18 December 1897.
121. *Morgans Courier*, W.A., 17 November 1906.
122. The *Sun*, W.A., 19 May 1907.
123. *Sunday Times*, W.A., 29 August 1909, 14 October 1909.
124. Ibid, 17 October 1909.
125. Ibid., 21 November 1909.
126. Ibid., 9 April 1911.
127. Letter from J.C. Kirby, Congregational Minister, Semaphore S.A., to Dept. of External Affairs, Correspondence Files, Series 1903-1938, regarding 'Marriage between British Women and Moslems, Hindus, Afghans', Australian Archives, CRS A1, Item 14/5188.
128. Ibid.
129. Rajkowski, P., *In the Tracks of the Camelmen*, op.
130. Noel Fullarton to Rajkowski, Camel Farm, Alice Springs, Northern Territory, September 1980.
131. Sallay Mahomet to Rajkowski, Alice Springs, Northern Territory, September 1980.
132. Receipt regarding Lal Mahomet's sale of camels to J. Akbar, in private collection of Mona Wilson, Inglewood, Victoria.
133. *Wise's Western Australian Post Office Directory*, 1915, Battye Library, Perth, W.A. This volume records that 'Silbert and Sharp', which was based on fruit merchandising, existed in Leonora in 1915. Also, the receipt is in the private collection of Mona Wilson, Victoria.
134. Mona Wilson to Rajkowski, 8 January 1988.
135. Ibid.
136. Letter from R. Cook to C.P.A., 4 August 1926, p. 6, DCS File 379/26.
137. This letter is in the private collection of Mona Wilson, Victoria.
138. Mona Wilson to Rajkowski, 8 January 1988, op. cit.
139. Morgan, M., op. cit., p. 6.
140. Mona Wilson to Rajkowski, 8 January 1988, op. cit.
141. Letter from R. Cook to C.P.A., 4 August 1926, p. 6, op. cit.
142. Mona Wilson to Rajkowski, op. cit.
143. This certificate of registration of a

commercial premise is in the private collection of Mona Wilson.
144. Mona Wilson to Rajkowski, op. cit.
145. Letter from Cook to C.P.A., 4 August 1926, DCS File 379/26.
146. Rajkowski, P., op. cit., p. 171.
147. Mona Wilson to Rajkowski, op. cit.
148. Letter from Police Constable S.E. Perks to Police Inspector Spedding Smith, Morgans station, 16 September 1926, Lallie's DCS file No. 379/26.

CHAPTER TWO

1. Verna Vos to Rajkowski, Aboriginal Affairs Planning Authority (AAPA), Perth, W.A., 22 May 1989.
2. Ibid.
3. 'Half caste Lallie Matbar - Marriage of to Jack Akbar', Chief Secretary of the Colonial Secretary's Department (CSO), ACC 993, File 379/26. - the Department of Community Services (DCS).
4. Verna Vos to Rajkowski, op. cit.
5. Bennett, M. M., Teaching the Aborigines; Data from Mount Margaret Mission', London, 1935, p. 28. In Battye Library, W.A.
6. Letter from Police Constable (P.C.) Perks to District Inspector of Police (D.I.P.) Spedding Smith, 26 August 1926, DCS File 379/26. and Letter from Chief Protector of Aborigines (C.P.A.) to C. in C. [the file does not provide the full names for these initials], 18 November 1926, File DCS 379/26. 7. Letter from P.C. Perks to D.I.P. Duncan, Kalgoorlie, 24 April 1923, Chief Secretary's Department, ACC 752, 931/21, Battye Library, Perth, W.A.
8. Margaret Morgan to Rajkowski, Perth, W.A., 26 May 1989.
9. Letter from P.C. Perks to D.I.P. Spedding Smith, 21 July 1926, DCS File 379/26.
10. Elkin. A.P., 'Aboriginal-European relations in Western Australia: an historical and personal record', in Berndt R.M. and C.H. (eds), *Aborigines of the West: Their Past and Present*, University of Western Australia., 1979, p. 294.
11. Biskup, P., *Not slaves not citizens; The Aboriginal Problem in Western Australia 1898-1945*, University of Queensland Press, 1973, p. 75.
12. Section 12, 1905 Aborigines Act, The Statutes of Western Australia, 1904-05.
13. Hasluck, P., *Mucking About; An Autobiography*, Melbourne University Press, Melbourne, 1977, pp. 211-2.
14. Section 37 and 38, 1905 Aborigines Act, op. cit.
15. The curfew times before or by sunset may have evolved from the terms of Section 40 of 1905 Aborigines Act, op. cit; and P. Biskup, op. cit., p. 146.
16. Morgan, M., op. cit, Chapter One.
17. Jacobs, P., *Mister Neville; A Biography*, Fremantle Arts Centre Press, Perth, Western Australia, p. 89.
18. Letter from Deputy Chief Protector of Aborigines Copping to Police Commissioner Connell, March 1921, from DCS File No. 931/21 to DCS File 379/26.
19. 'Aborigines - Native Matters - Laverton', Chief Secretary's Department. Acc. 752, File 931/21, in Battye Library, W.A.
20. Letter from P.C. Perks to D.I.P. Spedding Smith, 31 May 1923, DCS File 379/26.
21. Letter from P.C. Perks to D.I.P., March 1924, Acc 993, Police File, in Battye Library, W.A.
22. Ibid.
23. Gammage, W., and Markus, A. (eds.), *All That Dirt: Aborigines 1938*, Canberra, 1982, p. 87.

24. Morgan, M., op. cit., p. 21. Also, Gammage, W. and Markus, A (eds.), op. cit., pp. 86.
25. Morgan, M., op. cit., p. 103, 214 and 218.
26. Ibid, p. 9.
27. Biskup, P., op. cit., p. 77.
28. Letter from P.C. Thompson, Laverton, December 1921, Police File No. 931/21. In Battye Library, W.A.
29. Police File 931/21, op. cit.
30. 'List of Half castes in Mt. Margaret district, 5 March 1928', Acc. 993, File 484/26, Aboriginal Affairs Planning Authority (AAPA), W.A.
31. Letter from P.C. Perks to D.I.P. Spedding Smith, 26 August 1926, p. 6, DCS File 379/26.
32. 1905 Aborigines Act, W.A., Section 42, op. cit.
33. Ibid, Sections 43 and 36.
34. Letter from P.C. Perks to D.I.P. Spedding Smith, 31 July 1926, DCS File 379/26, p. 7.
35. Ibid.
36. Ibid.
37. Letter from Reg Cook to C.P.A., 4 August 1926, DCS File 379/26, p. 1, 2.
38. Letter from P.C. Perks to D.I.P. Spedding Smith, op. cit.
39. Ibid.
40. Letter from P.C. Perks to Deputy C.P.A. Copping, 10 August 1926, DCS File 379/26.
41. Letter from P. C. Perks to D.I.P. Spedding Smith, 5 August 1926, p. 8, DCS File 379/26.
42. Ibid.
43. Ibid.
44. Ibid.
45. See Biskup, P, op. cit., pp. 112-4.
46. Letter from P.C. Perks, 31 July 1926, op. cit.
47. Letter from D.I.P. Spedding Smith, 1 August 1926, p. 3, DCS File 379/26.
48. Letter from Sgt. McGuiniss to P.C. Perks, 3 August 1926, p. 8, DCS File 379/26.
49. Letter from D.I.P. Spedding Smith to P.C. Perks, 31 July 1926, DCS File 379/26.
50. Letter from R. Cook to C.P.A., 4 August 1926, DCS File 379/26.
51. Letter from R. Cook to C.P.A., 4 August 1926, op. cit.
52. Letter from P.C. Perks to D.I.P, 3 August 1926, p. 8,op. cit.
53. Ibid.
54. Letter from D.I.P. to Perks, 10 August 1926, p. 8, DCS File 379/26.
55. Letter from P.C. Perks to D.I.P., 26 August 1926, p. 10, DCS File 379/26.
56. Ibid, p. 10.
57. Ibid.
58. Ibid.
59. Ibid.
60. Whittington, Vera, *Two Fevers; Gold and Typhoid*: a social history of Western Australia, Bentley, W.A., 1986.
61. Letter from Perks to D.I.P. Spedding Smith, 26 August 1926, DCS File 379/26.

CHAPTER THREE

1. Jacobs, P., *Mister Neville;A Biography*, Fremantle Arts Centre Press, W.A., 1990, chapters one and two.
2. Ibid, p. 73.
3. Ibid, p. 63.
4. Letter from P.C. Perks to D.I.P. Spedding Smith, 26 August 1926, DCS File 379/26, p. 10.
5. Hasluck, P., *Mucking About; An Autobiography*, Melbourne University Press, Victoria, 1977, p. 211.
6. Ibid.
7. The Native Administration Act 1936 includes 'quadroons' in its definition of 'native'. Also, P. Jacobs, op. cit., p. 89.
8. Howard, M.C., 'Aboriginal society in south-western Australia, in Berndt, R. M. and C.H. (eds.), *Aborigines of the*

West; Their Past and Present, University of Western Australia Press, 1979, p. 94.
9. Hasluck, P., op cit., p. 210.
10. Jacobs, P., op cit., p. 62.
11. Annual Report of the Chief Protector of Aborigines, June 1915 to June 1916, AAPA, W.A.
12. Jacobs, P., op cit., p. 65.
13. This is the point of view of Margaret Morgan to whom her father Rod Schenk gave his impression of Neville when they met in 1921. Morgan to Rajkowski, Perth, 8 January 1989.
14. Biskup, P., op cit., p. 158.
15. Elkin, A.P., op. cit., p. 294.
16. Reece, B. and Stannage, T. (eds.), 'European-Aboriginal relations in Western Australian History', *Studies in Western Australian History VIII,* University of Western Australia, December 1984, p. 71.
17. Biskup, P., op. cit., p. 61.
18. Ibid, pp. 145-6.
19. Section 19, 20, 21 and 40, 1905 Aborigines Act, op. cit.
20. Biskup, P., op. cit., p. 144-5.
21. Neville, A.O., *Australia's Coloured Minority; Its Place in the Community,* Sydney, 1947. In the Battye Library, W.A.
22. Jacobs, P., op. cit., p. 82.
23. Comments by Auber Octavius Neville at the conference of Commonwealth and State Aboriginal authorities, Canberra, 1937, pp. 21 3.
24. Section 16 (a), (b), (c), 1937 Native Administration Act, the Statutes of Western Australia.
25. Gammage, Bill and Markus, Andrew (eds.), *All That Dirt; Aborigines 1938*, Canberra 1982, pp. 86-7.
26. Ibid., pp. 87-9.
27. Ibid, p. 90.
28. Morgan, M, op. cit., p. 218.
29. Neville, A.O., *Australia's Coloured Minority*, op. cit.
30. Ibid.
31. A paper by A.O. Neville, not dated, Battye Library, Perth, W.A.
32. Biskup, P., op. cit., p. 142.
33. Ibid, p. 157.
34. A paper by A.O. Neville, not dated, Battye Library, Perth. W.A.
35. Annual Report of Chief Protector of Aborigines (C.P.A.) ending 30 June 1917, Aboriginal Affairs Planning Authority (AAPA), W.A.
36. Annual Report of C.P.A., ending 30 June 1922, AAPA, W.A., and, Biskup, P., op. cit., p. 156, which says 400 inmates.
37. Acc 993, File 673/26, Annual Report of C.P.A.. ending 30 June 1926, AAPA, W.A.
38. Neville, A.O., *Australia's Coloured Minority; Its Place in the Community,* op.cit.
39. Annual Report of C.P.A., ending 30 June 1920, AAPA, W.A.
40. Comments by Auber O. Neville at the Conference of Commonwealth and State Aboriginal Authorities, Canberra, 1937, pp. 21-3.
41. Biskup, P., op. cit., p. 157.
42. Morgan, M., op. cit., p. 13.
43. Neville, A.O, *Australia's Coloured Minority; Its Place in the Community,* op. cit.
44. Ibid.
45. Letter from P.C. Perks to D.I.P. Spedding Smith, 26 August 1926, p. 16, File 379/26.
46. Letter from R. Cook to C.P.A., 19 August 1926, File 379/26.
47. Letter from R. Cook to Akbar, 19 September 1926, DCS File 379/26.
48. Letter from C.P.A. to R. Cook, 3 September 1926, p. 13, File 379/26.
49. Letter from J. Akbar to R. Cook, 16 September 1926, p. 21, File 379/26.
50. Letter from Perks to D.I.P. Spedding Smith, 26 August 1926, DCS File 379/26, p. 16.

51. Taped interview of Reggie Johnston of Menzies by Bill Bunbury, December 1986, Perth, ABC radio series, 'Out of sight, out of mind', Oral History Programme, Battye Library, W.A.
52. Davis, J., 'The First 150 Years', in Berndt R.M. and C. H. (eds.), op. cit., p. 59.

CHAPTER FOUR

1. See Morgan, M., *A Drop in a Bucket*, United Aborigines Mission, Melbourne, Victoria, 1986, p. 93.
2. Smith, H.P. (ed.), *The First Ten Years at Mount Margaret Mission*, Western Australia, Spectator Publishing Company, Melbourne, 1933, p. 58.
3. Morgan, M., op cit., pp. 45-7.
4. Ibid, pp. 1, 2. The author of this article is anonymous.
5. Smith, H.P. (ed.), op. cit., p. 51.
6. The Australian Aborigines Mission (A.A.M.) was established in 1894 at La Perouse in Sydney. It was re-organsed in 1928 when a split occurred amongst its ranks. This led to the foundation of the short-lived Melbourne-based Gospel Mission to the Australian Aborigines (G.M.A.A.). The changing of its name in 1929 to the United Aborigines Mission (U.A.M.) was permanent.
7. Margaret Morgan to Rajkowski, Perth, 26 May 1989; and Morgan, M., op.cit., p. 1.
8. Margaret Morgan (nee Schenk), Perth, W.A., to Rajkowski, 23 December 1993.
9. Section 5, 1905 Aborigines Act, The Statutes of Western Australia, 1904-05.
10. Comments by A.O. Neville at the Conference of Commonwealth and State Authorities, Canberra, April 1937, Battye Library, W.A.
11. Biskup, P., *Not Slaves not Citizens; The Aboriginal Problem in Western Australia 1898-1945*, University of Queensland Press, 1973, pp. 149, 152.
12. Morgan, M., *A Drop in a Bucket*, op. cit., pp. 27-8.
13. Ibid, p. 1.
14. Stanton,J., 'The Mount Margaret community', in Berndt R.M. and C.H. (eds.), *Aborigines of the West; Their Past and Present*, University of Western Australia, 1979, p. 132.
15. Annual Report of the C.P.A. ending 30 June 1919, AAPA, W.A.
16. Biskup, P., op. cit., p. 122.
17. Margaret Morgan to Rajkowski, Perth, 26 May 1989.
18. Morgan, M., op. cit., p. 1. Also, Margaret Morgan to Rajkowski, 23 December, 1993.
19. Morgan, M., op. cit., pp. 1-5.
20. Ibid.
21. Ibid.
22. Ibid., op. cit, p. 12.
23. Morgan, M. to Rajkowski, op. cit.
24. Morgan, M., op. cit., p. 6.
25. Ibid.
26. Taped interview of Reggie Johnston of Menzies, 1868, by Bill Bunbury, for ABC radio series, 'Out of Sight, Out of Mind', Oral History Programme, Battye Library, W.A.
27. Letter from R. Schenk to Copping, 27 June 1926, Acc 993, File 484/26.
28. 'Aborigines - Native affairs - Laverton', letter from Sergeant (Sgt.) Thompson to District Inspector Police (D.I.P.) Duncan, 24 March 1921, Acc 752, File No. 931/21, Chief Secretary's Dept., Battye Library, W.A.
29. Morgan, M., op. cit., p. 30.
30. Interview of Reggie Johnston of Menzies 1986, op. cit.
31. Stanton, J., 'The Mount Margaret community', op. cit., p. 119.
32. Elkin, A.P., 'Aboriginal-European relations in Western Australia; an his-

torical and personal record', in Berndt R.M. and C.H. (eds.), op. cit., p. 296.
33. Margaret Morgan and Shirley Wilson to Rajkowski, Armadale, W.A., 1990.
34. Smith, H.P. (ed.), op. cit., p. 14.
35. Ibid, p. 5.
36. Ibid, p. 14.
37. Biskup. P., op. cit., p. 123.
38. Swain, T., and Rose, D. (eds.), *Aboriginal Australians and Christian Missions*, Australian Association for the Study of Religions, S.A., 1988, p. 293.
39. Smith, H.P. (ed.), op. cit., p. 36.
40. Ranji McIntyre to Rajkowski, Kurrawang Mission via Kalgoorlie, W.A., 18 January 1989.
41. Morgan, M., op. cit., p. 28.
42. Stanton, J., 'The Mount Margaret community', op. cit., p. 119.
43. 'Aborigines - Australian Aborigines Mission - Morgans -Treatment and training of natives at Mount Margaret mission', Acc 993, File 484/26, Chief Secretary's Department, in Battye Library, W.A.
44. Smith, H.P. (ed.), op. cit., p. 44.
45. Elkin, A.P., 'Aboriginal European relations', op. cit., p. 301-2.
46. Marks, S.R., 'Mission Policy in Western Australia 1846-1959, *University Studies in Western Australian History*, Vol. 3, No. 4. 1960, p. 88.
47. Morgan, M., op. cit., p. 83.
48. Jeannie Patterson to Rajkowski, Perth, 7 January 1989.
49. Letter from Rod Schenk to A.O. Neville, 23 January 1923, ACC No. 993, 484/26, AAPA, Perth, W.A.
50. Police file papers, Laverton, 1920s, Battye Library, Perth W.A.
51. Taped interview with Reggie Johnston, op. cit.
52. Morgan, M., op. cit., p. 87.
53. Ibid, p. 48.
54. Ibid, p. 84.
55. Smith, H.P. (ed.), op. cit., p. 46.
56. Morgan. M., op. cit., p. 66.
57. Taped interview with Reggie Johnston, op. cit.
58. Ibid.
59. Ibid..
60. Ranji McIntyre to Rajkowski, op. cit., and taped interview with Reggie Johnston, op. cit.
61. Marks, S.R., op. cit., p. 90.
62. John Stanton to Rajkowski, Anthropological Research Museum, University of Western Australia, January 1989.
63. Morgan, M., op. cit., p. 120.andElkin, A.P., op. cit., pp. 300-1.
64. Matron Sadie Canning to Rajkowski, Leonora Hospital,W.A., 19 January 1989.
65. See Smith, H.P. (ed.), op. cit., p. 58 and Morgan, M., op. cit., p. 91.
66. Morgan, M., op. cit., p. 91.
67. Letter from P.C.Perks to D.I.P. Spedding Smith, 16 September 1926, DCS File 379/26, p. 17.
68. Letter from P.C. Perks to D.I.P., 16 September 1926, p. 17, DCS File 379/26.
69. Ibid.
70. Note from D.I.P. to C.P.A., 17 September 1926, p. 17, DCS File No. 379/26.
71. Letter from P.C. Perks to D.I.P. Spedding Smith, 14 October 1926, DCS File 379/26, p. 28.
72. Letter from C.P.A. to Under Secretary Colonial Secretary's Department (C.S.D.), 24 September 1926, p. 19, DCS File 379/26.
73. Letter from J. Akbar to R. Cook, 30 September 1926, p. 22, DCS File 379/26.
74. Letter from R. Cook to C.P.A., 1 October 1926, p. 23, DCS File 379/26.
75. Warrant for arrest of Lallie Matbar, 2 October 1926, p. 18, DCS File 379/26.

76. Letter from C.P.A. Neville to D.I.P. Spedding Smith, 4 October 1926, DCS File 379/26.
77. Letter from C.P.A. to R. Cook, 11 October 1926, p. 24, DCS File 379/26.
78. Report from P.C. Perks to D.I.P., 7 October 1926, p. 26, DCS File 379/26; and M. Morgan, op. cit., p. 91.
79. Letter from P.C. Perks to D.I.P., 7 October 1926, p. 26, DCS File 379/26.
80. Telegram from P.C. Perks to D.I.P., 12 October 1926, p. 28, DCS File 379/26.
81. Letter from P.C. Perks to D.I.P., 7 October 1926, p. 28, DCS File 379/26.
82. Police notes 19 to 23 October 1926, p. 29, DCS File 379/26.
83. Gaffy was Superintendent of Moore River Native Settlement (MRNS) from 1925 to 1927, *W.A. Government Gazette*, No. 14860, Colonial Secretary's Office, 17 July 1925, p. 1275.
84. Telegram from Police to Superintendent, Moore River Native Settlement (M.R.N.S.), 19 October 1926, p. 30, DCS File 379/26.
85. Note from C.P.A. to Police, 19 October 1926, p. 30, DCS File 379/26.
86. Inmate No. 873 for DCS File 379/26, MRNS, AAPA, W.A.
87. Letter from R. Schenk to P.C. Perks, between 7 and 14 October 1926, p. 27, DCS File 379/26.
88. Letter from Lallie Matbar to C.P.A., 14 October 1926, p. 27, DCS File 379/26.
89. Letter from P.C. Perks to D.I.P., 14 October 1926, p. 28, DCS File 379/26.
90. Letter from C.P.A. to C. in C. (MRNS), 18 November 1926, p. 33, DCS File 379/26.
91. Letter from C.P.A. to C. in C., 19 November 1926, p. 33, DCS File 379/26.
92. Biskup, P., op. cit., p. 160.

CHAPTER FIVE

1. Inmate No. 873 for DCS File 379/26, MRNS (Moore River Native Settlement), Mogumber, Aboriginal Affairs Planning Authority (AAPA), Perth, W.A.
2. Commissioner H.D. Moseley's Report, 24 January 1935, W.A. Parliamentary Votes and Proceedings, Vol. 1, 1935.
3. Haebich, A., 'On the Inside; Moore River Native Settlement in the 1930s', in Gammage, W. and Markus, A. (eds), *All That Dirt: Aborigines 1938*, Canberra, 1982. p. 53.
4. Ibid.
5. There are other books that describe in detail the conditions, way of life and physical surroundings of the Moore River Native Settlement.
6. Haebich, A., *For Their Own Good; Aborigines and Government in the South-west of Western Australia 1900-1940*, University of Western Australia Press, 1988, p. 190.
7. Ibid, p. 189.
8. Ibid, p. 190.
9. Clarke Rev., 'No More Fear at Native Settlement', *Express*, W.A., 11 August 1975. In Battye Library, W.A.
10. Haebich, A., op. cit., p. 210.
11. Dora and Claude Cotterill to Pamela Rajkowski, Leonora, W.A., 19 January 1989.
12. Mona Wilson to Rajkowski, Inglewood, Victoria, 8 January 1988.
13. Biskup, P., *Not Slaves, Not Citizens: The AboriginalProblem in Western Australia 1898-1954*, University of Queensland Press, 1973, p. 155.
14. Letter from District Inspector of Police (D.I.P.) to Police Commissioner, 6 April 1927, ACC 993 File 459/26.
15. Haebich, A., 'On the Inside', op.cit., p.60
16. Stone, N. (ed.), *Aborigines in White*

Australia: a documentary history of attitudes, affecting official policy and the Australian Aborigine, 1697-1973, Heinemann, London, 1974 p. 169.
17. Section 9, 1905 Aborigines Act, The Statutes of Western Australia 1904-05.
18. Haebich, A., 'On the Inside', op.cit., p.60.
19. Stone and Sharman, op. cit.,p. 169
20. DCS File 459/26 on 'Laura Quince'. The woman who is the subject of this file asked that her real name not be used. The contents quoted from the file in this text are true, accurate and contain the true names of the other people.
21. Card on 'Laura Quince' from MRNS, Mogumber, in DCS File 148/33, Department of Community Services (DCS), Perth, W.A.
22. Letter from Police Constable (P.C.) Goldie to Sergeant (Sgt), 2 April and 5 April, 1927 in DCS File 459/26 on 'Laura Quince'.
23. Haebich, A., 'On the Inside', op. cit., p. 51.
24. Letter from Inspector Mitchell to C.P.A., 7 February 1927, File No. 148/33.
25. Letter from C.P.A. to D.I.P. Spedding Smith, 1 March 1927, File No. 459/26, Dept. of Community Services, Perth, W.A.
26. Letter from C.P.A. to Under Secretary, 1 March 1927, p. 19, DCS File 459/26.
27. Warrant for the arrest of'Laura Quince's', 10 March 1927, DCS File 459/26.
28. Letter from C.P.A. to Superintendent Moore River Native Settlement (MRNS), 25 March 1927, DCS File 459/26.
29. Taped interview with Joyce Newland by Mona Wilson and Shirley Wilson, at Menzies, W.A., 1989. Joyce Newland is a daughter of Lallie's second family.
30. Ibid.
31. Morgan, M., *A Drop in a Bucket*, United Aborigines Mission, Melbourne, 1986, p. 92.
32. Ibid, pp. 83-8.
33. Ibid, p. 23.
34.Lallie's DCS file plus Morgan, M, op. cit., p. 21.
35. Morgan. M., op. cit., p. 23.
36. Letter from Neal to C.P.A., about 2 June, DCS File 379/26.
37. 10 June 1927, DCS File 379/26.
38. Jacobs, P., *Mr. Neville: A Biography*, Fremantle Arts Centre Press, W.A. 1990, p. 138.
39. Letter from C.P.A. to MRNS, [no date though mentions Lallie Matbar and her second abscondment], Aboriginal Affairs Planning Authority (AAPA).
40. Letter from MRNS to C.P.A., 31 October 1927, p. 44, DCS File 379/26, and p. 33, File 148/33.
41. Letter from C.P.A. to D.I.P., and to Northam Police, 2 November 1927, p. 39, DCS File 459/26.
42. Dora and Claude Cotterill to Rajkowski, Leonora, W.A., 19 January 1989.
43. Letter from C.P.A. to Police, 9 November 1927, op. cit., and p. 35, File 459/26.
44. Letter from Inspector Mitchell to C.P.A., 24 November 1927, p. 46, File 379/26.
45. Letter from P.C. Woods, 27 December 1927, p. 79, DCS File 379/26.
46. Letter from P.C. Polak, 10 January 1928, p. 79, DCS File 379/26.
47. Telegram from C.P.A. to D.I.P., 12 January 1928, p. 38, DCS File 459/26.
48. Letter from C.P.A. to R. Schenk, 12 January 1928, p. 38, DCS File 459/26.
49. Letter from R. Schenk to C.P.A., 12 January 1928, Acc.993, File 484/26, (AAPA), Perth, W.A.

50. Clarke Rev., 'No more Fear at Native Settlement', op cit.

CHAPTER SIX

1. Letter from C.P.A. to Police Commissioner Connell, 20 February 1928, DCS File 379/26, p. 57.
2. Ranji McIntyre to Rajkowski, Kurrawang Mission via Kalgoorlie, W.A., 18 January 1989.
3. Dora and Claude Cotterill to Rajkowski, Leonora, W.A., 19 January 1989.
4. Marks, S.R., 'Mission Policy in Western Australia 1846-1959', *University Studies in Western Australian History*, Vol. 3, No. 4, 1960, pp. 61-2.
5. Letter from R. Schenk to Chief Protector of Aborigines (C.P.A.)., 17 January 1928, p. 51-52, DCS File 379/26.
6. Margaret Morgan to Rajkowski, Perth, 23 December 1993.
7. Morgan, M., *A Drop in a Bucket*, United Aborigines Mission, Melbourne, 1986, p. 104.
8. Letter from R. Schenk to C.P.A., 5 April 1923, Acc. 993, DCS File 379/26.
9. Chief Secretary's Dept. Acc. 993 File 484/26, Battye Library, W.A.
10. Morgan. M., op. cit., pp. 57-8.
11. Letter from R. Schenk to C.P.A., 5 April 1923, op. cit.
12. Letter from R. Schenk to C.P.A., 19 April 1923, Acc 993, DCS File 379/26.
13. Morgan, M, op. cit., p. 105.
14. Bennett, M.M., *Teaching the Aborigines; Data from Mount Margaret Mission*, Perth, 1935.
15. Letter from Police Constable (P.C.) Warren to C.P.A., 1923, Acc 993, File 484/26.
16. Taped interview of Reggie Johnston of Menzies, W.A., by Bill Bunbury, December 1986, for ABC radio series, 'Out of sight, out of mind', Oral History Programme, Battye Library, W.A.
17. Smith, H.P. (ed.), *The First Ten Years of Mount Margaret Mission*, W.A., United Aborigines Mission, Melbourne, n.d., p. 30.
18. Wilf Douglas to Pamela Rajkowski, Kalgoorlie, W.A.,
21 January 1989.
19. Annual Report of C.P.A. ending 30 June 1928, AAPA, W.A.
20. Morgan, M, op. cit., p. 104; plus, Smith, H.P. (ed.), op. cit., p. 48.
21. The amount of meat is not identified in these statistics.
22. Morgan, M., op. cit., pp. 104-5.
23. Ibid.
24. Letter from C.P.A. to Inspector of Aborigines Mr Mitchell, 2 February 1928, DCS File 379/26, p. 54.
25. Letter from R. Schenk to C.P.A., 17 January 1928, p. 51-52, DCS File 379/26.
26. Letter from R. Schenk to C.P.A., 19 January 1928, DCS File 379/26.
27. Letter from R. Schenk to C.P.A., 12 January 1928, p. 49, DCS File 379/26.
28. Letter from C.P.A. to Mitchell, 2 February 1928, p. 54, File 459/26.
29. Letter from Mitchell to C.P.A., 11 February 1928, DCS File 379/26.
30. Ibid.
31. Letter from R. Schenk to C.P.A., 15 February 1928, DCS File 379/26.
32. Letter from P.C. White to District Inspector Police (D.I.P)., 9 February 1928, DCS File 379/26.
33. Letter from P.C. Allanson to D.I.P., 17 February 1928, DCS File 379/26.
34. Letter from P.C. Reilly, 3 March 1928, p. 80, DCS File 379/26.
35. Letter from C.P.A. to Police Commissioner Connell, 20 February 1928, p. 57, DCS File 379/26.
36. Letter from R. Schenk to C.P.A., 23 February 1928, p. 59, DCS File

379/26.

37. Letter from C.P.A. to Police Commissioner Connell, 20 February 1928, DCS File 379/26, p. 57.
38. Ibid.
39. Letter from P.C. Warren to D.I.P., 29 February 1928, p. 61, DCS File 379/26.
40. 'Not allowed to love', the *Mirror*, W.A., 5 October, 1928.
41. Letter from P.C. Warren to D.I.P., 29 February 1928, op. cit.
42. Letter from D.I.P. to Police Commissioner, 2 March 1928, p. 62, DCS File 379/26.
43. Note from Police Commissioner to C.P.A., 6 March 1928, p. 62, DCS File 379/26.
44. Letter from R. Schenk to C.P.A., 7 March 1928, p. 60, DCS File 379/26.
45. Letter from C.P.A. to Police Commissioner, 12 March 1928, p. 63, DCS File 379/26.
46. 'Deputation to Hon. Premier by Aborigines re amendments to 1905 Aborigines Act and criticising Dept.', 94/1928, State Archives, Alexander Building, Perth, W.A. Includes *West Australian* article, 9 March 1928.
47. Ibid.
48. Haebich, A., *For Their Own Good; Aborigines and Government in the South West of Western Australia 1900-1940*, University of Western Australia Press, 1988, p. 302.
49. Section 44, 1905 Aborigines Act, The Statutes of Western Australia, 1904-05.
50. Letter from C.P.A. to Police Commissioner, 12 March 1928, p. 63, DCS File 379/26.
51. Letter from R. Schenk to C.P.A., 27 March 1928, DCS File 379/26.
52. Letter from R. Schenk to P.C. Warren, 17 April 1928, p. 68, DCS File 379/26.

CHAPTER SEVEN

1. Letter from Chief Protector of Aborigines (C.P.A.) to Under Secretary, 30 August 1928, p. 88, DCS File 379/26.
2. Letter to Sergt. McGuiniss [no date], DCS File 379/26, p. 72, 73. This is written as a police report but there is not an author's name supplied on the report. Also, a telegram from Inspector Spedding Smith in Kalgoorlie to C.P.A., Perth, 24 April 1928, DCS File 379/26, p. 70
3. Letter from Schenk to C.P.A., 17 April 1928, DCS File 379/26.
4. Letter from Perks, 21 April 1928, p. 71, DCS File 379/26.
5. Note from Spedding Smith to Sgt. McGuiniss, 21 April 1928, p. 71, DCS File 379/26.
6. Will and Marjorie Sharpe, to Rajkowski, Esperance, W.A., 17 January 1989. This couple, who are ex-missionaries, were young adults at Mount Margaret mission for probationary training during the time when Jack Akbar took Lallie out of the district, and they recalled Schenk's reaction.
7. Gordon and Jennifer Leany to Rajkowski, Esperance, 19 January 1989. This couple who are retired missionaries knew Rod and Mysie Schenk at Mount Margaret mission in 1927-28.
8. Letter from P.C. Warren to Spedding Smith, Kalgoorlie,
5 May 1928, DCS File 379/26, p. 75
9. Telegram to Police, 23 April 1928, p. 70, DCS File 379/26.
10. Telegram from District Inspector of Police (D.I.P.) to C.P.A., 24 April 1928, p. 70, DCS File 379/26.
11. Police report to Sgt, McGuiniss, [no date], p. 72-3, DCS File 379/26.
12. Ibid.
13. Ibid.

14. Letter from P.C. Woodfin to D.I.P., 28 April 1928, p. 74, DCS File 379/26.
15. Letter from D.I.P. to Police Commissioner Connell, 1 May 1928, p. 76, DCS File 379/26.
16. Police Letter to C.P.A., 1 May 1928, DCS File 379/26, p. 76.
17. Letter from P.C. Warren to D.I.P., 12 June 1928, p. 87, DCS File 379/26.
18. Letter from D.I.P. to Police. Commissioner, 28 May 1928, p. 50, File 148/33, Aboriginal Affairs Planning Authority (AAPA), Perth, W.A.
19. Copy of Marriage Certificate, 23 May 1928, p. 87, DCS File 379/26.
20. Rajkowski, P., *In the Tracks of the Camelmen*, Angus and Robertson-Collins, Sydney, 1987, p. 115.
21. Sayira Todd (nee Mahomet) of Virginia, S.A., to Rajkowski, 1990. When asked if she could recall the visit of Jack and Lallie to her parents' home in Farina in 1928 just after their marriage in Adelaide, her response was that her father, Gool Mahomet, was a strict Moslem and according to tradition he did not share his business details with his daughters, nor allow his daughters to meet male visitors.
22. Rajkowski, P., op. cit., pp. 40-1.
23. Mona Wilson to Rajkowski, Inglewood, Victoria, 8 January 1988.
24. See Introduction for reference to terminology.
25. Letter from P.C. Warren to D.I.P., 21 August 1928, p.
87, DCS File 379/26.

CHAPTER EIGHT

1. 'Resolution by National Council of Women', Acc 993, File 337/27, AAPA, in State Archives, Alexander Building, Perth, W.A.
2. Jacobs, P., *Mr. Neville; A Biography*, Fremantle Arts Centre Press, Western Australia, 1980.
3. Section 9, 1905 Aborigines Act, The Statutes of Western Australia 1904-05.
4. Letter from Chief Protector of Aborigines (C.P.A.) to Police Commissioner, 14 August 1928, p. 85, DCS File 379/26.
5. Letter from C.P.A. to Under Secretary, 30 August 1928, p. 88, DCS File 379/26.
6. S.A. Police report, 31 August 1928, p. 92, DCS File 379/26.
7. Warrant for J. Akbar, 2 September 1928, p. 101, DCS File 379/26.
8. Letter from Crown Prosecutor to C.P.A., 12 September 1928, p. 89, DCS File 379/26.
9. Letter from C.P.A. to Under Secretary, 19 September 1928, p. 96, DCS File 379/26.
10. Form of Indemnity for J. Akbar, 2 October 1928, p. 98, and Note from Under Secretary to Crown Prosecutor, 27 September, 1928, p. 97, both of DCS File 379/26.
11. 'Law Courts: Alleged Illegal Removal of a Half caste', *Advertiser*, South Australia., 5 October 1928, p. 19.
12. Ibid.
13. Ibid.
14. Letter from K. McEntee to C.P.A., 8 October 1928, p. 132-3, DCS File 379/26.
15. Letter from Miss Smith to C.P.A., 1928, p. 128-31, DCS File 379/26.
16. Letter from C.P.A. to Police Commissioner Connell, 12 October 1928, p. 134, DCS File 379/26.
17. DCS File 379/26, p. 135
18. 'Not allowed to love', the *Mirror*, W.A., 13 October 1928.
19. Detective Parker, List of Expenses Incurred', re extradition of J. Akbar, DCS File 379/26, p. 173.
20. Re 'Pyrrhic victory' - Pyrrhus was

the greatest Molossian king of Epirus, a place in ancient Greece. He led thousands of troops into wars but every victory was at a great cost.
21. *West Australian*, W.A., 4 November 1928, State Archives, W.A.
22. Letter from Detective Parker, p. 156-7, DCS File 379/26.
23. Telephone message to C.P.A. from Detective Parker, 2 November 1928, p. 158, DCS File 379/26.
24. Note from A. Wolff to Police Commissioner, 6 November 1928, p. 116, DCS File 379/26.
25. Letter from Detective Parker to Detective Sergeant Frazer, Perth, 7 November 1928, DCS File 379/26, p. 167.
26. Ibid.
27. 'Not allowed to love', op. cit.
28. Letter from Det. Parker to Det, Sgt. Frazer, op. cit.
29. Note from J. Akbar to C.P.A. (witnessed by Greif), Mohammedan mosque, 9 November 1928, DCS File 379/26, p. 173.
30. Note from Detective Sergeant Frazer to Detective Parker, Perth, op. cit.
31. Letter from Greif to C.P.A., 7 November 1928, DCS File 379/26, p. 168.
32. Letter from Greif to C.P.A., 8 November 1928, DCS File 379/26, pp. 169-70.
33. Letter from C.P.A. to Kitson, 14 November 1928, DCS File 379/26, pp. 174 75.
34. Bond for J. Akbar, 9 November 1928, pp. 171-72, DCS File 379/26.
35. Note from J. Akbar to C.P.A. (witnessed by Greif), 9 November 1928, DCS File 379/26, p. 173.
36. Detective Parker, List of 'Expenses Incurred' op. cit.
37. Letter from C.P.A. to Kitson, 14 November 1928, DCS File 379/26, p. 174-75.
38. Note from 'Accountant' to C.P.A., 17 May 1929, DCS File 379/26, p. 189.

CHAPTER NINE

1. Mona Wilson to Rajkowski, Inglewood, Victoria, 5 September 1986.
2. Letter from R. Schenk to Chief Protector of Aborigines (C.P.A.), 7 December 1928, p. 178, DCS File 379/26.
3. Letter from C.P.A. to R. Schenk, 14 December 1928, p. 179, DCS File 379/26.
4. Note from C. in C. (complete words not provided in Lallie's DCS file) of Treasury Department to C.P.A., 19 June 1929, p. 189, DCS File 379/26.
5. Letter from C.P.A. to C. in C., 20 June 1929, p. 190, DCS File No. 379/26.
6. Letter from Police Commissioner to C.P.A., 18 July 1929, p. 191, DCS File 379/26.
7. Ibid.
8. Letter from C.P.A. to J. Akbar, 25 July 1929, p. 192, DCS File 379/26.
9. Letter from C.P.A. to J. Akbar, 20 September 1929, DCS File 379/26, p. 192.
10. Letter from C.P.A. to Police Commissioner, 4 November 1929, p. 194, File 379/26.
11. Letter from Police Commissioner to C.P.A., 26 November 1929, p. 195, DCS File 379/26.
12. Note from C.P.A., 26 November 1929, p. 195, DCS File 379/26.
13. Mrs Hagley to Rajkowski, Adelaide, 8 September 1986.
14. Letter from Police Commissioner. to C.P.A., 10 February 1931, p. 198, DCS File 379/26.
15. Ibid.
16. Letter from Police Commissioner to C.P.A., 14 November 1930, p. 200, DCS File 379/26.
17. Letter from Police Commissioner to

C.P.A., 5 January 1934, p. 202, DCS File 379/26.
18. Ibid.
19. Letter from police in S.A. to C.P.A. in W.A., 10 July 1934, p. 210, DCS File 379/26.
20. Letter from C.P.A. to J. Akbar, 16 November 1935, p. 226, DCS File 379/26.
21. Letter from J. Akbar to C.P.A., 18 November 1935, p. 227, DCS File 379/26.
22. Letter from Akbar to C.P.A., 30 November 1935, p. 229, DCS File 379/26.

EPILOGUE

1. Mona Wilson to Rajkowski, Inglewood, Victoria, 5 September 1986.
2. Ibid. ; and Reverend Glen and Mrs Roma Locke to Rajkowski, Armadale, W.A., 10 January 1989.
3. Hagley, Wattle Park, Adelaide, to Rajkowski, 1986.
4. Shirley Wilson to Rajkowski, Armadale, W.A., 25 May 1989.
5. Mona Wilson to Rajkowski, op. cit.; and Bill Summerfield to Rajkowski, Renmark, S.A., 1986.
6. Rajkowski, P., *In the Tracks of the Camelmen*, Angus and Robertson-Collins, Sydney, 1987, p. 173.
7. Mona Wilson to Rajkowski, op. cit.
8. Rajkowski, P., op. cit., p. 171.
9. Mona Wilson to Rajkowski, op. cit.
10. Vera Satour to Rajkowski, Alice Springs, Northern Territory.
11. Reverend G. and Mrs R. Locke to Rajkowski, op. cit.
12. Bill Summerfield to Rajkowski, op. cit.
13. Jim Locke to Rajkowski, Goolwa, S.A., 1986.
14. Ibid.
15. Bill Summerfield to Rajkowski, op. cit.
16. Mona Wilson, Victoria, to Rajkowski, 10 July 1994.
17. Bill Summerfield to Rajkowski, op. cit.
18. Mona Wilson to Rajkowski, 5 September 1986.
19. Jim Locke to Rajkowski, op. cit.
20. Mona Wilson to Rajkowski, op. cit.
21. Hagley to Rajkowski,, op. cit.
22. Bill Summerfield to Rajkowski, op.cit.
23. Letter from Mona Wilson to Rajkowski, 5 September 1988.
24. Rev. G. and Mrs R. Locke to Rajkowski, Armadale, W,A., 1989.
25. Bill Summerfield to Rajkowski, op. cit.
26. Mona Wilson to Rajkowski, op. cit.
27. Bill Summerfield to Rajkowski, op. cit.
28. Letter from Lallie Akbar to Mrs Schenk, 15 June 1939, DCS File 379/26, p. 237.
29. In 1936 the 1905 Aborigines Act was amended and its title was changed to the Native Administration Act. The Aborigines Department was now to be called the Department of Native Affairs and the Chief Protector of Aborigines was now to be called the Commissioner of Native Affairs.
30. Letter from R. Schenk to Commissioner of Native Affairs (C.N.A.), 27 June 1939, p. 233, DCS File 379/26.
31. Letter from C.N.A. to R. Schenk, 29 June 1939, p. 234, DCS File 379/26.
32. Letter from R. Schenk to C.N.A., 7 July 1939, p. 235, DCS File 379/26.
33. Letter from C.N.A. to R. Schenk, 19 July 1939, p. 336, DSC File 379/26.
34. Letter from R. Schenk to C.N.A., 1941, File 379/26.
35. Morgan, M., *A Drop in a Bucket*, United Aborigines Mission, Melbourne, 1986, p. 91.
36. Mona Wilson to Rajkowski, op. cit.
37. 'Half Caste - Snowy Bradley @

Lowe - Mount Magnet', Acc 993, File 74/34, Dept. of Community Services (DCS), Perth, W.A.
38. Mona Wilson to Rajkowski, op. cit.
39. Rajkowski, P., op. cit., p. 40, 41.
40. Mona Wilson to Rajkowski, op. cit. Also, Jan (nee Akbar) Van Nunen and Elaine (nee Akbar) McLean to Rajkowski, Adelaide, October, 1993. Jan and Elaine are daughters of Mona Wilson.
41. Mona Wilson to Rajkowski, op. cit.: and Jan and Elaine to Rajkowski, op cit.
42. Letter from R. Schenk to C.N.A., 3 January 1946, DCS File 379/26.
43. Letter from C.N.A. to R. Schenk, 22 January 1946, DCS File 379/26, p. 241.
44. From the collection of diaries of Frances Emma Jones dated 1888 to 1945, in the possession of the Jones family of Hampton Hill station near Kalgoorlie, W.A.
45. Death Notice for 'Newland; Akbar', *Kalgoorlie Miner*, W.A., 3 June 1970, p. 12.
46. Claim for Maternity Allowance, 17 May 1948, DCS File 379/26, p. 146.
47. A second Claim for Maternity Allowance, 1950, File 138/46 into DCS File 379/26, p. 17.
48. 'Brief Chronology of Aboriginal Affairs Planning Authority (AAPA)', Perth, W.A., February 1993.
49. Letter to C.N.A., 21 March 1956, from File 138/46 to DCS File 379/26.
50. Funeral Notice for 'Akbar, J.', *Murray Pioneer*, S.A., 30 September 1954.
51. To the Wongai, and other Aboriginal people, the word 'aunty' is used to denote a female who is an important relative in a family or member of a community.
52. Jeannie Patterson to Rajkowski, Perth, W.A., 8 January 1989.
53. Richard 'Splinter' Akbar, son of Shirley Wilson, Armadale, W.A., 1989.
54. Shirley Wilson to Rajkowski, Armadale, W.A., 8 January 1989.
55. Mona Wilson to Rajkowski, op. cit.
56. Ibid.
57. Ibid.
58. Funeral Notice for 'Newland, Akbar', *Kalgoorlie Miner*, W.A., 4 June 1970.
59. Letter from Mona Wilson to Rajkowski, 14 May 1987.
60. Letter written by Mona Wilson to Shirley Wilson, 12 June 1970, in possession of Shirley Wilson, Armadale, W.A.

INDEX